PROSPECTS FOR THE EUROPEAN MONETARY SYSTEM

Also by Piero Ferri

ADJUSTING TO SHOCKS: A North–South Perspective (*co-editor*)
THE LABOUR MARKET AND BUSINESS CYCLE THEORIES (*with E. Greenberg*)

Prospects for the European Monetary System

Edited by
Piero Ferri
Professor of Economics
University of Bergamo, Italy

St. Martin's Press New York

First published in the United States of America in 1990

Printed in Great Britain

ISBN 0-312-05351-7

Library of Congress Cataloging-in-Publication Data
Prospects for the European monetary system/ edited by Piero Ferri.
p. cm.
Papers presented at a conference held in May 1989 at the
University of Bergamo, Italy.
Includes index.
ISBN 0-312-05351-7
1. Monetary policy—European Economic Community countries—Congresses. 2. Monetary unions—European Economic Community countries—Congresses. 3. Capital movements—European Economic Community countries—Congresses. 4. Euro-dollar market—Congresses.
I. Ferri, Piero.
HG925.P76 1990
332.4'566'094—dc20 90-44601
CIP

Contents

List of Tables

List of Figures

Acknowledgements

This volume contains the papers from a conference ('The EMS, Ten Years Later') held in Bergamo in May 1989 to honour the twentieth anniversary of the foundation of the University of Bergamo, which culminated with the *Laurea Honoris Causa*, attributed to Helmut Schmidt, Former Chancellor of the Federal Republic of Germany and one of the founders of the EMS. Special thanks are due to Filippo Maria Pandolfi, Vice President of the European Commission and Chairman of the committee for the celebrations, who promoted the initiative, and Professor Luigi Spaventa whose advice was most useful.

Generous support was given by the local public institutions, including the Comune, the Provincia and the Camera di Commercio. Financial contributions by Banca Popolare di Bergamo, Credito Bergamasco, Banca Provinciale Lombarda, Italcementi and Unione degli Industriali are gratefully acknowledged.

Abbreviations and Acronyms

CAP	Common Agricultural Policy
ECU	European Currency Unit
EEC (EC)	European Economic Community
EMS	European Monetary System
ERM	Exchange Rate Mechanism
FRG	Federal Republic of Germany
IM	Single Internal Market
IMF	International Monetary Fund
NICs	Newly Integrating Countries
OECD	Organisation for Economic Cooperation and Development

Notes on the Contributors

Jacques Le Cacheux is Deputy Director of the Departement des Etudes of the Observatoire Français des Conjunctures Economiques in Paris. He has written on macroeconomic themes.

Marcello de Cecco is Professor of Economics at the University of Rome, La Sapienza. He was formerly a Professor at the European University Institute, Florence. He held the Chair of Italian Culture at the University of California (Berkeley). He has written extensively on national and international money and finance.

Piero Ferri is Rector of the University of Bergamo, and Professor of Economics. He has published books on labour market themes and macroeconomic topics. Among his recent publications is, in collaboration with E. Greenberg, *The Labor Market and Business Cycle Theories*.

Jean-Paul Fitoussi is Professor of Economics at the Institut d'Etudes Politiques de Paris and External Professor at the European University Institute of Florence. He is also the director of the Research Department of the OFCE. He has published books on inflation, unemployment and macroeconomic theory.

Francesco Giavazzi is Professor of Economics at the University of Bologna, a CEPR research fellow, and research associate at the National Bureau of Economic Research. His main fields of interest are economic policy and international economics.

Paul De Grauwe is Professor of Economics at the Katholieke Universiteit, Leuven. He is also a senior research fellow at the Centre for European Policy Studies in Brussels and a CEPR research fellow, London. He has published extensively on international economics.

J.A. Kregel is Professor of Political Economy at the University of Bologna, Italy. He has taught in many American and European universities. He has published extensively on the theory of economic growth and on post-Keynesian economics.

Jorge Braga de Macedo is the Director of National Economies at the Directorate General for Economic and Financial Affairs of the EEC Commission. He is on leave as Associate Professor of Economics at the New University of Lisbon. He has written numerous articles on international trade and finance.

Rainer S. Masera is the General Director of the Istituto Mobiliare Italiano, Rome. He was formerly Director of the Research Department of the Bank of Italy. He has worked in many international committees during and since the creation of the EMS. In this area he has published widely.

David Metcalf is Professor of Industrial Relations at the London School of Economics. He is the editor of the *British Journal of Industrial Relations*. Recently he was a consultant to the OECD in connection with their work on labour market flexibility.

Richard Portes is Director of the CEPR in London and Professor of Economics at Birkbeck College, University of London. He has written extensively on sovereign borrowing and debt, central planning, macro-economic disequilibrium, and East–West economic relations.

Pippo Ranci is Professor of Economic Policy at the University of Bergamo. He is also a researcher at IRS. He has published many books on industrial theory and policy.

Stefano Vona is Assistant Director in the Research Department of the Bank of Italy. He has published many works on the labour market and on international trade.

List of Participants

J. Braga de Macedo, University of Lisbon

M. Casari, University of Bergamo

M. de Cecco, University of Rome

P. De Grauwe, University of Leuven

P. Ferri, University of Bergamo

F. Giavazzi, University of Bologna

J. Kregel, Johns Hopkins University, Bologna

J. Le Cacheux, OFCE, Paris

R. Masera, IMI, Rome

H.P. Minsky, Washington University, St Louis

D. Metcalf, London School of Economics

F.M. Pandolfi, Economic Commission, Brussels

R. Portes, Birkbeck College, London

P. Ranci, University of Bergamo

S. Vona, Bank of Italy, Rome

Preface

One may well wonder whether the European Monetary System deserves a high place on an agenda of problems that faces the European Economic Community, as the Report on the Economic and Monetary Union envisages the creation of a Federal Central Bank and a full monetary union. If the programme of the report is realised, then the EMS will disappear. However, for the present, the EMS remains a central pillar of the European system, which needs to be adapted to accommodate to the liberalisation of capital movements that is scheduled for July 1990.

The schedule for liberalising capital movements is set out in the Single Act, which aims to achieve a complete economic integration of Europe. In the programme laid out by the Single Act, the EMS is a bridge between national monetary autonomy and European monetary union. Because the future is going to be built on the reality of the EMS as an existing institution, it is important to know its history, to understand the reasons underlying the successes attributed to it, the problems that it created and possible evolutionary trajectories for the European monetary structure.

In the post-second World War era there has been a cyclical movement between emphasising real and monetary aspects of the international economy. The Treaty of Rome was signed in a period of fixed exchange rates, when the Bretton Woods agreements were still working smoothly. As a result, the Treaty dealt mainly with real economic problems and was abstracted from the monetary and financial aspects of economic integration. The EMS focused on achieving agreed exchange rates, postponing to an indeterminate date the implementation of phase two, which involved a full utilisation of the ECU and of a European Monetary Fund. At the time the EMS was set up, flexible exchange rates were widely believed to be a cure for the weakness that had been revealed in the dollar-centred system to which the Bretton Woods structure had evolved. The Single Act stressed the importance of economic integration and the steps to reach it. Perhaps the time has now come when it is necessary to consider real and monetary aspects jointly.

Two tendencies are revealed in the literature on the EMS. One stresses inflation, speculation and exchange rate volatility which are related to macroeconomic and monetary developments. This leads to policies that stress monetary and fiscal discipline. The other emphasises long-run real phenomena such as differentials in economic growth and productivity which are imputed to structural characteristics that are barriers to economic efficiency. This leads to policies that are oriented to achieving competitive markets and social institutions that are not barriers to mobility. The aim of this book is to bridge the gap between the two approaches. In trying to identify the lessons that can be drawn from the ten years of the EMS which will help us to mould the future we need to consider:

1. The integration of monetary with real aspects: exchange rate movements are mainly attributed to unanticipated monetary disturbances and, more accurately, to unanticipated shifts in the demand for one country's currency by others. In an integrated approach, real aspects must additionally be considered.
2. This approach applies to short-run as well as to medium- and long-run aspects. In fact, some concern centres on the capacity of the EMS to limit not only short-run volatility, but also longer-term misalignment, i.e., departure from a structure of intra-EMS exchange rates consistent with macroeconomic equilibria.
3. A reconsideration of the objectives to be reached: if a stagflationary environment conditioned priorities when the EMS was initiated, the necessity of a return to full employment in a world with differing degrees of imbalances must now be kept in particular consideration.
4. An evaluation of the challenges deriving from the implementation of the Single Act which aims at creating a unified market for goods, services and capitals and which allows, starting from July 1990, for a complete liberalisation of capital movements.
5. A discussion of institutional reforms which are either a pre-requisite or a necessary aspect of the evolution of the monetary system.

Some of these aspects have been dealt in the Delors Report which has fixed a long-run profile of this economic and monetary union and has identified the role of the EMS in the transitory phase. This does not mean that the problems that the EMS has dealt with will be overcome by institutional changes. For these reasons, it is important to study the role of the EMS during the process of economic and monetary integration, i.e. between the Single Act and monetary union.

In the Introduction, Piero Ferri considers the genesis of the EMS, its nature and the challenges that it must face in the transitory phase which goes from the implementation of the Single Act to the reaching of a full monetary union. A review of the main problems and of the different interpretations is offered. This chapter also introduces the main themes developed in the book.

In trying to identify the nature of the European Monetary System, Marcello de Cecco in Chapter 2 compares the EMS to other international monetary regimes from a historical point of view. In particular, he examines the relationships between the gold and silver standard countries from the nineteenth century up to the decades before the first World War. He considers the Latin Monetary Union, which can be considered a forerunner of the EMS. He also examines the national interests of the main countries participating in the Bretton Woods System, and he examines the EMS from the same point of view.

In Chapter 3, Francesco Giavazzi analyses the main lessons of the EMS experience from two general points of view that are typical of any international monetary systems, i.e. the issues of symmetry and of discipline. From both points of view, the EMS provides an important case study. Ten years of operation of the system have witnessed a dramatic convergence of inflation rates across members. The question that is addressed is whether the decision to join an exchange rate system centred around a low-inflation country affected price and wage expectations, and thus made the output cost of disinflation lower. Professor Giavazzi argues that, despite its popularity, the view that European countries may have joined the EMS simply to buy the anti-inflationary reputation of the Bundesbank is quite narrow. The EMS is just one of a much richer set of agreements among European countries in the trade, industrial and agricultural areas. These aspects are essential when one considers which lessons can be drawn from Europe in order to face the wider question of world monetary arrangements.

Furthermore, Chapter 3 looks ahead in Europe, asking whether the EMS can survive the current process of rapid financial integration, and what the prospects are for monetary unification. Financial integration and further progress toward monetary unification will not succeed unless they are accompanied by sweeping fiscal reforms.

Stefano Vona studies the relationship between real exchange rates and trade imbalances in Chapter 4. Having identified three phases in the working of the EMS, he draws two main conclusions. The first is that the EMS has a deflationary bias not owing to its intrinsic nature as a fixed but adjustable exchange rate agreement, but rather because of the way it has been implemented. Secondly, that monetary union based on one single currency is the only feasible long-run solution to the intra-EMS imbalances.

Jean-Paul Fitoussi and Jacques Le Cacheux stress the asymmetric nature of the EMS and the role of international transmission mechanisms. Chapter 5 is designed to emphasise some rather unorthodox channels of international transmission policy disturbances inducing real shocks that affect open economies through supply responses. When plausible asymmetries in the policies of European countries are introduced, unbalanced consequences of external real shocks are the likely outcome. Financial factors in causing European unemployment are strengthened and the likely relationship between the process of 'Eurosclerosis' and the actual working of the EMS is also stressed.

In Chapter 6 Pippo Ranci answers two questions and then considers a long-run problem. The questions are: is exchange-rate stability good for commercial integration? Is the Single Internal Market good for maintaining fixed exchange rates? After giving a positive answer, with some caveats, to the first question, and a more problematic one to the second, the author faces the long-run problem of exchange-rate stability. This can be maintained only if the sources of divergent behaviour by the current account and by capital flows are either sufficiently reduced or adequately compensated. To this purpose, the role of fiscal stabilisers is stressed.

In Chapter 7 David Metcalf, after identifying the most important aspects of the labour market in European countries, reaches the conclusion that the divergence in institutions, processes and outcomes is far more noticeable than the points of similarity across the various labour markets (see for instance, unionisation, labour mobility, market flexibility, wage determination). Finally, the social dimension of 1992 is brought into the analysis in order to consider the stalled industrial relations initiatives on industrial democracy and working time. Professor Metcalf raises doubts about the possibility of reaching a Europe-wide approach to social policy on the 'harmonisation upwards' lines normally advanced by the EC.

Paul De Grauwe, in Chapter 8, studies the relationship between capital liberalisation, asymmetric functioning of the EMS and the role of coordination policies. After challenging the thesis according to which capital controls have favoured the success of the EMS, he identifies the existence of two regimes in the working of the EMS: the German–Dutch regime, and the one referring to the remaining countries. After arguing that liberalisation of capital movements will significantly increase the pressure to coordinate, he stresses that the real question is whether the EMS countries will be able to devise more symmetric decision rules in the system.

In Chapter 9 Jorge Braga de Macedo argues that specific and exchange rate arrangements among the 'newly integrating countries' (NICs) may be desirable, as long as they do not run counter to the ultimate objective of economic integration and are open to other member countries. The idea of an as-if joining of the EMS seems to be the most attractive during the time before the removal of capital controls or before consolidation of public finance. This desirable caution should never be used as a defence of the existing financial structure in the NICs. It is difficult to attain a cohesive EC without broadening financial development. In turn, a cohesive EC would allow a smoother transition towards a monetary union.

Rainer Masera focuses in Chapter 10 on three problems that have to be tackled in the short term to enable the financial integration of Europe to proceed in an orderly manner: national regulatory systems, the taxation of financial assets and enhanced exchange rate stability in a context of closely coordinated monetary policies. In order to obtain a system characterised by greater exchange rate cohesion and monetary stability which is rigorous but nonetheless able to forestall and counter destabilising currency speculation, it is important to have a greater convergence of economic fundamentals. In other words, domestic costs will have to be stable if integration is to provide the foundation for economic growth.

In Chapter 11 Richard Portes considers both 'relative coordination' (which focuses on exchange rate relationships and balance of payments interactions) and 'absolute coordination' (which refers to the overall stance of policy) and refers them to the EMS in transition. In a monetary union with irrevocably fixed parities and a common currency, fiscal policy coordination is strictly unnecessary. After considering the policy coordination discussed in the Delors Report, the author stresses the role of asymmetry among countries in raising important problems. However, whatever policy coordination is required internally, the EC will still be only a coalition of players in a broader game, the world economy.

This global perspective is also considered in Chapter 12 by J.A. Kregel, who says that the EMS can be considered most realistically as an institutional response to changing conditions concerning the position of the US in the world economy as much as an independent design for an ideal European monetary union. Despite this fact, the recent discussions of monetary union seem to be more concerned with internal imbalances than the conditioning effect of international imbalances and the likely behaviour of the dollar. He believes that there can be a 'common European dollar policy' but that it is not the only one being discussed.

PIERO FERRI

Introduction

1 The EMS, the Single Market and Monetary Union: An Overview*

Piero Ferri

1 INTRODUCTION

On 13 March 1979 the European Monetary System (EMS) came into operation. In the inflationary context that then ruled, the experience with exchange rate flexibility that had been inauguarated when Bretton Woods was set aside in 1971 was not the success that some economists had predicted.[1] Furthermore, in the political environment of the time any move that called for broad reforms of the world's monetary system was neither fashionable nor feasible. In this environment, the EMS was born as a practical answer to two problems that the European Economic Community (EEC) had to face: to constrain exchange rate uncertainty and to reduce the divergence of inflation rates that could undermine trade among EEC countries. The two problems were related, for variable and divergent inflation rates give rise to exchange rate uncertainty.

The EMS was born out of the experience with 'the Snake', which tied together some of the EEC currencies. The EMS differed from 'the Snake' in that it included more of the EEC countries, provided agreement upon bands within which the currencies were allowed to fluctuate and had mechanisms to promote policy coordination (see Masera, 1987).

On the whole, in the past ten years the two limited objectives of the EMS have been accomplished: exchange rates, which have been adjusted intermittently and by agreement, have been more stable than hitherto and inflation rates have converged to lower, more tolerable levels. However, the EMS is a 'monetary system' in which the underlying financial structures are not integrated: there are barriers to capital movements and portfolio diversification among the members of the

*I wish to thank H.P. Minsky (Washington University) for stimulating comments and discussions.

system and between members of the system and the rest of the world. In the near future, in 1990 and in 1992, barriers to the movement of firms, labour and capital, as well as to portfolio diversification, will be removed.

To date, the EMS has worked because surplus countries in the trade imbalances that arise have been willing to acquire assets based upon the economies of deficit countries. The next step in the evolution of the European Economic Community and the European Monetary System will be to adjust to the liberalisation of capital movements and to the subsequent full integration of the financial structures. The test of the system as it now stands and the determination of whether the system needs to evolve in the direction of a common currency and a unified Central Bank will emerge out of the experience with capital and money market integration that is now on the immediate horizon.

It is in the light of the problems that are sure to confront the Community and the System that the problems and experience of the past decade are reviewed here. It seems clear that within the overriding vision of a unified Europe, the success of the Community and the System rests upon the pragmatic approach to problems that has generally ruled. Adaptation and adjustment rather than bold, ideologically driven reforms have served Europe well in the past three decades. If the approach of the past is a guide as to how the future will be faced then the future of the EMS and its successors may be assured.

2 THE BEGINNING AND SOME BACKGROUND

When in 1977 and 1978 the German Chancellor, Helmut Schmidt, and the French President, Valéry Giscard d'Estaing, agreed on the desirability of greater monetary and exchange integration, impetus was given to the development of a new framework for exchange rates as an improvement upon 'the Snake'. As Masera (1987) put it:

> The fall in the dollar during that period, coupled with exchange rate fluctuations, was threatening the cohesion of the Community by tempting countries to undertake competitive devaluations. The view that the weakness of the US currency should be countered by an area of monetary stability in Europe gathered strength: a new Bretton Woods on the other side of the Atlantic (p. 2).

The remote genesis of the monetary agreement can be found in the history of the European economy. The competitive devaluations of the 1930s were a negative experience with fluctuating rates (see Chapter 3). More recently, the process of economic integration formalised in the Treaty of Rome of 1957 set a well-defined first task and a precise timetable: the removal of tariffs and quotas amongst European countries within twelve years. Two aspects are worth stressing. First, the approach was in keeping with the pragmatic spirit of the founders: Robert Schuman remarked that 'Europe will not be made all at once or according to a single plan. It will be built through concrete achievements, which first create de facto solidarity' (*The Economist*, 9 July 1988, p. 6). Secondly, the Treaty did not mention a European Monetary System. The Treaty was mainly concerned with real aspects. Since then an oscillation between essentially real formulations and fundamentally monetary proposals has taken place.

3 THE POLITICAL ECONOMY OF THE AGREEMENTS

One important element setting the stage for the EMS was the Common Agricultural Policy (CAP), the maintenance of which was challenged by exchange rate flexibility. The safeguard of the CAP (a French objective) and the avoidance of competitive devaluations (a German target) were at the root of a political exchange that offered to the other EEC partners the public good of monetary stability.

A consideration of the documents of the meetings in Bremem, first, and in Bruxelles, later, when the EMS was set up on 5 December 1978, reveals that the ambitions were greater than the announced stabilisation goals. The breadth of political vision and the implications of the project resulted in the creation of a European monetary unit – the ECU – and a monetary fund which involved sharing reserves. These measures were supposed to be the cornerstone for promoting growth, restoring full employment, reducing regional disparities and completing the integration of the Community. In particular, redistributive measures in favour of the less developed regions were to be undertaken.

The ambitious proposals for the EMS were circumscribed by the committees of experts that worked out the details of the system. For instance, an important target of the political decision was to devise a system which worked more symmetrically than 'the Snake'. (The so called 'divergence indicator' was considered an important tool for achieving a symmetric functioning of the system.)

4 THE NATURE OF THE EMS

Symmetry was not achieved. The divergence indicator is unbalanced, contains currencies outside the EMS, and does not bind member central banks to any action. The provision for marginal intervention, although symmetric, is rarely resorted to effectively since the largest fraction of EMS intervention is infra-marginal. Furthermore, Italy negotiated a 6 per cent fluctuation band, while Great Britain did not participate in the exchange rate agreements.

The EMS has in fact worked asymmetrically in the sense that German economic policy objectives have conditioned the working of the system (Wyplosz, 1988). It is important to stress that German dominance has not been due to the size of her economy but rather to her economic policy targets. The Bundesbank's low inflation targets have de facto constituted the monetary anchor for the whole system. German economic policy has had to face the trade-off between growth and monetary stability, whereas the other countries have had to choose between growth and the balance of payments equilibrium. The Bundesbank has pursued a low inflation rate and a low oscillation of real exchange rates. This strategy has been called the 'Strong Currency Option' in other countries. The result has been the process of creation of a public good, monetary stability for the members of the EMS (see Padoan, 1988, p. 76).

Furthermore, 'Phase Two', which was expected to take place two years after the inception of the EMS and which was to bring about a full utilisation of the ECU and the development of a European Monetary Fund, has not taken place. As a result, the EMS worked fundamentally as an exchange rate agreement. This does not mean that the EMS has been static. On the contrary, it has shown a great capacity for change and adaptation to different environments (ibid., p. 8).

The EMS incorporates mechanisms necessary to stabilise intra-European exchange rates, while allowing for realignments in response to fundamental disequilibria. Relative stability within a framework that allows for adaptability may account for much of the success of the EMS.

When the EMS is compared with other international monetary systems both with respect to the kind of exchange rate mechanism prevailing, and the underlying power relations (see Russo and Tullio, 1988), one can say that the EMS is:

1. a managed exchange rate variety,
2. based upon asymmetric relations (see Williamson and Miller, 1988).

This latter point is one way of solving the so called *n*-1 problem that arises where *n* interdependent countries exist, while only *n*-1 policies can be set independently (see Mundell, 1968). To have symmetry, one needs agreement on targets. The institutional characteristics and the working of the EMS are such as to differentiate its nature both from past experiences (De Cecco, in Chapter 2, stresses the analogies with the Latin League) and recent proposals for reforming the international monetary system (see Von Furstenberg, 1983, and Williamson and Miller, 1988).

5 THE PERFORMANCE

According to some findings (see Bewley and Kearney, 1988), the EMS as a whole, although becoming more responsive to changes in the major external currencies, has succeeded in reducing the variability of its participating members' bilateral exchange rates.

These results reflect both a greater economic policy coordination and a decreased inflationary differential. From these points of view, the EMS experience has been acknowledged as a success. In order to understand these achievements, two further (institutional) aspects should be mentioned (see Giavazzi, 1988):

a) Inter-relations with other political arrangements: the EMS is just one element of a much wider set of agreements among European countries in the trade, industrial and agricultural areas. These agreements imply an exchange rate stability and thus lend credibility to exchange rate targets.
b) The control of capital mobility: these controls avoided realignments during periods of crisis and enabled banks to delay parity realignments during the disinflation.

As Rogoff (1985) pointed out, if monetary policy coordination is the main explanation for the convergence of nominal and real exchange rates, one would expect to observe a corresponding degree of convergence of nominal and real interest rates in these countries. The continued existence of high onshore–offshore interest differentials suggests that capital controls have played a significant role in the achievement of exchange rate convergence. (For a criticism to this conclusion, see Chapter 8.) This circumstance has been exploited by some Community members (particularly the UK) who continue to remain outside the EMS, while justifying their position by arguing that the existence of capital controls renders the system a flawed model of international economic policy coordination.

Undoubtedly, the most remarkable result obtained by the EMS has been its contributions to bridging the inflationary gap within the EEC countries. In fact, asymmetry can be an efficient way of providing the so called 'nominal anchor' for the whole system in the sense that the country with the highest anti-inflationary reputation sets a discipline for all the participants. As Giavazzi (1988) has pointed out:

> Inflation is simply the inefficient outcome of a non-cooperative game between the public and monetary authorities. If inflation is just a source of inefficiency, then the inflation standard in an international monetary system should be set by the country where the game produces the least inefficiency.... The view rests on the assumption that the exchange rate can influence inflationary expectations, because exchange rate targets are more credible than monetary targets (p. 9) (see also Horn and Persson, 1988).

According to this theory, the response of the economy to particular shocks or policy actions will depend on the expectations held by the public which in turn depend on what regime the public believes to be in effect. And according to Leijonhufvud (1987): 'a monetary regime is a system of expectations that governs the behavior of the public and that is sustained by the consistent behavior of the policy-making authorities' (p. 44).

Three aspects should be mentioned. The first is that realignments were quite substantial, at least in the initial phase.[2] However, one can say that in spite of numerous realignments, the EMS cannot be considered a crawling peg system. Secondly, the discipline imposed by the system, which has made itself felt in the determination of nominal incomes and the planning of budget balances, has encouraged the acceptance of changes in central rates that did not fully accommodate inflation differentials. Thirdly, one must consider that it took some time before the credibility of the agreements became accepted. For France, the turning point was 1983, while in Italy one often refers to the agreements on the '*scala mobile*' (1984).

The inflationary performance of the EEC countries, however, cannot be attributed solely to the working of the EMS. Favourable factors which contributed to the fall in the inflation rate at the world level were the strong dollar and the fall in the price of oil. Both elements contain some paradoxical aspects. With respect to the pattern of the dollar, it should be noted that the setting up of the EMS was a partial defence against a falling dollar. For a long time the appreciation of the dollar and the growing US deficit on the current account mitigated tensions within the system, both by weakening competitive pressures and by boosting exports. As far as the price of oil is concerned, an opposition exists between the working of the two institutions established during the turbulent 1970s, the EMS and OPEC. A weaker OPEC seems to be more favourable to the working of the EMS. Actually, one can identify three periods in the working of the EMS (see also Vona, Chapter 4) which are strongly correlated with the oil shocks.

6 TEN YEARS LATER

When the EMS was launched, it was regarded with much scepticism. Now it is considered a success (see Giavazzi, Micossi and Miller, 1988). The evaluation depends both on the targets and the period of time considered.

There appears to have been three stages in the EMS working. In the initial stage, which goes from the inception to the second oil crisis, the behaviour of the authorities was modified because the policy instruments available to them worked differently in a regime with more stable exchange rates. In the second period, which goes from 1981–2 to the oil counter-shock, the disinflationary commitment became more credible to the public. The last phase is the present one characterised by an increased intra-trade, renewed interest in growth and less favourable external developments. Judgements on the performance depend very much on the period of time taken into consideration.

If one considers the whole period, one can say that the system has evolved in two directions:

a) exchange rate discipline has become tighter;
b) policy coordination has increased.[3]

The system has evolved along practical lines and the realignments can be considered as a form of indirect macroeconomic cooperation (see Padoan, 1988, p. 23). After a decade, however, account should be taken not only of how effective the system has been in reaching the monetary targets, but also of those aspects neglected because of the particular economic environment prevailing at the start, and of new targets which have become important meanwhile: questions which should be raised are not restricted to the monetary short run domain.

In particular, four aspects are relevant:

a) The relationship between the EMS, real exchange rates and trade imbalances (see Bini-Smaghi and Vona, 1988).
b) The pattern of real exchange rates and hence of competitiveness implies an inquiry into the medium-run differences in the dynamics of prices, wages and productivity among the various countries. With this perspective, inflation is not simply the inefficient outcome of a non-cooperative game between the public and monetary authorities: there are structural differences in productivity growth and in nominal income formation.
c) A clarification as to whether or not the EMS is biased towards deflation and slow growth (on these aspects, see Fitoussi and Phelps, 1988). This has a bearing on the fourth aspect.
d) The extent to which full employment remains an economic policy target to be effectively pursued.

7 MEDIUM- AND LONG-RUN PROBLEMS

In the medium- to long-run perspective, the economic problems belong to either of the following categories:

i) the engine for growth
ii) the convergence of economic fundamentals.

The EMS is a hierarchical system with the German economy at the apex: while the degree of asymmetry existing in the system has decreased, it is still correct to stress the importance of the German economy for the system. Unfortunately its growth rate has been low for a long time, and what is worse is export-led. This double characteristic is a cause for concern. Since the EEC countries have benefited from growth in the US, it is important to understand what happens when US performance deteriorates.

The potential for Germany to act as a locomotive depends very much on the evolution of the East European economies.

As far as the second aspect is concerned, it is necessary to consider that the reduction of costs associated with balance of payments problems cannot be achieved exclusively by exploiting the mobility of factors of production. Masera has pointed out that the EMS 'should be supported by a parallel explicit undertaking to modify and correct domestic factors of cost/price pressure, notably in respect of wages and the budget' (Masera, 1987, p. 10). However, these divergences cannot be easily overcome because they are inevitably created by structural dynamics and therefore fixed exchange rates must rely on adequate compensation mechanisms (See Chapter 6).

8 THE SINGLE EUROPEAN ACT

With a long-run perspective, one also has to consider both the recent and the possible evolution of the institutional setting which has thus far characterised the working of the EMS in order to understand how far these changes can deal with the problems we have identified. One of these changes in the institutional setting refers to the Single European Act. This new phase appears promising, in view of attaining a faster growth, but is not without dangers and tensions requiring the adaptation and strengthening of the system.

The Single European Act of 17 February 1986 (see EEC, 1987, and Padoa-Schioppa, 1987) aims at the establishment of an area without internal frontiers permitting the free movement of goods, persons, services and capital by 1992 so as to improve the allocation of resources, and to put a seal, thirty-five years after the signing of the Treaty of Rome, on the integration of Europe.

The expected effect on employment due to the completion of the internal market has three dimensions (see Catinat, Donni and Italianer, 1988): temporal, geographical and sectoral. The eventual outcome depends very much on the extent to which the proposals are adhered to and on the macroeconomic environment in which they take place. The process of trade creation deriving from the reaching of a greater market is sometimes supposed to be the potential engine for growth that the Community is looking for. Finally, it is worth mentioning that the Single European Act, although strictly confined to the real aspects of the economy, opens the door to the consideration of monetary aspects when dealing with the liberalisation of capital movements.

The 1992 plans for removing trade barriers within the EEC countries are not, however, the most important pressure toward a monetary reform; 1990 is important because of the liberalisation of capital movements due in that year. This liberalisation and the creation of a European financial market are key objectives that will influence not only the conduct of monetary and credit policies in the coming years but also the structure of financial systems.

The trade and capital market reforms have strong implications for the working of the EMS. In fact, it needs to be recognised that complete integration of national financial markets entails exchange rates remaining fixed, otherwise financial assets held in different currencies will not be perfect substitutes. Financial integration calls for monetary convergence:

> In principle, sovereignty in monetary matters, which takes the form of autonomy in controlling the money supply and the exchange rate, is not compatible with the objective of creating a single European financial market. On the other hand, the benefits associated with currency integration depend in the final analysis on the ability to ensure, after a period of steady convergence, permanently stable exchange rates within the area and, ultimately, a single currency (Masera, 1987, p. 6).

Once money is free to flow anywhere within the Community's borders, any fear that EMS parities might need to be changed would send investors fleeing from weak currencies to strong ones, unless governments in the weak currency countries tolerated disruptive swings in interest rates. A way out of this dilemma is to pursue a common monetary policy. On the other hand, liberalisation of capital movements also raises a problem for the real side of the economy. It has been described as the 'order of liberalisation' (see CER, 1988, p. 58), meaning the pressure that capital liberalisation puts on the other sectors of the economy to follow the same pattern.

The major change with which the EMS will have to contend in a period of liberalisation of capital movements is the gradual loss of national monetary autonomy. This in turn implies a series of related problems. One refers to the need for participation in the exchange rate mechanism to be extended to all countries belonging to the EMS. The question does not arise only with the pound sterling but also with currencies of the other countries about to join the EMS. The entry of Greece, Spain and Portugal into the EEC calls for an extension of the area of exchange rate stability to these new members: exchange rate stability is a necessary condition for a smooth functioning of the EEC.

There are two difficulties. The first is related to the nature of the EMS agreement which is characterised by the absence of a hegemonic country. As has been pointed out (see Padoan, 1988, p. 77), the process of cooperation (i.e., the production of collective goods) is possible in this context only when i) the pay-off matrix can be changed, ii) the time horizon of the agents is lengthened, and iii) the number of players is minimised. It follows that an increased number of participants can make the game infeasible.

The second aspect is that the entry of the three new countries makes the EEC much less homogeneous. An acceleration of growth and the process of financial integration could avoid the danger of having a 'two-speed' Europe. In an integrated financial market, regional current account imbalances are automatically accommodated by private capital flows. In this sense, financial integration could remove the bias that now prevents some European countries from growing as fast as they should.

9 THE CHALLENGES

One must wonder how successful the EMS will be in meeting future challenges. These challenges will come from internal and external factors and will test its ability to constrain exchange rate fluctuations even as the financial system evolves so as to facilitate economic growth.

The most important internal factor that challenges the EMS is to accommodate to institutional changes that will accelerate the process of economic integration of the European Economic Community and deal with the greater economic interdependence that will result. The challenge emanating from the 'Single European Act' is based upon the paradox of complexity: more integration is called for in order to overcome monetary and real instability. The strategy using legislation to create 'dynamic disequilibria' (see Micossi, 1988), which force markets and official authorities to react, raises many questions about the stability and efficiency of the process. In particular, the integration of the European financial markets by liberalising capital markets will force changes in the EMS. The equilibrating process in the monetary structure will become more dependent upon short-run portfolio choices by private agents and may well force central banks to act in order to constrain instability. As a minimum, central banks may be required to deal in different types of assets (see Chapter 12) and the power of the central banks to make individual units behave so as to aid the maintenance of exchange stability will be tested.

A main external challenge facing the EMS comes from the potential instability of the world financial structure. It is not clear whether the

EMS is sufficiently resilient to adjust to an explosion of inflation or to a fall in the value of the dollar.

10 DIFFERENT STRATEGIES

The economic and social model of an emerging bloc, such as the European Community, may be defined concretely in terms of three broad categories of public policy (see Emerson, 1988, p. 2):

i) the regime for goods, services and capital markets
ii) the regime for macroeconomic policy management, and
iii) the regime for labour market and social policy.

Each of these aspects is relevant for the assessment of results thus far obtained, of targets to be pursued and strategies to be followed. Opinions may differ depending on which particular aspect is considered.

The plan to make Europe a fully-integrated trading area – a single market – has important monetary implications. Two contradictory propositions appear to emerge. First, the single market will imply less exchange rate stability because of the abolition of capital controls. After 1990 agents will be entirely free to transfer assets among different countries so that the balance of currency demand and supply will become more volatile and the exchange rate tend to fluctuate more, *ceteris paribus*. On the other hand, the full benefit of a single market will be realised only if greater exchange rate stability is achieved. Exchange rate instability is a bar to competition.

Three ways out of this contradiction can be identified. Each has its own costs and benefits. However, they are not easily comparable because, as has been pointed out earlier, both economic and political spheres are implicated.

These strategies are considered below:

a) The status quo

The alternative to greater potential volatility in currencies is a greater volatility of interest rates. Once liberalisation of capital movements is effective, expectations of currency realignments will cause a bigger rise in interest rates in the countries whose currencies come under pressure, and both interest rate and exchange rate volatility diminish the benefits of the single market. In the long run, a separate currency creates a separate economy, and economic integration between the various parts is bound to diminish. In analytical terms, one may say that maintenance of the status quo does not ensure stability for the system.

Only in a credible fixed exchange system is there no expectation of a currency realignment, so that there is no need for any change in the interest rate. This result can be achieved either by very strict monetary policy coordination or by a monetary union. The cost is the loss of independent monetary policy.

The limit of a convergent monetary policy is to adopt a common currency. If governments pursue this goal, they surrender national monetary control altogether and replace it with a uniform, region-wide policy. A merger-by-monies would bring about benefits to Europe of both a micro and a macro nature. In micro terms, a single currency is convenient and convenience breeds efficiency. The macro advantage would be the achievement of a lower inflation rate and greater financial stability.

However, another problem would arise. As *The Economist* (25 June 1988) has suggested:

> The present EMS leaves a member government the option of restoring a loss of competitiveness by devaluing its exchange rate.... Without national currencies, governments would have to do the same thing by letting market forces cut wages, or by letting labour migrate to more prosperous regions, or by some mixture of the two.... Tempting though the gains from a single currency are, irresistible though the capital market pressures may anyhow prove, Europe's single market adventure could crash for lack of new, Community-wide economic shock-absorbers. Without them, the strains of adjustment inside a one-currency zone might prove politically unbearable. Monetary integration, which is already underway, must henceforth go hand-in-hand with measures to improve mobility of labour within Europe and with procedures (preferably automatic) for letting resources flow from high- to low-growth parts of the EEC (p. 14).

There are two alternative strategies. One is pragmatic: developing what exists already. The other one is offered by the Federalists.

b) A pragmatic approach

Masera (1987)[4] identifies three main paths for the transition to a single market and a single currency, namely (see also Chapter 10 below):

i) the inclusion of all the countries participating in the EMS in a stricter, but not yet rigid, exchange rate mechanism that would promote the gradual stabilisation of exchange relations in Europe;
ii) a closer monetary policy and interest rate coordination, with the monetary effects of intervention not being sterilised;
iii) the integration of private and official markets for the ECU, which would come to play the role of real European currency both inside the area and in international relations, under the supervision and control of a European Monetary Fund.

In this strategy the distinction between forward and intermediate steps (towards a fuller union) remains blurred. It is based on the development of what already exists and it is in keeping with the EEC tradition. As *The Economist* (9 July 1988) has pointed out:

> Such a parallel ECU could provide the EEC with the appropriate, transitional money-system. There would be national, smoothly adjustable, means of payment for static workforces of differing greed and productivity. But there would also be an EEC-wide accounting unit (and store of value) that would make Europe-wide price lists and price comparisons easier, and afford protection, by averaging to those who used it. Until European central government has evolved a lot more, that will be about as far towards one-money America as the EEC can hope to move (p. 52).

The discipline of tighter monetary formation in the EMS will prove difficult for economically weak countries. In theory, their workforce might migrate, but this is not likely to happen. These countries could borrow, but not by printing their own money, and only from a world that has learnt about sovereign credit risk. This is the cost of the pragmatic approach.

c) The federalist approach

In federal countries, like the US for example, two mechanisms relieve the strain on the poorer states. People move out and fiscal relief moves in automatically. Somehow the EEC has to follow the same lines. Indeed, as *The Economist* (9 July 1988) put it: 'the extent to which this happens is probably the ultimate constraint on the degree of economic integration that Europe will find it politically possible to achieve' (p. 52).

Too diverse to become a federal community, too complex to remain only a simple exchange rate agreement, the European Community is looking for its identity in a pragmatic and innovative way.

11 THE DELORS REPORT

The final document of the Committee for the Study of Economic and Monetary Union, known as the Delors Report (1989), accepts the thesis that monetary union must be implemented in parallel with economic union.

> Monetary union without a sufficient degree of convergence of economic policies is unlikely to be durable and could be damaging to the Community. Parallel advancements in economic and monetary integration would be indispensable in order to avoid imbalances which could cause economic strains and loss of political support for developing the Community further into the economic and monetary union (para. 42).

The report proposes that this union should be achieved gradually in three stages. Only the first stage, the liberalisation of capital movements, has a precise date, i.e. July 1990. At this stage, governments would improve their policy coordination (on this point, see also Chapter 11 below) and the EEC countries not at present in the EMS would become full members. The second stage would see the building of a European central bank. This would require a change in the Treaty of Rome, and the EMS would become a more binding force on national monetary and fiscal policy. The final stage involves the fixing of exchange rates, i.e. the virtual elimination of national currencies. When this happens monetary policy passes to the new European central bank.

Two aspects of the process being set in motion should be mentioned. The first is that the EMS remains an important corner stone in the development of full economic integration. The second is that the remaining two steps, although temporally indeterminate, need to be implemented in order to demonstrate the irreversible nature of the move towards monetary union.

The Delors Report is a compromise between the so called 'institutionalist approach', which holds that changes in institutions must lead the process of economic integration, and the 'market approach', represented by the British government, which holds that monetary and political union are not necessary in order to achieve an economic union.

12 AN ASSESSMENT

Stage one of the Delors Report includes many of the suggestions that were listed under the gradualist approach. The first steps centre on completing the freeing of the internal market and the reduction of income and inflation disparities among the members. The monetary first steps emphasise 'removing all obstacles to financial integration and on intensifying co-operation and the co-ordination of monetary policies'. However, one important difference must be stressed between the Delors Report and the gradualist approach. The Delors Report contrasts its recommended sequence of steps leading to full integration with the 'parallel-currency' view of the gradualist approach which holds that the pace of transition to monetary union should be driven by the demand side. The Delors Report argues that the demand driven approach must be ruled out because 'an additional source of money creation without a precise linkage to economic activity could jeopardize price stability' (see also *The Economist*, 22 April 1989).

Even after attaining economic and monetary union, the Community would continue to consist of individual nations. For this reason it would not be possible simply to follow the example of federal states, such as the United States. The Delors Report recognises that it 'is necessary to develop an innovative and unique approach' for, as Jean Monnet pointed out long ago, 'the problem is not so much to identify the objective as to govern a process'.

It seems clear that the success of the EC and the monetary system rests upon the pragmatic approach to problems that have arisen. Adaptation and adjustment, rather than ideologically driven reforms, have served Europe well in the past thirty years. In the light of that pragmatic approach the future success of the EMS and its successors may be assured. The process of unification may well consist of steps that strengthen the cohesion of the system while gradually moving towards full economic and monetary union. This approach was confirmed by the summit held in Madrid in June 1989 where only the first step of the Delors Report was given a precise date – July 1990, i.e. simultaneously with the liberalisation of capital movements – without the irreversible nature of the other two steps having been accepted.

But monetary union is not an inevitable result of the process that is now in motion. Where the process leads will depend upon both the internal and the external factors. The internal factors that will affect the outcome mainly refer to distributive impacts that are linked to the process of creating a single market and to the ability of the Community to develop a social consensus on the targets of the process. The external factors depend upon the international environment within which the European Community will operate.

Whether the European Economic Community will be a protectionist fortress or a major building block of a multipolar open world[5] depends on what happens in the rest of the world and in particular in the Eastern European countries. Likewise it is difficult to foresee whether the evolutionary process now in motion will lead to a full monetary union, some intermediate partially integrated system, some form of national currency competition, as suggested by the British position, or a breakdown into national systems dominated by a unified Germany. Historical indeterminacy is nothing new. As we know, there has been a multitude of explanations offered to explain the fall of the Roman empire. It is no wonder that there are different opinions and many question marks about the economy and the monetary system of European in the near future.

Notes

1. For a discussion of this point see Bhandari and Putnam (1984).
2. Dates of realignments of the EMS are the following:
   13 March 1979, 24 September 1979, 30 November 1979, 23 March 1981, 5 October 1981, 22 February 1982, 14 June 1982, 21 March 1983, 22 July 1985, 7 April 1986, 4 August 1986, 12 January 1987. On 5 January a EMS realignment took place in the form of a restriction of the margins within which the lira could fluctuate relative to other currencies in the system (the band was narrowed to 2.25 per cent from 6 per cent).

   It is important to stress that when a realignment occurs, a currency's ECU central rate is redefined, and that the revaluations or devaluations of the currencies are designed to offset some or all of the changes in relative price levels. A recomposition of the ECU is different from a realignment; a

recomposition involves changing the actual number of units of each currency in defining the ECU.
3. A significant step towards this goal came with changes in the EMS mechanisms decided in September 1987 by the Committee of the EEC Central Bank Governors, and presented by the EEC Ministers of Finance at the informal meeting in Nyborg on 12 September 1987.
4. A survey of the various proposals for the transitional phase is to be found in CER (1988).
5. In this perspective, one can consider the EMS experience within the broader issues associated with the theory of optimum currency areas, started by Mundell (see De Cecco and Giovannini, 1989).

References

Bewley, R. and Kearney, C. (1988) 'A System Approach to Modelling the EMS Exchange Rate Mechanism', Paper presented at the European Economic Association, Bologna.

Bhandari, J.S. and Putnam, B.H. (eds) (1984) *Economic Interdependence and Exchange Rates* (Boston: MIT Press).

Bini Smaghi, L. and Vona, S. (1988) 'La coesione dello SME e il ruolo dei fattori esterni: un'analisi in termini di commercio estero', *Temi di Discussione*, Bank of Italy.

Catinat, M., Donni, E. and Italianer, A. (1988) 'The Completion of the Internal Market: Results of Macroeconomic Model Simulations', *EEC Economic Papers*, no. 65.

CER (1988) 'Lo SME 10 Anni Dopo', Rapporto, Rome.

Commission of the European Communities (1987) 'Second Report on the Implementation of the White Paper on the Completion of the Internal Market', COM(87), 203.

Committee For The Study of Economic and Monetary Union (1989) Report on the Economic and Monetary Union in the European Community, April.

De Cecco, M. and Giovannini, A. (eds) (1989) *A European Central Bank?* (Cambridge University Press).

Emerson, M. (1988) *What Model for Europe* (Boston: MIT Press).

Fitoussi, J.P. and Phelps, E.S. (1988) *The Slump in Europe* (Oxford: Blackwell).

Giavazzi, F. (1988) 'The European Monetary System. Lessons from Europe and Perspectives in Europe', mimeo.

Giavazzi, F., Micossi, S. and Miller, M. (eds) (1988) *The European Monetary System* (Cambridge: MIT Press).

Guerrieri, P. and Padoan, P.C. (eds) (1988) *L'Economia Politica dell'Integrazione Europea* (Bologna: Il Mulino).

Horn, H. and Persson, T. (1988) 'Exchange Rate Policy, Wage Formation and Credibility', *European Economic Review*, 32, 1621–36.

Leijonhufvud, A. (1987) 'Rational Expectations and Monetary Institutions' in M. de Cecco and J.-P. Fitoussi (eds) *Monetary Theory and Economic Institutions* (London: Macmillan).

Masera, R. (1986) 'An Increasing Role for The ECU', *Temi di Discussione*, no. 65, Bank of Italy.

Masera, R. (1987) *L'unificazione Monetaria e lo SME* (Bologna: Il Mulino).

Masera, R. (1987) 'European Currency: an Italian View', Strasbourg, mimeo.

Micossi, S. (1988) 'The Single European Market: Finance', *Banca Nazionale del Lavoro Quarterly Review*, 135–46.

Mundell, R.A. (1968) *International Economics* (New York: Macmillan).

Padoa Schioppa, T. (ed) (1987) *Efficiency, Stability and Equity. A strategy for the evolution of the economic system of the European Community* (Paris: Economica).

Padoan, P.C. (ed.) (1988) *Politiche Monetarie e Politiche di Bilancio nella CEE* (Bologna: Il Mulino).

Rogoff, K. (1985) 'Can Exchange Rate Predictability Be Achieved Without Monetary Convergence? Evidence from the EMS', *European Economic Review*, vol. 28, 93–115.

Russo, M. and Tullio, G. (1988) 'Monetary Policy Coordination Within the EMS: It There a Rule?', *Economic Papers*, no. 63.

The Economist (1988) 'A Survey of Europe's Internal Market', 9 July.

Von Furstenberg, G.M. (ed) (1983) *International Money and Credit: The Policy Roles* (Washington: International Monetary Fund).

Williamson, J. and Miller, M. (1988) 'The International Monetary System: An Analysis of Alternative Regimes', *European Economic Review*, vol. 32, 1031–47.

Wyplosz, C. (1988) 'Asymmetry in the EMS: Intentional or Systemic', European Economic Association, Bologna.

Part I
The Nature of the EMS

2 The EMS and other International Monetary Regimes Compared

Marcello de Cecco

> It was not the absence of historical records that left so many other chapters of English economic history to be first dealt with by foreigners. The main cause is to be found in the anti-historical bias of the dominant school of English official economists, most of them avowed disciples of that most unhistorical writer, David Ricardo. Their doctrinaire habits of thought, and their belief that they were in the possession of a set of 'principles' of universal application, led them to frown on historical research as at best a mere waste of time. No physician, worthy of the name, will prescribe without some knowledge, direct or inferred, of the history of the case under treatment. To the typical English economist, however, who claimed that his 'laws' were, would or should be (he was not quite clear about the tense) of world-wide pertinence, historical differences had no interest, and he relegated history to the antiquary. This, as we now see, is really the attitude of the quack.
>
> H.S. Foxwell; Preface to A. Andreades, *History of the Bank of England*, London, 1909.

The EMS is ten years old. Since its inception it has been subjected to intense scrutiny, which was at first aimed at discovering how it would influence national and international economic affairs, and whether the influence it would exercise would be good, bad or negligible. Most German academic and banking observers saw it as likely to wreak havoc in Europe and in the world. Some of them, like Roland Vaubel, attained heights of Wagnerian lyricism in describing the ways in which the EMS would corrupt German monetary virtue. Others, in other countries, were more dismissive. They thought the EMS would soon fail, not being able to stand the test of diverging monetary policies in its member countries.

After ten years, the EMS is alive and well. The fashionable question has thus become: Why did it succeed? And what exactly did it succeed in doing, beyond staying alive?

It thus becomes imperative to determine how the System works. This is mostly done these days by comparative analysis. The EMS, that is to say, is compared to other international monetary regimes. It seems to be convenient to compare it to the International Gold Standard and to the Bretton Woods system, on the strength of the fact that all three are managed exchange rate regimes, which emphasise exchange rate stability. To use an anthropomorphic simile, the question is: does this 10-year-old boy look like his father, the Bretton Woods system, or his great grandfather, the International Gold Standard? Or does it rather have the likeness of the family 'baddies', the Interwar system or Benign Neglect?

Writers usually begin by discarding the last two hypotheses, which have associations with very negative world events. And, having found to their satisfaction that the boy indeed resembles his more virtuous forebears (virtue obviously has something to do with luck, the luck of having coincided with two long periods of world economic prosperity, and 'therefore' of having contributed to them), they then begin to ask themselves whether the boy also shows signs of possessing some rather unsavoury features notoriously displayed by his two ancestors.

There is basically nothing very harmful in these exercises, in which most families find honest entertainment, and which can therefore be tolerated even when it is economists that indulge in them. The problem is, however, that the method used by economists for their comparative exercises is the one chastised by Foxwell in the above quotation, which reduces real life phenomena to stereotypes or even caricatures.

In what follows I shall attempt to compare these stereotypes, more nobly called logico-deductive models of alternative international monetary regimes, with what can be considered as more realistic images of how the latter really worked. I shall then proceed to compare my own images of the world with one another, and with others which may be thought to be more relevant.

It is necessary to begin by finding out what the EMS has been really like, how it has worked. Unlike the pre-1914 Gold Standard, but more like the inter-war Gold Standard, the Bretton Woods system, and the Latin Monetary Union (about all these regimes I shall have more to say later), the EMS can be defined as a cooperative effort, a negotiated international monetary system. It is the result of conscious drawing-board planning, implemented by international agreement. It is quite clear, however, that the original design of the EMS, the one contained in the articles of agreement establishing it, turned out to be very different from its real-world realisation, the EMS as we have seen it working in the last ten years.

It has been correctly pointed out that the designers of the EMS wanted it to be a symmetrical arrangement. This is clearly shown by the preoccupation with the ECU and the Divergence Indicator. Even the Italian insistence on a wide fluctuation band for the lira can be interpreted as an attempt to re-establish symmetry against the backdrop of other much stronger member economies. And Britain's decision to stay out can be seen as a deliberate decision not to join a club where there would be too much interference with one another's affairs, and where she could not lead.

As it turned out, reality has been very different from the scenario sketched in the Agreement. We know that official ECUs have been created in only very small amounts. That the Divergence Indicator has never come into real life. That the only thing that has counted have been bilateral exchange rates. That the D-Mark, far from being too strong for other and weaker members' currencies to bear, has experienced heavy real depreciation against them.

The divergence between the EMS of the Agreement and that of ten years of real life reinforces the opinion that an international monetary system must be considered as a process, which evolves from the time when the Agreement that establishes it is signed, sometimes taking completely unforeseen directions from those programmed for it by its planners. This is certainly a unifying feature of all systems which emerged as the result of conscious planning and formal agreement among states. Thus the EMS was consciously launched as an exercise in symmetry. It would have not been acceptable had it been otherwise. The balance of power in the European Community would not have allowed it.

The most popular exercise economists have engaged in since the EMS seemed to succeed as an exchange rate convergence mechanism has been to establish whether it developed from symmetry into asymmetry. Symmetrical international monetary systems are those where no country can be seen as the leader, the conductor of an ideal international orchestra, whose will must be forcibly accepted by other members of the system. Symmetrical systems derive their numeraire and their supply of liquidity either from the outside, as in metallic systems, or from an international agreement on liquidity creation. The proponents of the hypothesis which sees the EMS as an asymmetrical system, see it as a D-Mark area, one where the Deutsche Bundesbank establishes its own monetary objectives in total autonomy and other member countries accept them. Why they do is open to interpretation. Some writers maintain that they act in their own self-interest, because they want an anti-inflationary anchor, and their central banks not having sufficient international reputation as inflation fighters, they must borrow credibility from the Bundesbank. Others think that Europe more closely resembles the Bretton Woods system of the 1950s, with the Federal Republic having as much power in Europe now as the US used to have over the world then, and thus ruling by sheer market weight. It is also suggested that this was the way Great Britain ruled over the pre-1914 international monetary system, and that it was her relative economic decline that brought crisis and instability to the last decades of that period.

With reference to the first hypothesis, it can be said (and has been said) that many other countries, in Europe and elsewhere, have obtained results even superior to those obtained by the EMS countries without being part of it, and with the same level of sacrifice of real variables' growth. These countries did not borrow credibility or reputation from the Bundesbank, nor can their central banks be considered more credible as inflation fighters than those of the EMS members.

Has the Federal Republic ruled over the EMS by sheer displacement power? Did it make its wish the other EMS countries' command just by doing its own thing? This can hardly be the case. The economic size of the FRG, relative to that of its major EMS partners, is not large enough. It is not nearly similar to that of Britain in the 1870s or the US in the 1950s. And the percentage of its total exports to the other large EMS partners makes it much more vulnerable to the latters' economic policies, if we also remember how much larger a percentage of German GNP trade is, compared to the US.

Furthermore, while the US and Britain were the financial centres of their respective systems, this can hardly be said of Germany. Germany still has an intensely domestic financial system, one which is heterogeneous with respect to those of other EMS members and which Germany seems firmly intentioned to keep that way. To add even greater difference between the EMS, the Gold Standard and Bretton Woods, we must consider that both Britain and the US had sizeable trade deficits with the rest of the system, while they ran current account surpluses with it. The opposite seems to happen in the EMS. The FRG has huge trade surpluses with its EMS partners, and is only now experiencing a current account deficit. Previously it ran a surplus with the EMS on both accounts. The EMS thus cannot be said to have functioned as a solar system, run by a very powerful centre which keeps it together by its sheer power of attraction. It is much more appropriate to consider it as a regional joint-float agreement. It is much more a reaction than an alternative to something.

It would be thoroughly unrealistic to think that the numeraire of the EMS has been the D-Mark. While D-Mark reserves kept by EMS members have increased, so have those held in US dollars by the same countries, which were much larger than the D-Mark ones to begin with. Thus the *primum mobile* of the international monetary system has still firmly remained the US dollar, and the US monetary policy has firmly remained the monetary policy of the whole system. Evidence of this, of the subjection of EMS monetary policy to US monetary policy is the coincidence of business cycle phases of the two areas. The EMS had deflation when the US exported deflation, and began to revive and then bloom when the US began exporting the revival of demand it had originated within its own economic system by its own policy measures. We cannot say that we have noticed any real decoupling of EMS countries' main economic variables from the dynamics of US and world main economic variables. The US is still, during the ten years of EMS life, very much in charge of global (including the EMS) economic policy.

What has not been very clear in the analysis of those who have studied the EMS experience, is that the EMS countries had mainly regional objectives in mind when they agreed on a European joint float, to harmonise their reactions to the stimuli imparted to their economies and to the world economy, by US economic policies. After rather disastrous experiences in the decade of dollar devaluations and oil price shocks, when the large EMS countries had separate exchange rate policies, the centrifugal forces liberated by different exchange rate dynamics were threatening to scatter all the common policies of the European community, which were based on fixed exchange rates, thus dissolving twenty-five years of European trade integration. This was the real determinant of the EMS. Its member countries did not even consider the possibility that they would be able to go against the prevailing trends of the world economy, which were still set by US policy. They wanted only to organise a joint float against the dollar to keep the level of mutual integration they had achieved in twenty-five years of operation of the EEC free trade area. Their declared aim 'to create an area of monetary stability in Europe' meant just that. It was an important but limited target. And it succeeded only because thoroughly domestic considerations induced the American economic authorities to impose first deflation and then reflation on their own, and on the world, economy.

We cannot detect any real decrease in the degree of asymmetry which characterises the international monetary system that can be said to have occurred since, and because of, the inception of the EMS. The EMS countries cannot say that they have regained monetary sovereignty. Their monetary numeraire is still the dollar and is still as exogenous to their own sphere of decision as it ever was. If the US imposes deflation on itself, deflation it will bring to the rest of the world, including the EMS countries. When it brings expansion on itself, the world economy will expand, and the EMS countries will go along. All the EMS has managed to achieve is not to allow the very high level of trade integration that exists among its members and the common policies they have adopted, like the CAP, to be totally disrupted by an uncoordinated float of EMS currencies against the dollar, which would set in motion, as it did in the 1970s, a giant wave of arbitrage among all European markets, with a trail of instability resulting from it for the whole European economic system.

The EMS agreement, therefore, marked the end, rather than the beginning, of an independent European policy against the dollar. Before the EMS inception, the FRG had tried its solitary confrontation against US economic policy, and had, after a few years of interest rate wars, revaluation and the defeat represented by the locomotive experiment, decided that it could not risk a repetition of the attempt to have an independent economic policy. The EMS was ostracised by the Bundesbank and imposed by the German political authorities exactly because it represented the end of monetary autonomy vis-à-vis US monetary policy, not that of other European countries. The German political authorities, by starting the EMS, demonstrated that they had become aware that they could not have an independent monetary authority, when other large European countries pegged their currencies to the dollar. By forming the EMS the German political authorities accepted again the dollar as the numeraire, renounced to push the D-Mark in the role of global alternative to the dollar, as they had done in the seventies, and hid their defeat by agreeing with the French on a joint European float which would diminish the danger of disrupting the European Community implicit in the D-Mark policy of the 1970s.

With the EMS agreement, therefore, the German political authorities climbed down from a global monetary role to a regional one. They stopped their policy of confrontation against the dollar, agreed to go along the direction shown by US economic policy-makers, and concentrated on a monetary policy vis-à-vis other European countries which would allow them to keep their share of the European and world market for industrial products.

To get confirmation of this, let us just consider Italian exchange-rate policy before and after 1979. In the second half of the 1970s, the lira floated jointly with the dollar against the D-Mark. Italy maintained employment and investment levels and increased its share of exports. It had a trade surplus with Germany. After 1979, the lira was revalued against the mark, as was the dollar. The same happened to the French franc, but to a smaller degree. We could say that the French and the Italians never left the dollar area. It was Germany which, after the EMS agreement, re-entered it and accepted the hegemony of US economic policy. By letting the mark float jointly with the lira and the franc, German monetary authorities definitely closed their flirt with monetary independence. The relative up-valuations experienced by the lira and the franc in recent years only occurred because of the different sizes of the German, French and Italian foreign exchange markets, given the continuous presence of exchange controls in France and Italy. Had there been free capital movements, the lira and the franc would have certainly not up-valued against the mark as they did. Exchange controls were therefore very beneficial to the German competitive position in Europe. Their recent abolition, which has been acclaimed by Germany ought, on the contrary, to be seen with some dislike by the economic authorities of that country.

It is extremely unclear, therefore, whether the French and Italian monetary authorities have traded off their monetary independence from the Bundesbank against the latter's credibility and reputation. The French and the Italians inflated with the US and deflated with them when Volcker started his wild squeeze. They borrowed, like everybody else in the West, their credibility and reputation from the Federal Reserve, as they had done for the previous forty years. And they allowed themselves to reflate when the Fed inverted its policy stance. So did the much vaunted Bundesbank, which in the 1970s had tried to navigate independently and almost sank in a sea of unemployment and falling world export shares. This is, I believe, a more realistic interpretation of EMS history than the ones which circulate more widely. The EMS marked the surrender of the neo-Faustian German dream to have a world role again and its demotion to the rank of regional power. The same did not happen to Japan, which has kept growing into its new world role by accepting to up-value the yen against the dollar and by conditioning the US through its holdings of short- and long-term US government and private assets. It would be interesting to make a comparative analysis of German and Japanese economic policies in the 1970s and in the 1980s.

Having restored the EMS (and the mark) to a less inflated role in the world, we may now be able to compare it with other international monetary systems with a chance of being more realistic. From what I have said above it must be clear that I do not believe the EMS can be usefully compared to a global monetary system like the Bretton Woods system. The EMS is based on stable exchange rates among its members. So was the Bretton Woods system. But, unlike Bretton Woods, the EMS is a regional system, while Bretton Woods covered the whole non-communist world. It is true that many countries in the Bretton Woods system did not manage to keep their currencies stable against the dollar, but all those of the industrial world pretty much did, if we disregard the isolated devaluations of the French franc and the British pound, and the one revaluation of the mark.

The Bretton Woods system was nominally based on gold, but in reality only the dollar was pegged to gold, while all other currencies were pegged to the dollar. The dollar was thus the *de facto* numeraire of the system, which rendered the world liquidity supply endogenous. But, *de jure*, the final numeraire was still gold, and countries could still hold gold reserves. I am not going to examine the internal contradictions which beleaguered that system and brought it to its final demise in 1971.I only want to emphasise its 'global' span.

The EMS is on the contrary a regional monetary system, spanning a Community of nations highly integrated by trade and common economic policies, like the CAP. It is a system which was born with the potential for a numeraire, the ECU, and a central bank, the Fecom, but which in reality has continued to use an exogenous numeraire, the dollar, supplied by an exogenous central bank, the United States Federal Reserve. The EMS was founded to stabilise its members' exchange rates against one another, because it was felt that, by floating independently against the traditional numeraire, they were disrupting the real integration of the European economies, obtained as a result of twenty-five years of efforts. The joint European float (alias the EMS) was thus formed to save the Common Market and the common policies of the EC.

As a result of the EMS, the international monetary world of the last ten years has curiously come to resemble that of the last three decades of the nineteenth century. The gradual weakening of British power rendered that world much more symmetrical than it used to be. Gold and silver were fighting to determine which one of them would become the global numeraire. This had been a perennial fight lasting literally thousands of years, but in the last decades of the nineteenth century the fight looked like coming to a definitive conclusion, as silver started what looked like an irreversible fall.

In the 1860s things had looked very different. Silver had been revaluing against gold, because of the gold sales effected by the United States civil war governments. Four European countries, France, Italy, Belgium and Switzerland, which had enjoyed a very high degree of trade, financial and monetary integration, had reacted differently to the depreciation of gold by decreasing in different degrees the silver content of their subsidiary coins. This resulted in huge arbitrage, with a tendency for good coins to disappear, leaving the countries which coined them in a state of currency shortage. Economic integration was thus threatened by policies which were independent national reactions to an exogenous problem, the fall of the gold–silver parity, over which individual nations had no control.

The Latin Monetary Union was the joint solution found to the problem by the four countries. They thought that by reiterating their stance on the 1 to $15\frac{1}{2}$ gold/silver parity, by agreeing on a uniform silver content for all their national divisional coins, and by fixing the respective national supplies of divisional coins, they would manage to save their long dated *de facto* economic and monetary integration. The treaty establishing the Latin Monetary Union, signed in 1865, was to last until the 1920s. It created an asymmetrical system, in the sense that France was, as it had been before, the centre country of the Union, and that the Bank of France was the lender of last resort for the whole Union. By the formation of the Union, Europe was divided into two halves, one monometallic based on gold and centred around Great Britain, the other based on silver monometallism and consisting of the Russian and Hapsburg Empires, united by the Latin Union, which was bimetallic. For five years it looked like the bimetallic solution might be extended to the monometallic halves, but the French defeat at Sedan put a stop to that trend, and ushered in an era of gradual gold prevalence, especially after Germany, reinforced by the French war indemnity, adopted the Gold Standard and started selling massive amounts of silver. This caused the price of silver to precipitate, because the selling occurred just when new silver mines were discovered in the United States and technical progress reduced the cost of silver extraction.

Ever since 1870 current historical interpretation has seen the Gold Standard as going from strength to strength, gradually conquering the whole civilised world. That is not exactly what happened. The world experienced in the next three decades a veritable flood of silver, coming from the American mines, and a ruinous fall of its market price. The two main monetary areas of Europe reacted differently to this structural and continuous fall of the gold/silver parity. The gold standard area, led by Britain, adopted a policy of benign neglect with respect to the price of silver. The bimetallic area, led by France, attempted to regulate the fall, by a series of *ad hoc* policies, which were adopted in agreements achieved with difficulty among the members of the Latin Union. The best-known of these policies was the decision, taken in the second half of the 1870s, to close the mints to the private coinage of silver. This measure effectively managed to bring to a halt the German sales of silver, by inflicting terrible losses on the German Exchequer, which had to sell silver at heavily reduced prices. Thus the German policy of adopting a pure gold standard was stopped in its tracks. Germany, though it formally was on gold, kept a very large silver circulation.

As was clear to contemporary observers, the Latin Monetary Union policies to amortise the fall of silver by providing a series of successive shock absorbers were a very important parachute to the ruinous fall of prices which characterised the two decades of the world depression, a depression from which Europe was not to emerge before the middle 1890s. Had the Latin Union also adopted a benign neglect attitude towards the gold/silver parity, world prices would have slumped much more heavily. When, in the last twenty years of the pre-1914 international monetary system, there was a world convergence towards gold, it was left to India and China to absorb the whole of world silver, and those stocks were forcibly imposed on them by the developed world. Deflation was avoided only because gold started being mined in South Africa in huge amounts.

The persistence of two monetary blocs in the last decades of the nineteenth century seems to bear an interesting resemblance to the most recent ten years of international monetary history. We have a regional monetary union forming to protect the economic integration of its members against recurrent fluctuations in the gold/silver parity, i.e. against exogenous shocks which threaten the stability of economic relations among the Union members. The depth and recurrence of these shocks, moreover, exercise strong centrifugal forces on the Union, which manages, however, to survive into the twentieth century by a series of ad hoc measures and by the preparedness of the Bank of France to serve as lender of last resort for other members, and to try to smooth the fluctuations of the price of silver. Another interesting feature of the world monetary system of those decades is the role played by the United States. Even then, it was a heavily destabilising factor in the world economy, because it flooded the world with agricultural produce and silver, and adopted mutually contradictory policies, like going on the gold standard and conducting stop and go official silver purchases at the same time. Another interesting feature of that period is the behaviour of Germany, which wanted to adopt the Gold Standard to form a monetary bloc with Great Britain, but could only half do so, because France very effectively sabotaged German silver sales and managed to induce Bismarck to stop them.

The Latin Union, however, was rather different from the EMS. The Bank of France came to the rescue of member central banks by accepting to provide them with gold against their silver whenever they felt pressure on their reserves and ought to have raised their discount rates, thus sacrificing, by the resulting decrease in their loans, the level of economic activity in their countries. Moreover, France had a visible trade deficit with the other member countries of the Union matched by a current account surplus with them. Finally, France fully accepted, for an extended period, lower silver content Italian coins on her territory, thus giving Italy the power of determining, to a certain extent, French money supply.

The comparison with the German role in the EMS is somewhat damning for Germany. France can be said to have headed a Union which helped, through its silver policies, to head off the worst effect of the world depression which lasted almost twenty years, and which would have been far worse if the inconsiderate policies of the two main gold countries, Britain and Germany, had been left to work themselves out unfettered on the European and world economy. The famed stability of exchange rates which characterised the European currencies in the second half of the nineteenth century would probably not have been achieved had the Latin Union not been there to stabilise silver prices and to prevent silver countries, like the Russian and Hapsburg Empires, from adopting monetary policies even more drastic than the ones they were compelled to take because of the fall in the price of silver.

The Latin Monetary Union, in conclusion, played a very positive role in the international monetary world of the late nineteenth century. Can the same be said of the EMS? I leave the answer to this last question to other authors.

3 The EMS: Lessons from Europe and Perspectives in Europe*

Francesco Giavazzi

1 INTRODUCTION

When the EMS was launched in 1978, the new plan for exchange rate stability in Europe was accepted with much scepticism. Policy-makers were still influenced by the collapse of Bretton Woods, and concentrated on learning how to live with flexible exchange rates. Because economists were also attempting to understand the working of flexible exchange rates, there was no analysis of the EMS until the mid-1980s. Now the situation is quite different. The conventional wisdom is that the EMS has been a success, and the debate in Europe has moved on to the issue of monetary unification and the European central bank. Outside Europe, the reform of the international monetary system is no longer an unfashionable topic: 'target zones', and the simple return to fixed exchange rates, have taken centre stage in policy discussions and, to some extent, in economic analysis.[1]

There are three views on the future of the international monetary system. Two of them advocate reforms which would limit the degree of exchange rate flexibility; a third concentrates on 'fundamentals', and rules out the active management of exchange rates. Ronald McKinnon (see for example McKinnon, 1988) is responsible for the first set of proposals. He argues for fixed nominal exchange rates. The system he envisages is very similar to a symmetric gold standard: central banks would use domestic credit policies to peg the price of a common basket of internationally traded goods. Fiscal policy would target external balance: deficits and surpluses would be corrected by changes in the level of spending in the various countries, at given relative prices.

The second proposal, 'target zones', was originally formulated by John Williamson (1985), and later elaborated in Miller and Williamson

*I am especially indebted to Alberto Giovannini, for I draw freely in this chapter on material contained in our book (1989a).

(1988) and the Croham Committee (1988). The central point of the plan is the assignment of monetary policy to a real exchange rate target: interest rate differences among countries keep the real effective exchange rate of each country within a preassigned band. Nominal variables (nominal GDP) are controlled by the average level of world real interest rates, and by domestic fiscal policy in each country.

A radically different view seems to be favoured by the staff of the International Monetary Fund. It begins with the premise that 'a reform of the international monetary system should be viewed as a constitutional change that should not be taken lightly, [... and] not viewed as an instrument for crisis management' (Frenkel, 1987, p. 11). Policy-makers should concentrate on eliminating the 'fundamental' sources of imbalance in the world economy: 'the use of monetary policy to sustain exchange rate stability has definite drawbacks as a longer term strategy, and monetary policy is no more than a temporary substitute for changes in underlying fiscal positions' (IMF, 1987, p. 17).

In the debate that surrounds these proposals, the EMS experience is often referenced. Some – McKinnon, for instance – point to the success of the system at limiting exchange rate volatility. Others – Miller and Williamson – point to the evidence indicating that the EMS has operated as a DM-zone demonstrating how difficult it is to build symmetric exchange rate regimes. Still others – Fischer (1987a) – point to the apparently crucial role played by capital controls in keeping the system together.

These frequent references to the EMS have lacked so far a review of the system aimed at identifying which lessons – if any – one can draw from this experiment at limiting exchange rate flexibility. Analyses of the EMS have been limited to Europe, and have never been brought to bear on the wider question of world monetary arrangements. This is one of the aims of this chapter.

Two issues seem of particular relevance. First is the issue of symmetry, that is the formal resolution of the so-called *n*-1 problem. Mundell (1968, p. 195) pointed out the importance of this problem in any plan for the reform of the international monetary system, and Frenkel (1987) has recently reminded us: 'it is essential to ask how the various proposals, including those for target zones, deal with the extra degree of freedom.' The second issue is the contraints – if any – that the exchange rate system imposes upon domestic policies, and upon inflation in particular. The issue of 'discipline' was central in discussions over the reform of the Bretton Woods system in the 1960s, and has been raised recently by Fischer (1988).

This chapter is divided into two parts. In the first I ask what lessons can we draw from the EMS experience that may be relevant for the reform of the international monetary system. Sections 2.1 and 2.2 discuss symmetry and discipline, respectively; Section 2.3 draws the main conclusions. The second part of the chapter looks at the prospects in Europe; in Section 3.1 I discuss European public finances; in Section 3.2 I analyse the effects of the two major developments in Europe since the beginning of the EMS: the enlargement of the Community and the Single European Act.

2 CAN THE EMS SERVE AS A BLUEPRINT FOR THE REFORM OF THE INTERNATIONAL MONETARY SYSTEM?

2.1 The gold standard, Bretton Woods and the EMS

A central feature of any operational monetary system must be a solution of the n-1 problem – namely a solution for the problem that in a system of n interdependent countries (and n currencies), only N-1 policies can be set independently, and therefore one policy instrument is redundant. The problem has a symmetric and an asymmetric solution. The symmetric solution *par excellence* is flexible exchange rates: each country sets its own monetary policy independently, and exchange rates are endogenous. Whenever countries actively manage their exchange rates, the consistency between the n-1 targets and the n instruments can be achieved symmetrically or asymmetrically. In the symmetric solution, each central bank uses domestic credit policies to peg the price of a basket of goods in units of domestic currency, and abstains from sterilising reserve flows. If exchange rates are fixed, central banks must peg similar baskets, ideally to the price of a single good – for example, gold.

In an asymmetric system, the centre country pegs the price of a good (or a basket) in units of its own currency: all other countries peg the bilateral exchange rate vis-à-vis the centre country. If exchange rates are fixed, the peripheral countries relinquish all monetary autonomy. In a managed exchange rate system, the possibility of changing the bilateral exchange rate vis-à-vis the centre country gives the others some leeway in the pursuit of independent monetary policy.[2]

The current proposals for reform of the international monetary system all envisage symmetric solutions to the n-1 problem. The McKinnon plan resembles a symmetric gold standard. The 'target zones' proposal also calls for symmetry in the management of world monetary policy: 'We reject both the idea that any one country should in effect use the level of world interest rates solely for its own purposes, or that the latter should emerge as a result of a set of decentralized decisions by separate countries' (Croham Committee, 1988, p. 50). These blueprints of symmetric exchange rate systems contrast sharply with the historical experience.

Bretton Woods

In the Bretton Woods system the *n*-1 problem was solved asymmetrically. Although the numeraire of the system was gold, and thus there was the theoretical possibility of affecting all countries' exchange rates independently by changing their gold price, the *dollar* price of gold was very much regarded as the cornerstone of the system. A change in the dollar/gold parity was considered a *de facto* abandonment of the system. The role of the dollar contrasted with the ability that countries other than the United States had to change their exchange rates. After the abandonment of the 'gold pool', in 1968, the Bretton Woods system evolved into a *dollar standard*: a system in which the United States would choose domestic policies with a view to domestic objectives, while the other countries pegged to the dollar, retaining the right to change their peg.

The International Gold Standard

The gold standard that operated from the late 1870s to World War I also worked asymmetrically. Triffin (1947, pp. 58–64) argues that the system was less similar to the classical gold standard than it was to a sterling-exchange standard managed by the Bank of England – at least in the years from 1870 to 1890. The 1931 Committee on Finance and Industry concluded that Britain could 'by operation of her bank rate almost immediately adjust her reserve position. Other countries had, therefore, in the main to adjust their conditions to hers.' In an econometric study of the international gold standard Giovannini (1986) also shows that the data are not consistent with the hypothesis that the Bank of England followed the 'rules of the game' by using domestic credit policies to minimise the volatility of international gold flows. In the case of the Reichsbank, on the contrary, the hypothesis that it followed the rules of the game can not be rejected.

The European Monetary System

The EMS provides one more example of a managed exchange rate regime that has worked asymmetrically. Although 'symmetry' was the word most frequently pronounced at the Bremen and Brussels summits of June and December 1978 where the EMS was created, and notwithstanding rules designed with the explicit purpose of 'sharing the burden of adjustment', the system has worked effectively as a DM-zone. Germany by and large has retained the ability to set monetary policy independently; the other countries have pegged to the DM. The conclusion that the EMS has worked as a DM-zone is supported by four empirical observations:[3]

i) The institutional features that were designed to achieve symmetry in the exchange rate mechanism of the EMS did not work appropriately. The *divergence indicator* is unbalanced, contains currencies outside the EMS and, most importantly, it does not bind member central banks to any action.[4]

ii) The *rules for exchange market intervention* were designed with the explicit purpose of 'sharing the burden of adjustment': intervention at the margin – when two currencies reach the limit of the bilateral fluctuation band – is compulsory, it has to be carried out by both central banks involved, using each other's currency, and is supported by the Very Short Term Financing Facility. Table 3.1 reports cumulative intervention figures as percentages of total intervention by all countries, in the period from January 1983 to April 1986. From January 1983 to March 1985, there was a general appreciation of the dollar on an effective basis.[5] In the second period, from April 1985 to April 1986, there was a downward trend of the dollar effective exchange rate index.[6] The three panels of the table contain data on intervention at the margin of bilateral fluctuation bands (which is carried out in EMS currencies), on intramarginal intervention in EMS currencies, and on dollar intervention, respectively. The table shows that the two countries most involved in intervention at the margin were Belgium and France. The negative signs in Table 3.1 indicate a *sale* of foreign exchange by the central bank: for example, the first figure for Belgium [(—)0.554] indicates that the Belgian central bank undertook 55.4 per cent of all marginal interventions carried out between January 1983 and March 1985. The sign is negative, indicating that during this period the Belgian franc frequently hit the bottom of the band relative to another currency in the system. This currency was often the French franc: over the same

Table 3.1 Central bank intervention in the EMS

	Jan. 1983–Mar. 1985	*Apr. 1985–Apr. 1986*
Marginal intervention (in EMS currencies)		
Germany	(−)0.093	(−)0.031
Netherlands	(−)0.039	(−)0.108
France	0.313	0.861
Italy	0.000	0.000
Belgium	(−)0.554	0.000
Intramarginal intervention (in EMS currencies)		
Germany	0.000	0.000
Netherlands	0.006	0.051
France	0.637	(−)0.647
Italy	0.073	(−)0.079
Belgium	0.283	(−)0.224
Intervention in $US		
Germany	(−)0.645	(−)0.076
Netherlands	(−)0.009	0.092
France	(−)0.303	0.142
Italy	0.012	(−)0.592
Belgium	(−)0.030	(−)0.097
Summary		
Intervention at margin	0.196	0.429
Intramarginal intervention	0.196	0.250
Dollar intervention	0.608	0.321

Notes: The data used to construct this table are cumulative intervention figures expressed in $US. Negative signs indicate foreign exchange sales by the central bank of the corresponding country. Each entry represents the share of intervention of that country in the total volume of intervention during the given interval, that is in the sum of the absolute values of the entries of that column.

Source: Giavazzi and Giovannini (1988a, ch. 4).

period the *Banque de France* was responsible for sizeable interventions (31.3 per cent of the total) in the opposite direction. Notice that the Bank of Italy, which enjoyed a wider fluctuation band, never intervened at the margin.

The second panel reports data on intramarginal intervention. It shows that on average Germany – at least during the years reported in our table – has kept no positions in other EMS currencies for the purpose of intervention. This strongly suggests that Germany might not intervene in the EMS when the DM is within the bilateral fluctuation bands of its partner currencies.

The other important piece of evidence on intramarginal intervention comes from the bottom panel of the table: intramarginal intervention is as significant in volume as intervention at the margin, and intervention *vis-à-vis* the dollar.[7] In the second panel, we can see that the direction of intramarginal intervention changed between the first and the second sub-periods. The strength of the dollar between 1983 and 1985 was associated with a weak D-mark within the EMS: Table 3.1 shows that all the other central banks in the system were purchasing D-marks. After April 1985, when the dollar started falling, the signs in the table change: a weak dollar was associated with a strong DM inside the EMS; all other central banks (with the exception of the Netherlands) intervened selling D-marks.

The third panel of the table reports dollar intervention. The large dollar sales by the Bundesbank, especially during the period of dollar appreciation, might have been motivated by the objective of avoiding the strains within the EMS associated with fluctuations of the dollar exchange rate.[8] With the data in Table 3.1, however, we cannot determine whether dollar intervention by the Bundesbank was motivated by the desire to avoid exchange rate strains in the EMS or by the desire to avoid big fluctuations in relative prices with a large trading partner – the United States – along with the assumption that other European authorities would accommodate.

The important lesson from Table 3.1 is that the burden of EMS-related intervention was shared very unevenly among EMS countries: most of the intramarginal intervention was carried out by countries other than Germany, while Germany intervened only when bilateral fluctuation margins were reached.

iii) The strongest evidence in support of the hypothesis that the EMS actually worked as a DM area comes from the study of *interest rates*. West German interest rates are unaffected by most intra-EMS shocks, like the expectations of parity realignments, while interest rates denominated in other currencies are those that suffer the full impact of intra-EMS portfolio disturbances. Countries like Italy and France, however, have prevented the wide fluctuations in their own interest rates observed in the (unregulated) Euro-markets from affecting their domestic economies by imposing capital controls. This evidence is similar to that of the gold standard and the Bretton Woods period, when countries other than Great Britain and the United States, respectively, sought to defend their policies from the influence of the 'centre' country by imposing various forms of regulatory hurdles on the international transmission of monetary policies.

iv) The data on *exchange rate movements around EMS realignments* show that at the time of a realignment the DM appreciates vis-à-vis its EMS partners in the majority of cases. However, the DM value outside of the EMS is hardly affected by what happens within Europe. This is consistent with the view that EMS realignments – to the extent that they affect spot exchange rates – are centred around the DM.

2.2 Inflation and the exchange rate regime

An international monetary system may work asymmetrically because of the efficiency of solving the overdeterminacy associated with the *n*-1 problem by allocating to one country the task of providing the 'nominal anchor' for the whole system. The centre country should be chosen from those whose monetary authorities have the highest 'anti-inflationary reputation'. This often is referred to as the 'discipline' argument for fixed exchange rates.

The 'discipline' argument dates back to Mundell's (1968) 'optimal burden of adjustment' argument.[9] More recently, it has acquired new fame – along with the emergence of a new and influential view of the inflation process. Inflation is simply the inefficient outcome of a non-cooperative 'game' between the public and the monetary authorities. If inflation is just a source of inefficiency, then the inflation standard in an international monetary system should be set by the country where the 'game' produces the least inefficiency: that is the lowest equilibrium rate of inflation. Thus there is an incentive to build monetary areas centred around low inflation countries.

The view rests on the assumption that the exchange rate system can influence inflationary expectations, because exchange rate targets are more credible than monetary targets. This remains an empirical question. Professional views of the role of the exchange rate regime in a disinflation, and the actual experiences, differ widely. On one hand, experiences such as the Latin American 'new style' IMF plans, where the exchange rate was used to stop very high inflation rates, were viewed as negative. Critics (for example Dornbusch, 1982) pointed to the disruptive effects of the large appreciation of the real exchange rate, that eventually became unsustainable, and to the lack of credibility of the exchange rate targets. On the other hand, Bruno (1986) suggests that exchange rate policy might have had an important role in the successful Israeli stabilisation. The positive role of exchange rate policy in the Bolivian stabilisation is also stressed by Sachs (1986).

In the case of the EMS experience, the general perception is that the exchange rate regime helped the high-inflation countries. Fischer (1987) describcs the EMS as 'an arrangement for France and Italy to purchase a commitment to low inflation by accepting German monetary policy'. Even in countries considering EMS membership, the main advantages of membership are associated with Germany's reputation. *The Economist* (21 September 1985) wirtes: 'If sterling does join, the biggest change will be the transfer of responsibility for Britain's monetary policy from the Bank of England to the Bundesbank which, as the central bank keenest on sound money, sets the pace for others to follow. This would be a blessing: Tory governments may like appointing City gents as governors of the Bank, but Mr. Karl Otto Poehl would do a better job.' The *Financial Times* (28 September 1987) writes: 'In place of money supply targetry, long since discredited, we would have that unflinching guardian of monetary rectitude, the Bundesbank, standing as guarantor against Britain's endemic propensity to generate double-figure rates of inflation.'

What is the evidence? The EMS has worked as a DM-zone: according to the 'discipline view' we would expect the low inflation propensity of the Bundesbank to have shifted inflation expectations downward in the other countries. Table 3.2 compares inflation rates of various European countries at the start of the EMS with the present. The table suggests both the presence of significant convergence of European inflation rates towards the West German levels, and a general decrease of inflation, which is not limited to the countries belonging to the EMS. Since the conclusion of the preceding section is that West Germany's

Table 3.2 European disinflation (GDP deflator: annual growth, percentage)

	1978	*1987*
Belgium	4.3	2.1
Denmark	9.9	4.6
France	9.5	3.3
Germany	4.3	2.1
Ireland	10.5	2.9
Italy	13.9	5.5
Netherlands	5.4	− 1.0
United Kingdom	11.3	4.0

Source: *European Economy*.

monetary policy has been at the centre of the EMS, and since West German authorities built a wide reputation as 'inflation fighters' in the second postwar period, the natural question raised by this experience is whether the structure and working of the EMS, and in particular the central role played by the German monetary authorities, have played any role in the disinflation experience of countries as different as Denmark, France and Italy. In Giavazzi and Giovannini (1988a, ch. 5) we have attempted to measure empirically the effects of the EMS on the dynamics of inflation in member countries. The results appear to broadly agree with the popular presumptions, but the evidence of a shift in expectations associated with the institution of the EMS is very weak. Inflationary expectations seem to have adjusted with a long lag: two to three years. One explanation might be that learning takes time. Another and more appealing explanation is that some European governments used the EMS to justify unpopular domestic policies. These policies, in turn, shifted expectations.

Using the exchange rate regime to justify being tough is an indirect, albeit effective, way to impose discipline. If it worked in Europe – and our evidence suggests that it might have – then it did so under two *very special* circumstances. First, the EMS is just one element of a much richer set of agreements among European countries in the trade, industrial, and agricultural areas. As I discuss in Section 3.2 these agreements rest on exchange rate stability, and thus lend credibility to exchange rate targets.

The other reason why the EMS may have shifted inflationary expectations is capital controls. By allowing 'weak-currency' countries to fend off speculative attacks against the reserves of the central bank, capital controls have performed two important functions in the EMS. They have avoided realignments during periods of crisis in the system – for example, when the dollar falls. Episodes of dollar weakness are often associated with a crisis in the EMS: in the absence of capital controls, it would be difficult to sustain existing parities. Second, capital controls have enabled central banks to delay parity realignments during the disinflation. This has been a crucial factor in forcing inflation convergence, because the discipline that the EMS imposes upon its high inflation members depends crucially on the interval between successive realignments being sufficiently long. If high inflation countries had been forced to realign as soon as higher-than-average inflation (combined with the rigidity of the nominal exchange rate) started hurting competitiveness, then the system would have been indistinguishable from a crawling-peg: all discipline gains would have vanished.[10]

We conclude that despite its popularity, the view that European countries may have joined the EMS simply to buy the anti-inflationary reputation of the Bundesbank is quite narrow. First of all, the discipline argument certainly was not prominent when the EMS was designed. By neglecting the incentives to stabilise intra-European exchange rates, the reputation view overlooks the main motivations that brought about the establishment of the EMS.

Moreover, the reputation view fails to explain Germany's incentives. What did Germany gain from the discipline it provided to the rest of Europe? There is no general explanation for the incentives of the centre country. Models of credibility and reputation are suggestive of the reasons why inflation-prone countries may want to belong to a monetary area centred around a low-inflation country, but do not explain the incentives of the centre country. A tentative explanation for why Germany might have accepted this role is suggested by the observation of real exchange rates. By joining the EMS, Germany seems to have achieved more stability in its real effective exchange rate. EMS membership has dampened the effects on the German economy of extreme dollar–DM fluctuations. This has happened because, since the beginning of the EMS, European currencies on average have kept closer to the DM, thus contributing to the stabilisation of Germany's global competitiveness. This is the opposite of what happened in the early 1970s, when the fall of Bretton Woods was accompanied by an appreciation of the Deutsche mark *both* in Europe and *vis-à-vis* the United States. This evidence provides some support for the 'European Alliance' view of the EMS: the interest that Germany had in the creation of the system was 'to limit the detrimental effects of dollar disturbances' (Thiel, 1987, p. 17).

2.3 Summing up: is the EMS exportable?

In this section I have reviewed the experience of the EMS to identify the lessons that this experiment in monetary coordination could provide to those who are considering a reform of the international monetary system. Policy coordination, and the successful attempt at making exchange rate targets credible, are sometimes hailed as important European achievements and examples for experiments outside of Europe as well. This view should be taken with caution:

1. The degree of *policy coordination* probably has been higher in the EMS than under Bretton Woods, particularly during realignments

However, coordination has never been extended to the area of monetary policy targets. As a result, the EMS operates essentially as a Deutsche mark zone, in a way that is not very different from the Bretton Woods system.

2. The *credibility of exchange rate targets* has been enhanced under two very special conditions, unlikely to be reproduced outside Europe:

(i) intra-European agreements, and the EC common agricultural policy in particular, rely on the stability of intra-European exchange rates. Leaving the EMS is perceived in Europe as a move that would question the survival of other EC institutions as well. These institutions have played an important part in lending credibility to exchange rate targets;
(ii) capital controls also have played a major role in making exchange rate targets credible, by severely limiting the possibility of speculative attacks against central banks' reserves.

3. WHAT NEXT FOR EUROPE?

3.1 European public finances and the exchange rate regime

The imported reputation argument discussed in Section 2.2 relies on the assumption that inflation is only a source of inefficiency, arising from the information costs of nominal price volatility. However, there are other important aspects of the cost-benefit analysis of inflation. One is the role of inflation in public finance, which might be particularly relevant for European countries.[11]

Inflation is an important source of government revenue. Inflation should thus be thought of as one element in an optimal tax problem, namely the problem of raising a given amount of revenue at the lowest cost in terms of welfare. In solving this problem, the distortions induced by inflation should be traded off with those induced by regular taxes.

The extent to which governments generate revenue through the seignorage attached to money creation varies across Europe. Table 3.3

Table 3.3 The importance of seignorage among total tax revenues in Europe

	Tax revenues excluding seignorage (% GDP)		*Seignorage (% of seignorage plus total tax revenues)*	
	1979–86	*1986*	*1979–86*	*1986*
Portugal	30.6	32.4	10.0	4.2
Greece	32.2	36.7	9.6	7.3
Spain	2.9	30.4	9.3	4.9
Italy	32.9	36.2	6.4	3.5
Ireland	36.8	40.2	2.3	0.9
France	42.9	44.2	1.3	−0.6
Germany	37.6	37.5	0.7	1.4
Belgium	45.2	45.4	0.4	0.8
Netherlands	45.5	45.5	0.9	0.6
Denmark	46.7	50.6	0.9	−4.9
U.K.	37.2	39.0	0.8	0.3

Sources and definitions:
Seignorage is the change in the monetary base (line 14 from: International Monetary Fund, *International Financial Statistics*), as in Fischer (1983). *Tax revenues* are from the OECD: *Revenue Statistics of OECD Member Countries*, Paris, OECD, 1988. They refer to total tax revenues, including taxes on personal and corporation income, employers' and employees' Social Security contributions, property taxes, consumption taxes, and excises.

documents the importance of seignorage among the sources of government revenue in the EC. The data show clearly that the countries where seignorage revenue is the highest are also the countries where the revenue from other forms of taxation is the lowest. Seignorage accounts for 10 per cent of total government revenue in Portugal, 9 per cent in Greece and Spain, 6 per cent in Italy, 2.3 per cent in Ireland; these are also the countries where the share of tax revenue (net of seignorage) in GDP is the lowest. In the rest of Europe, seignorage accounts for one per cent at most of the total revenue.

Low tax revenues often reflect the structure of the economy; it is not clear that they could be raised very fast. They are often associated with a narrow tax base, rather than with lower-than-average tax rates. In discussing the Greek economy, for example, the OECD writes:

> There is [in Greece] a relatively heavy tax burden on incomes and transactions that are easily taxable (wages and salaries, purchases of cars and some consumer durables, real estate and inheritance transactions). Tax evasion and avoidance are partly responsible,

but the most important factor is the structure of the economy characterised by a large share of agriculture in GDP (18%), and of self-employment in the non-agricultural labour force (33%) (OECD, *Economic Survey of Greece*, 1987).

The case of Portugal is similar: 'Low tax yield is attributable to the narrowness of the tax-base, which is not unrelated to the high marginal tax-rates' (OECD, *Economic Survey of Portugal*, 1986). The inflation tax may also be the only way of taxing economic activity in the underground economy. In some countries a substitution of seignorage for other forms of taxation may not be possible without further adding to the distortions of the tax system. Differences in fiscal structures thus justify differences in the 'optimal' revenue from seignorage. It is unlikely that with an unchanged fiscal structure and in the absence of fiscal redistributions, the 'optimal' inflation rate may be the same across Europe.

3.2 Which exchange rate regime for the single European financial market?

The major development in Europe since the EMS began was the decision – made in 1985 – to 'complete the internal market': that is, to eliminate by 1992 a variety of practices that cause frontiers to matter still in the EC. The plan (as set out in the *Single European Act* of 1986, see Commission of the European Communities, 1985, 1987) would create a truly unified market, comparable to that which exists in the United States. Its motivation is the widespread impression that notwithstanding the EC, European markets remain less than fully integrated in ways that may not be explained by visible obstacles.[12] Market segmentation is particularly evident in the banking and insurance industries: in fact, the high point of the Single European Act is the establishment of a common market for financial services. However, the plan for integrating European financial markets comes up against the inconsistency between full financial integration and the current working of the EMS.

The recent experiences of liberalisation have had mixed outcomes. No sooner had the Italian monetary authorities removed controls on 'leads and lags' (in May 1987) than they were faced with a severe speculative attack. Because of the level and maturity structure of the Italian public debt, the authorities could not accept a rise in domestic interest rates large enough to stop the capital outflow. The Bank of Italy was thus forced to choose between giving in, and accepting a realignment that it viewed as unwarranted by 'fundamentals', or reintroducing administrative controls. And so went (at least temporarily) the attempted liberalisation of leads and lags. The French experience has been more successful so far, notwithstanding a sequence of attacks on the French franc. There are two likely explanations for such success. The first is that France does not have a public debt problem, so that the French authorities have been more prepared than the Italian to let domestic interest rates bear the burden of adjustment. The other important reason is that foreign lending in domestic currency is still controlled, so that the volume of funds that can be mobilised to stage an attack is limited.

If full financial integration remains the primary political objective in Europe, and if the current system of fixed but adjustable parities cannot survive full financial liberalisation, the choice is between allowing greater exchange rate flexibility, or giving up realignments altogether, moving toward a system of credible, and thus irrevocably fixed rates – that is a monetary union. I believe that greater exchange rate flexibility is not a viable option in Europe today. Since the mid-1950s Europeans have attempted to limit intra-EC exchange rate fluctuations, for three main reasons. First, European countries are all relatively open. Second, many in Europe hold the floating rates of the 1920s and 1930s responsible for the ensuing collapse of national economies and of the international trading and monetary systems. Third, postwar European institutions – particularly the common agricultural market – depend for their survival on exchange rate stability.[13]

Analysing the exchange rate question in Europe without considering why Europeans are particularly averse to exchange rate fluctuations would not give a clear picture of the problem. As mentioned above, the EMS is just one element of a much richer set of agreements among European countries in the trade, industrial, and agricultural areas. These agreements rest on exchange rate stability.

In Europe financial integration thus calls for more – rather than less – exchange rate stability. This explains why the viability of irrevocably fixed exchange rates, reserve pooling and the setting of monetary targets by a supernational institution have become prominent issues on the European agenda.[14]

3.4 Financial integration and fiscal reform

The risk of the financial integration *cum* monetary unification strategy is that it will not work in the absence of a fiscal reform. There are two reasons why fiscal reform is a *prerequisite* for financial integration:

i) Fiscal structures, as documented in Section 3.1, differ across Europe: tax systems are less efficient in the southern countries, and, as a consequence, governments there 'optimally' rely more on the inflation tax than northern countries do;
ii) A monetary union implies giving up exchange rate realignments as a tool of economic policy. The loss of the exchange rate instrument may be compensated either by *fiscal transfers* across countries (centralising some revenues and redistributing them throughout Europe, along the example of the US Federal government), or by an active use of *differentiated fiscal policies*. One option requires building new fiscal institutions in Europe. The other may not be easy, since in an integrated market the only transactions and the only factors that can be taxed differently across countries are those that can not be relocated at low cost.

A note of caution on the 'financial integration strategy' is also suggested by the situation of some current members of the EMS. The three OECD countries characterised by the highest ratio of public debt-to-GDP are also members of the EMS. In these countries, the debt problem has emerged during the EMS years and is far from being solved. From 1981 to 1988, the ratio of public sector debt-to-GDP has increased from 61 to 97 per cent in Italy, from 88 to 130 per cent in Belgium, and from 90 to 145 per cent in Ireland. While Belgium and Ireland have a primary budget surplus – and thus have gone some way toward stabilising the budget – Italy still has a primary deficit equal to 3 per cent of GDP. Unemployment however is close to 20 per cent in Ireland, 12 per cent in Belgium and Italy. When fiscal policy turns around, will the optimal inflation rate still be the same in Ireland, Italy, and Germany? Once again, further steps toward financial integration and monetary unification in Europe are closely linked to the issue of fiscal reform.

Notes

1. See for instance, Krugman (1988a).
2. If countries retain some policy independence, as in the case of flexible and managed rates, the shortage of independent instruments gives rise to policy conflicts. In the managed exchange rate regime, the possibility of international conflicts can make the regime unstable, because managed rates give peripheral countries the ability to control the exchange rate in their own interest – and thus against the interest of the centre country (see for example Giavazzi and Giovannini, 1989b).
3. This evidence is presented in Giavazzi and Giovannini (1987; and 1989a, ch. 4).

4. For a discussion of the properties of the divergence indicator see Spaventa (1982) and Masera (1987).
5. During that interval there was one EMS realignment which took place in March 1983 and involved a revaluation of the DM vis-à-vis all EMS partners.
6. In that period there were two realignments: July 1985 (lira devalued) and April 1986 (general D-mark revaluation).
7. For discussion of the growing importance of intramarginal intervention, see also Ungerer *et al.* (1986).
8. Notice that the dollar interventions by the other central banks are generally consistent with their intramarginal interventions. When the dollar starts falling, for example France sells D-marks and buys dollars: the DM sale supports the franc inside the EMS, and the dollar purchase is an attempt at slowing down the fall in the dollar that is ultimately responsible for the weakness of the French franc relative to the DM. Italy is an exception: when the dollar starts falling, the Bank of Italy intervenes, selling *both* dollars and EMS currencies (presumably D-marks and Dutch guilders).
9. There is also an influential view maintaining that the Bretton Woods system collapsed when the United States stopped providing price stability to the world economy. See for example Johnson (1973).
10. For an analysis of the role of capital controls in the European disinflation see Giavazzi and Pagano (1988a, b). For an analysis of the effects of dollar fluctuations on intra-European exchange rates, see Giavazzi and Giovannini (1986).
11. Dornbusch (1988a, b) and Giavazzi (1988) point to the public finance role of inflation as an important factor in choosing an exchange rate regime for Europe. Seignorage and fixed exchange rates are discussed in Fischer (1983).
12. For a discussion of market segmentation in the EC, see Krugman (1988b) and Smith and Venables (1988).
13. In Giavazzi and Giovannini (1989a, ch. 1) we describe in detail the effects of exchange rate realignments on European institutions and in particular on the common agricultural market and on the EC budget.
14. The issue of a 'European Central Bank' is analysed in Cohen (1989) and Thygesen (1987). The prospects of the EMS after financial liberalisation are discussed in Padoa-Schioppa (1988).

References

Bruno, M. (1986) 'Sharp Disinflation Strategy: Israel 1985', *Economic Policy*, 2, 379–408.

Cohen, D. (1989) 'Problems of a European Central Bank', in M. de Cecco and A. Giovannini (eds) *A European Central Bank?* (Cambridge University Press).

Commission of the European Communities (1985) 'Completing the Internal Market', White Paper from the Commission to the European Council, COM(85) 310.

Commission of the European Communities (1987) 'Second Report on the Implementation of the White Paper on the Completion of the Internal Market', COM(87) 203.

Committee on Finance and Industry (1931) *Report* (London: HMSO).

Croham Committee (1988) 'After the Louvre: Promoting Exchange Rate Stability' (London: Public Policy Centre).

Dornbusch, R. (1982) 'Stabilisation Policies in Developing Countries: What Have We Learned?', *World Development*, 10, 701–8.

Dornbusch, R. (1988a) 'The EMS, the Dollar and the Yen', in F. Giavazzi, S. Micossi and M. Miller (eds) *The European Monetary System* (Cambridge University Press).

Dornbusch, R. (1988b) 'Money and Finance in European Integration', in *Money and Finance in European Integration* (Geneva: EFTA).

Dreze, J., Wyplosz, C., Bean, C., Giavazzi F. and Giersch, H. (1987) 'The Two-Handed Growth Strategy for Europe: Autonomy through Flexible Coordination', 1987 Report of the CEPS Macroeconomic Policy Group, EC, *Economic Papers*, no. 60.

Fischer, S. (1983) 'Seignorage and Fixed Exchange Rates', in P. Aspe, R. Dornbusch and M. Obstfeld (eds) *Developing Countries in the World Financial Market* (Chicago University Press).

Fischer, S. (1987a) 'International Macroeconomic Policy Coordination', NBER WP no. 2244.

Fischer, S. (1987b) 'British Monetary Policy', in R. Dornbusch and R. Layard (eds) *The Performance of the British Economy* (Oxford University Press).

Fischer, S. (1988) 'Comments to Miller and Williamson', *European Economic Review*, vol. 32, pp. 1048–51.

Frenkel, J. A. (1987) 'The International Monetary System: Should it be Reformed?', NBER WP no. 2163.

Giavazzi, F. (1988) 'The Exchange-Rate Question in Europe', EC, *Economic Papers*.

Giavazzi, F. and Giovannini A. (1986) 'The Dollar and the EMS', *Economic Policy*, no. 2.

Giavazzi, F. and Giovannini A. (1987) 'Models of the EMS: Is Europe a Greater Deutsche Mark Monetary Area?', in *Global Macroeconomics: Policy Conflicts and Cooperation*, in R. Bryant and R. Portes (eds) (London: Macmillan).

Giavazzi, F. and Giovannini A. (1989a) *Limiting Exchange-rate Flexibility: The European Monetary System* (Cambridge: MIT Press).

Giavazzi, F. and Giovannini A. (1989b) 'Monetary Policy Interactions Under Managed Exchange Rates', *Economica*, vol. 56, pp. 199–213.

Giavazzi, F. and Pagano, M. (1988a) 'Capital Controls and the European Monetary System', in D.E. Fair and C. de Boisseau, (eds) *International Monetary and Financial Integration* (Dordrecht: Martinus Nijhoff).

Giavazzi, F. and Pagano, M. (1988b) 'The Advantage of Tying One's Hands: EMS Discipline and Central Bank Credibility', *European Economic Review*, 32, 5, pp. 1055–75.

Giovannini, A. (1986) 'Rules of the Game during the International Gold Standard: England and Germany', *Journal of International Money and Finance*, 5, pp. 467–83.

International Monetary Fund (1987) *World Economic Outlook*, October.

Johnson, H. (1973) 'The Exchange-rate Question for a United Europe', in M.B. Krause (ed.) *The Economics of Integration* (London: George Allen and Unwin).

Krugman, P. (1988a) 'Target Zones and Exchange Rate Dynamics', NBER WP no. 2481.

Krugman, P. (1988b) 'EFTA and 1992', mimeo.

McKinnon, R.I. (1988) 'Monetary and Exchange Rate Policies for International Financial Stability: A Proposal', *Journal of Economic Perspectives*, 2, 1, pp. 83–104.

Masera R. (1987) *L'Unificazione Monetaria e lo SME* (Bologna: Il Mulino).

Miller, M. and Williamson, J. (1988) 'The International Monetary System: An Analysis of Alternative Regimes', *European Economic Review*, vol. 32, pp. 1031–54.

Mundell, R.A. (1968) *International Economics* (New York: Macmillan).

Padoa-Schioppa, T. (1988) 'The EMS: A Long-Term View', in F. Giavazzi, S. Micossi, and M. Miller (eds) *The European Monetary System* (Cambridge University Press).

Sachs, J. (1986) 'The Bolivian Hyperinflation and Stabilisation', NBER WP no. 2073.

Smith, M.A.M. and Venables, A. (1988) 'Completing the Internal Market in the European Community: some Industry Simulations', CEPR discussion paper no. 233.

Spaventa, L. (1982) 'Algebraic Properties and Economic Improperties of the "Indicator of Divergence" in the European Monetary System', in R. Cooper *et al.* (eds) *The International Monetary System under Flexible Exchange Rates – Essays in Honor of Robert Triffin* (Cambridge, Mass.: Ballinger).

Thiel, E. (1987) 'Macroeconomic Policy and Coordination: A View from Germany', Paper presented at the NBER Interdisciplinary Conference on the Political Economy of International Macroeconomic Policy Coordination, November.

Thygesen, N. (1987) 'Decentralisation and Accountability within the Central Bank: Any Lessons from the US Experience for the Potential Organisation of a European Central Bank Institution', University of Copenhagen, mimeo.

Triffin, R. (1947) 'National Central Banking and the International Economy', in L.A. Metzler, R. Triffin and G. Haberler (eds) *International Monetary Policies* (Washington D.C.: Board of Governors of the Federal Reserve System).

Ungerer, H., Evans, O. and Young, P. (1986) 'The European Monetary System: Recent Developments', Occasional Paper no. 48, Washington, D.C.: International Monetary Fund.

Williamson, J. (1985) *The Exchange Rate System* (Washington, D.C.: Institute for International Economics).

Part II
The EMS and Real Adjustments

4 Real Exchange Rates and Trade Imbalances in the EMS

Stefano Vona[1]

1 INTRODUCTION

Perhaps in reaction to the scepticism with which the establishment of the EMS was greeted by many economists and by most European central banks, celebrations of the ten years of the EMS tend to magnify the System's virtues and successes. In this chapter, I have tried to follow a more balanced approach in analysing the relatively neglected effects of the EMS on real economic variables.[2]

In this area the achievements appear less exciting, both because the performance of member countries has generally been poorer than that of non-members and because intra-area trade relations have resulted in large and increasing imbalances. In this chapter, attention is mainly given to the latter phenomenon and its relation to real exchange rate developments. Although the topic appears increasingly important in the discussions on the EMS, the study has not been confined to it; rather, a more general approach has been chosen in order not only to examine the developments of the trade imbalances and their causes, but also to explain why these imbalances require attention and need to be corrected. In turn, this last argument has called for a short discussion of the policy options available.

This chapter is organised as follows. Section 2 briefly reviews the main monetary aspects of the EMS examined in the literature. The real aspects are considered in Sections 3 and 4. In the former, the issue of growth and growth convergence is discussed and the performance of the countries participating in the exchange rate mechanism (ERM) compared with that of the other OECD countries. In the latter, the trade issue is taken up, considering the 'trade creation' effect of exchange rate stabilisation in the ERM, introducing the problem of intra-ERM trade imbalances, and showing its quantitative relevance. In Section 5 it is argued that those imbalances are a problem that requires corrective policy action. Before addressing the issue of the policy instruments to be used, the causes of the increase in intra-ERM imbalances in trade in manufactures are investigated. On the basis of this analysis, Section 7 tentatively addresses the question of what policy should be followed. Here a set of interpretations and points of view are presented but not thoroughly elaborated upon. Nevertheless, they are helpful in focusing on the most important aspects of the problem of policy options within the EMS for demand management and growth promotion. In this respect, particular attention is paid to fiscal policy. In conclusion, Section 8 elaborates upon the feasible strategies for dealing with the intra-ERM imbalances in a growth-oriented environment.

2 THE EMS: THE MONETARY ASPECTS

There is an extensive literature on the monetary aspects and achievements of the EMS, and although this chapter is concerned with other aspects of the System, it is worth recalling the main themes of this literature. On the one hand, attention has been paid to the monetary policy coordination arrangements that came to prevail in the course of time. The central role of the DM has been stressed, as well as the pyramidal organisation of economic policy coordination, whereby the Bundesbank has the power to affect the DM's exchange rate vis-à-vis the dollar and to pursue a monetary policy independent from the other participants in the ERM, while the latter followed the German policy by linking their currencies to the DM (Basevi *et al.*, 1983; Micossi and Padoa-Schioppa, 1984; Kaufman, 1985). Three questions have been asked in this context: (i) whether the System's organisation is exportable to the entire world (Padoa-Schioppa, 1988b; Bofinger and Gerberding, 1988); (ii) whether it can survive the recent changes, especially capital liberalisation (Rogoff, 1985; Giavazzi and Pagano, 1985); and (iii) what the conditions for its survival and development in the new environment are (Dini, 1988).

On the other hand, the crucial question has been the causal relation between ERM membership and the success in reducing inflation (Table 4.1). Basically the question has been whether 'tying one's hands' through such an exchange rate arrangement has been helpful in fighting inflation and in reducing inflation differentials among member countries. Although the authorities tend to reply in the affirmative (see EEC, 1989, p. 5), this question has far-reaching implications and is not at all easy to answer, since the reply must inevitably be based on some

Table 4.1 Consumer prices

	1968–73	*1973–78*	*1978–83*	*1983–88*	*1988*
Germany	4.6	4.8	4.9	1.2	1.1
France	6.1	10.7	11.8	4.3	2.7
Italy	5.7	16.4	17.0	7.1	5.0
Netherlands	6.8	7.8	5.2	1.1	0.7
Belgium	4.9	9.2	6.9	3.0	1.2
Denmark	6.4	11.0	10.1	4.6	4.5
Ireland	8.9	15.3	15.9	4.6	2.1
ERM (*)	5.6	9.6	9.8	3.5	2.4
	(6.2)	(10.7)	(10.3)	(3.7)	(2.5)
Standard deviation	1.42	4.06	4.92	2.12	1.70
Coefficient of variation	0.23	0.38	0.48	0.57	0.68
Spread min–max	2.20	9.60	12.10	6.00	4.30
Spread min–max average	0.69	1.08	1.17	1.60	1.56
United Kingdom	7.5	16.0	11.2	4.7	4.9
EEC	6.0	11.5	10.5	4.5	3.3
United States	5.0	8.0	8.8	3.5	4.1
Japan	7.0	11.3	4.2	1.0	0.5
OECD	5.7	10.0	9.2	3.9	3.9

Note: Data for ERM have been calculated both as a weighted average (first line) and as simple average (second line, data in parenthesis).

Source: OECD, *Main Economic Indicators.*

sort of counterfactual analysis, which is extremely hard to conduct in a reliable way (Collins, 1988).

3 EMS, THE REAL ASPECTS: GROWTH

In assessing the performance, careful attention must be paid to the fact that the EMS has continuously evolved both on the 'institutional front' and in the area of practical management. This has rightly been seen as one of the System's strengths (see Micossi, 1985; Padoan, 1988, p. 17). Transformation in both areas is also under way at the time of writing, as capital liberalisation is progressing and the *Report on Economic and Monetary Union in the EEC* has been distributed to the public for some time.

Hence, the literature on the EMS has often distinguished different periods (see Masera, 1987, ch. 4). In my view, three phases can be clearly singled out. The first ran from the inception of the EMS to 1981–2. This was a 'learning' period for both authorities and market participants in a hostile international economic environment (the second oil shock). The second phase, up to 1986, was characterised by substantial disinflation and, above all, by the narrowing of inflation differentials while realignment became a collective decision. Overall, external factors such as the strong dollar (up to March 1985), fast economic growth in the US, and the oil countershock (in 1986) contributed to the important achievements of this period. The last phase is the present one, characterised by capital liberalisation, a decisive effort towards exchange rate stabilisation as a step in the process of monetary unification, renewed interest in growth and less favourable external developments (dollar weakness and slowdown in US domestic demand growth).

Although the above periodisation seems appropriate for the general analysis of the EMS, for the assessment of the growth performance of the member countries it is better to divide the ten years of existence of the EMS into two five-year periods, the former being generally characterised by the stagnation of economic activity as a consequence of the disinflationary policy adopted, the second by sustained growth.

Table 4.2 GDP/GNP growth (percentage changes, annual rates)

	1968–73	*1973–78*	*1978–83*	*1983–88*
Germany	4.9	1.9	1.3	2.5
France	5.5	2.7	1.9	2.1
Italy	4.6	2.1	2.2	3.2
Netherlands	4.9	2.7	0.5	2.4
Belgium	5.6	2.3	1.3	2.1
Denmark	4.0	1.5	1.5	2.1
Ireland	4.8	4.9	2.3	2.2
ERM	5.1	2.3	1.6	2.5
Standard deviation	0.54	1.11	0.62	0.40
Coefficient of variation	0.11	0.48	0.39	0.16
Spread min–max	1.6	3.4	1.8	1.1
Spread min–max average	0.31	1.48	1.13	0.44
United Kingdom	3.3	1.3	0.8	3.3
EEC	4.8	2.2	1.4	2.7
United States	3.1	2.5	1.1	4.3
Japan	8.7	3.3	3.9	4.4
OECD	4.7	2.5	1.7	3.6

Source: OECD, *National Accounts*, 1989.

Table 4.3 Total domestic demand growth (percentage changes, annual rates)

	1968–73	*1973–78*	*1978–83*	*1983–88*
Germany	5.3	1.9	0.8	2.6
France	5.6	2.1	1.6	2.7
Italy	5.3	1.2	2.3	3.8
Netherlands	4.2	3.0	−0.4	2.5
Belgium	6.2	2.6	−0.1	2.6
Denmark	4.4	1.3	−0.3	2.2
Ireland	6.6	3.7	0.6	0
ERM	5.4	2.0	1.2	2.9
Standard deviation	0.87	0.91	1.02	1.15
Coefficient of variation	0.16	0.46	0.85	0.40
Spread min–max	2.4	2.5	2.7	3.8
Spread min–max average	0.44	1.25	2.25	1.31
United Kingdom	3.3	0.5	1.2	3.9
EEC	5.1	1.7	1.1	3.2
United States	3.0	2.5	1.0	4.4
Japan	9.3	2.4	2.8	4.9
OECD	4.6	2.2	1.4	4.1

Source: OECD, *National Accounts*, 1989.

These have also been compared with the two immediately preceding five-year non-EMS periods. In each of the four periods the performance of the ERM countries has been compared with that of the three major non-ERM countries and to conventional groups of countries (EEC and OECD). Both GDP/GNP and total domestic demand developments have been considered (Tables 4.2 and 4.3). Going by the former variable, the EMS decade, in particular the second five years, has been characterised by a much slower growth of the ERM countries vis-à-vis both the other major industrial countries and the OECD area as a whole, including the ERM group. In the previous decade, by contrast, the ERM area grew at the same rate as the OECD overall.

Moreover, the various measures of dispersion reported in Table 4.2 show that a significant convergence has taken place in the EMS period. In particular, if the country with the highest rate (Italy) is excluded, it is striking that the difference between the highest and the lowest rate of growth of GDP/GNP between 1983 and 1988 has been only 0.4 per cent.[3] For inflation (consumer prices), and again excluding Italy as the highest inflation country, the spread is 3.5 percentage points. All the indicators of dispersion considered confirm that convergence in growth rates was more pronounced than in inflation.

Of course, these data cannot say the final word in assessing whether growth has converged towards the minimum or, rather, towards the maximum, which would help us to reach a judgment on the EMS's performance. Nonetheless, taking into account the results cited above, i.e. the particularly slow growth of the ERM area vis-à-vis the other OECD countries, a feature of the EMS period only, one gets the impression that convergence has not occurred towards the highest possible rate.

Some interesting differences emerge when the performance of real domestic demand is evaluated (Table 4.3). In fact, although it is confirmed that in the EMS period, in particular in the most recent sub-period, the ERM countries grew less than the other industrial countries, it is far less clear that there was convergence, as in the GDP/GNP case. On the contrary, indicators of dispersion not normalised for the average tend to show divergence. In particular, in the most recent period, even neglecting Italy which is again the highest growth country, the difference between the maximum and the minimum growth rates in the area is 2.7 percentage points. In this period, in fact, there are two outliers, Italy and Ireland, at the opposite extremes. The difference in the remaining five countries narrows to 0.5 percentage points.

A further consideration on this topic is that, in the 1983–8 period, Italy's growth in both GNP/GDP and domestic demand was fast for ERM standards, but below the average rate achieved by the OECD area as a whole. Finally, combined investigation into the data of Tables 4.2 and 4.3 reveals the different growth models of the ERM countries. In the 1978–83 period, all member countries but Italy received a significant external contribution to growth (slower expansion of domestic demand than of GDP/GNP). In the 1983–8 period, domestic demand grew faster than GDP in Italy and France, with both countries experiencing a significant deterioration of the foreign balance in real terms.

Yet it would not be correct to attribute these somewhat disappointing developments entirely to the EMS. Surely, at any rate, they do not derive from the structure of the System, i.e. its rules and obligations, but if anything from the way it has been managed in practice.[4] A more close examination of this aspect will be undertaken in Section 6.

4 EMS, THE REAL ASPECTS: TRADE

Other achievements of the EMS are, in my opinion, more clear-cut. First of all, with respect to the main objective of the System, i.e. the creation of an area of monetary stability, a 'first level' but important and relatively uncontroversial achievement has been the reduction of exchange rate volatility and the avoidance of wide fluctuations and 'misalignments' of real exchange rates, which have been common to the main non-ERM currencies (Ungerer *et al.*, 1986; Artis and Taylor, 1988).

According to the Founding Fathers of the EMS, exchange rate stability, by reducing uncertainty, would spur integration in the area, especially in the form of increasing intra-ERM trade. In fact, as shown in De Grauwe (1987), trade integration in the area, measured in real terms, slowed down after the inception of the EMS. Because the growth rate of the participating countries declined sharply, however, only a complete model of trade determination can convincingly assess whether intra-ERM trade was stimulated by the greater exchange rate stability. De Grauwe's findings, obtained by using an equation which captures the income as well as other important effects, support this thesis. Nonetheless, the quantitative importance of the 'trade creation' due to exchange rate stability proved to be small. Bini Smaghi (1988), working with a more detailed trade model and more sophisticated data, also found evidence of moderate trade creation induced by lower variability of real exchange rates.

An issue closely related to the EMS's trade creation effect is that of the allocation of trade flows across member countries. This allocation, especially in the case of manufactured goods, is determined by the exchange rate policies and the development of total domestic demand in the ERM countries, i.e. the classical price and income effects of standard trade analysis. Before embarking on an explanation of intra-ERM trade flows, it is worth providing a brief account of the main trends.

The pre-1979 imbalances in intra-ERM trade have widened sharply in the past decade. In this respect two points must be stressed:

1. the aggravation of the imbalances has involved most notably France and Germany but also Italy and the Netherlands (see Table 4.4). The former country in each pair has recorded deficits, the latter surpluses;
2. these developments were mostly due to trade in manufactures, which is also the most responsive to real exchange rate changes, since agricultural prices in the EEC are administered, not market determined, while primary commodities trade between ERM countries is negligible (see Table 4.4).

As regards the first aspect, Germany's surplus with its ERM partners in 1988 is estimated at about \$26.5 billion, i.e. more than four times

Table 4.4 Trade balance (fob) intra-ERM countries of the EMS (US $ billions)

	1979	*1983*	*1986*	*1987*	*1988*[1]
ALL SECTORS[2]					
Belgium	−0.8 (0.7)	−0.8	−0.6	−0.7 (0.49)	−3.4
Denmark	−2.2 (3.4)	−1.1	−3.4	−2.8 (2.9)	−1.8
France	−7.0 (1.2)	−12.4	−17.0	−20.7 (2.3)	−21.9
Germany	5.7 (0.7)	4.1	15.4	22.3 (2.0)	26.5
Ireland	0.3 (8.1)	0.9	1.8	3.0 (24.9)	3.4
Italy	−0.9 (0.3)	−1.3	−3.4	−6.1 (0.8)	−8.6
Netherlands	4.9 (3.1)	10.6	7.3	5.0 (2.3)	5.7
MANUFACTURED PRODUCTS[3]					
Belgium	1.1	1.1	1.4	1.2	
Denmark	−2.1	−1.7	−4.4	−3.9	
France	−8.3	−13.5	−19.4	−23.8	
Germany	13.3	13.8	25.1	32.2	
Ireland	0.3	0.9	1.8	2.9	
Italy	−0.3	0.6	−0.5	−3.2	
Netherlands	−3.8	−1.2	−3.9	−5.4	
MINERAL FUELS, LUBRIFICANT AND RELATED MATERIALS					
Belgium	−1.2	−1.2	−1.2	−0.9	
Denmark	−0.7	0.0	0.0	0.1	
France	−1.4	−2.0	−1.2	−1.2	
Germany	−3.5	−5.9	−5.7	−4.7	
Ireland	−0.1	−0.1	−0.1	0.0	
Italy	0.8	−0.6	−0.4	−0.2	
Netherlands	6.1	9.8	8.6	6.9	
RAW MATERIALS (AGRICULTURAL AND MINERALS)					
Belgium	−0.3	−0.2	−0.2	−0.5	
Denmark	0.3	0.3	0.4	0.4	
France	0.3	0.8	0.7	1.0	
Germany	−0.9	−1.1	−1.2	−1.6	
Ireland	0.1	0.1	0.1	0.1	
Italy	−0.7	−0.5	−0.9	−0.9	
Netherlands	1.1	0.7	1.2	1.6	
FOOD (UNPROCESSED)					
Belgium	−0.5	−0.5	−0.6	−0.5	
Denmark	0.3	0.3	0.5	0.7	
France	2.8	2.4	3.2	3.6	
Germany	−3.3	−2.7	−2.9	−3.8	
Ireland	−0.1	−0.1	−0.1	0.0	
Italy	−0.6	−0.8	−1.5	−1.8	
Netherlands	1.4	1.3	1.4	2.0	

Notes: (1) Estimates based on date concerning three quarters only. (2) In parenthesis the percentage on current prices GDP. (3) Including processed food but excluding oil and gas derivatives.
Source: OECD, *Foreign Trade by Commodities*.

the 1979 surplus. In the same period the French deficit increased threefold to about $22 billion in 1988. The Italian deficit has also increased considerably in the last three years, but is still well below the French one. The Dutch surplus, by contrast, has been diminishing over the last few years.

Also in relation to GNP/GDP, the intra-ERM imbalances are far from negligible. In 1987 the highest was the Danish deficit (about 3 per cent of GDP), while the German surplus was 2 per cent and the French deficit 2.3 per cent, like the Dutch surplus. Hence, these imbalances are significant both in absolute values and in relation to the size of the economies.

As concerns the second aspect, the data in Table 4.4 show that virtually the entire variation of the trade balances of Germany and France, over the 1979–87 period, was accounted for by manufactures, which caused 50 per cent of the overall deterioration in the case of Italy. Finally, for the Netherlands, the surplus stems from trade in the other commodities, especially energy.

Disaggregation of trade flows by sectors thus reveals that trade in manufactures is the main source of the trade imbalances in the ERM area, at least for the three largest countries, Germany, France and Italy, on which the following analysis will be centred.

5 ARE INTRA-ERM TRADE IMBALANCES A PROBLEM?

The existence of these large and increasing imbalances poses two questions. First, are they a reason for concern? And, if so, how can they be reduced or even eliminated? This obviously brings up the issue of their causes, which will be examined in the next section.

As regards the first question, it is increasingly argued that the imbalances are no great worry. The rationale is that current accounts no longer matter. In fact, financial capital has become much more mobile in Europe with recent liberalisation, especially by France and Italy, and this can only intensify since in July 1990 full freedom of capital movements will prevail in all the ERM countries. Moreover, with 1992, the creation of a large and unified European financial market will facilitate any reallocation of capital that is required in the EEC area. Financing current account imbalances will thus be much easier, which, according to this argument, will virtually eliminate the problem of sustainability. This is admittedly an extreme characterisation of this position, but I believe it is fundamentally accurate.

There is also a more cautious version of this view. It stresses the need for using in a 'productive way' the capital attracted to a country to finance its current account deficit. That is, it must be employed to improve productive potential and competitiveness. Hence, it must finance investment, not private consumption or public expenditure.

The former position is not founded in economic theory but has been used by the authorities of the countries concerned to justify or defend the persistence of large surpluses. It completely neglects the role of the current account in the formation of exchange rate expectations and the need for a deficit country to counter deteriorating expectations by raising interest rates. This means that a persistent deficit can only be financed by incurring increasing costs, unless the exchange rate is allowed to depreciate. This is clearly contrary to the EMS philosophy as it has emerged in the last few years. The exchange rate is increasingly viewed as fixed, and especially after the Basel–Nyborg Agreement, adjustments – to be made only when absolutely needed – are supposed to be 'small and infrequent' and aimed only at compensating (possibly not in full) for inflation differentials.

In such circumstances, a current account deficit may, if continuously financed instead of reduced, lead to the rapid expansion of a country's external debt, with the interest burden becoming potentially explosive.

Although it is very difficult, in practice, to gauge to what extent a current account deficit is transitory, due to a momentary rise of investment above saving, or a permanent feature of the economy calling for corrective policies, the more cautious, investment-oriented version of the argument that intra-ERM trade and current account imbalances do not matter seems sounder. Nonetheless, it cannot justify neglect of current account developments. In fact, even in the favourable situation in which capital inflows, compensating for the current account deficit, are used entirely to finance new investment, sustainability is guaranteed by the expectation of foreign investors that the consequent increase in productive capacity and competitiveness will bring about the required adjustment in the current account by enhancing export growth and restraining import penetration. Hence, not even this argument can support the view that a persistent current account deficit is no problem.

All in all, there is no clear theoretical case for dismissing current account equilibrium as a long-run condition for sound growth and exchange rate stability.

The experience of the 1980s supports this view. The large and persistent US deficit has been the main issue in economic policy coordination in the G-7 and remains one of the most acute problems the international economy has to deal with. Thus, not even the United States can disregard its current account performance, although it is in the unique position of being able to finance its external deficit with liabilities denominated in its own currency.

These arguments in support of the relevance of long-run current account equilibrium, however, are still not enough to show that intra-EMS trade imbalances are reason for concern. ERM countries are part of a much wider multilateral trade network and therefore may well compensate, in the aggregate, for the disequilibria between them. These, in turn, might be justified on grounds of comparative advantages. In the end, what really matters is the development of the overall current account balance of each member country.

Although I agree with this view, the point I want to stress is that the process of adjusting the current account disequilibria at the world level, which is now under way, combined with the developments within the ERM in terms of price competitiveness and relative real demand growth, is turning the intra-ERM deficits of some countries into overall current account deficits. In other words, the appreciation of the dollar and the oil countershock, which had permitted some EMS members to offset intra-area trade deficits with external surpluses, have played themselves out. The ERM countries, excluding Germany, recorded (declining) surpluses in trade with the US until the end of 1987. In the first half of 1988 they recorded a deficit with the US.

More important is that Italy and France, after recording current account surpluses in 1986 for the first time in the 1980s, witnessed a deterioration in the following two years of about $7 billion each, producing significant deficits of about $4 billion respectively in 1988. For both countries the deterioration of the intra-ERM trade balance between 1986 and 1988 can be estimated at about $5 billion (see Table 4.4), i.e. roughly two-thirds of the overall deterioration of the current account. Nevertheless, especially for France, the recent changes in the international environment have only revealed a phenomenon, i.e., the intra-ERM trade imbalances, that was already a significant factor in the overall current account difficulties in the first half of this decade.

Hence, intra-ERM trade imbalances are a significant problem that warrants careful consideration.[5] De Cecco (1988) also argued that growing intra-ERM trade imbalances have to be interpreted as a disequilibrating force in the System. In the *Report on Economic and Monetary Union in the European Community* (1989), the existence of trade imbalances is cited as one of the phenomena that call for a stricter convergence in economic performances (p. 5).

6 THE REASONS FOR THE INCREASING INTRA-ERM TRADE IMBALANCES

Determining how the imbalances could be reduced requires some understanding of the reasons for their formation. Here I shall draw heavily on my work with L. Bini Smaghi (Vona and Bini Smaghi, 1988; Bini Smaghi and Vona, 1989). The 1988 work, in particular, which was published first although prepared later, uses a partial equilibrium model of trade and inflation that distinguished between the intra- and extra-ERM trade flows of Germany, France and Italy (see Table 4.5), to show that the main cause of the growing trade imbalances in manufactures is the different rates of domestic demand growth (see Figures 4.1 and 4.2). The effects of demand on trade flows have been reinforced by the high levels of expenditure elasticities, which in no case are below 1.5 and, often, are above 2 (see Table 4.6).

Price competitiveness, measured by wholesale/producer prices of manufactures, by contrast, is of minor importance, not because the 'Marshall–Lerner' conditions are not satisfied[6] but because the System was characterised by the absence of significant real exchange rate changes. In fact, of the three major currencies, only the Italian lira has appreciated in real terms over the entire EMS period, despite fears that its wider fluctuation band would have allowed a more relaxed attitude towards exchange rate discipline (see Figure 4.3).[7]

During the EMS period the total exchange rate of the French franc remained below the 1980 level in 1982–4. After some appreciation in 1986 it has fallen again in the last two years to the levels of the beginning of the 1980s.

Broadening the analysis to include the exchange rates of the other ERM countries (except Ireland), a picture emerges that contradicts some of the standard views on the working of the EMS. In fact, it is evident from the development of the real and nominal exchange rates of the Belgian franc that nominal exchange rate depreciation has been used to get gains in price competitiveness, while the Dutch guilder has not been allowed to appreciate as much as would have been needed to avoid the significant lowering of the real exchange rate that has occurred in the last few years. Denmark, by contrast, followed the 'orthodox' prescription for a higher inflation country and, like Italy, devalued the currency less than enough to avoid a rise in the real exchange rate.

Since many different measures of real exchange rates are available, it could be argued that other indicators, either calculated through a different methodology or based on different price/cost indices, would

Table 4.5 Model for analysis of manufacturing trade flows

Model		*Variables*
$X_i^A = X(DA_i, CX_i^A \ldots)$	(6.1)	X_i^A = Exports of country i to A
$M_i^A = M(D_i, CM^A \ldots)$	(6.2)	M_i^A = Imports of country i from A
$PX_i^A = PX(PAX_i^A, PI_i \ldots)$	(6.3)	DA_i = Domestic demand of A calculated as in (6.10)
$PI_i = PI(CL_i, MAT_i, PM_i, GAP_i \ldots)$	(6.4)	D_i = Domestic demand of country i
$CX_i^A = PX_i^A / PAX_i^A$	(6.5)	PX_i^A = Export prices of country i to A
$CM_i^A = (PI_i^{\lambda} + PM_i^{NA^{1-\lambda}}) / PM_i^A$	(6.6)	CX^A = Export competitiveness, calculated as shown in (6.5)
$B_i^A = PX_i^A \cdot X_i^A - PM_i^A \cdot M^A$	(6.7)	CM^A = Import competitiveness, calculated as shown in (6.6)
$PM_i = PM_i^{A^{\alpha}} + PM_i^{NA^{1-\alpha}}$	(6.8)	PAX_i^A = Prices of competitors of country i in A, calculated as shown in (6.9)
$PAX_i^A = \sum_{j \neq i} w_j PX_j^A + \sum_{j \neq i} z_j PI_j + \sum_{k \neq i \neq j} v_k PX_k^A$	(6.9)	PI_i = Prices of domestic producer of country i
$DA_i = \sum_{j \neq i} z_j D_j$	(6.10)	CL_i = Unit labour costs of country i
$0 < \alpha, \lambda < 1; j \in A; k \in NA; \Sigma w_j + \Sigma z_j + \Sigma v_k = 1$		PM_i^A = Import prices of country i from A
		PM_i^{NA} = Import prices of country i from NA
		MAT_i = Raw materials import prices of country i
		GAP_i = Domestic demand deviation from trend of country i
		w = Multilateral competitive weights
		z = Bilateral export weights

Note: A, NA = ERM or non-ERM, respectively.
Source: Vona and Bini Smaghi (1988).

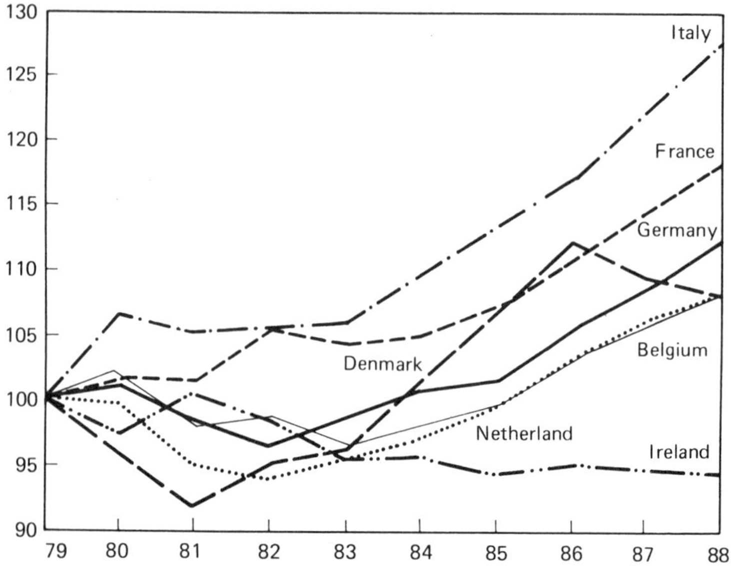

Figure 4.1 Domestic demand (index 1979 = 100)

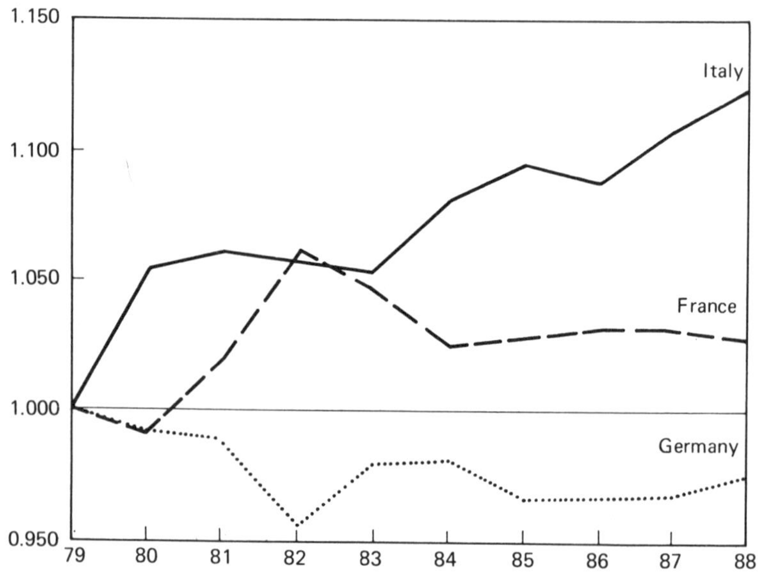

*Ratio between domestic demand and that of other ERM countries; weights based on the country's export shares.

Figure 4.2 Relative domestic demand* (index 1979 = 1)

Table 4.6 Price and expenditure 'equilibrium' elasticities of manufacturing export and import volumes

Exports to:	*ERM countries*		*Non-ERM OECD countries*	
From:	*Price*	*Expenditure*	*Price*	*Expenditure*
Italy	−0.82	2.21	−1.04	2.40
Germany	−0.97	1.88	−0.68	1.66
France	−0.57	1.90	−0.57	1.71
Imports from:	*ERM countries*		*Non-ERM OECD countries*	
To:	*Price*	*Expenditure*	*Price*	*Expenditure*
Italy	0.98	2.16	1.23	2.32
Germany	0.89	1.64	1.23	1.89
France	0.58	2.74	0.95	2.73

Source: S. Vona and L. Bini Smaghi, 1988.

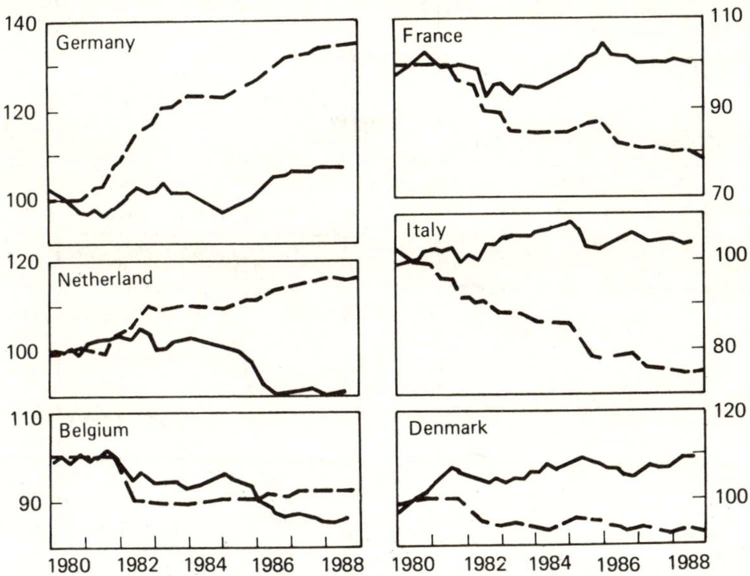

Key: Nominal – – – Real ——

Source: Bank of Italy; *Economic Bulletin* no. 8, February 1989.

Note: Increases (decreases) of the indices indicate appreciations (depreciations) of the currency of the country concerned.

Figure 4.3 Effective exchange rates of the ERM countries vis-à-vis the other members (quarterly figures, index 1980 = 100)

provide a different picture. To make sure that this is not so, the data in Figure 4.4 have also been used. The source is not the Bank of Italy but the Commission Services (European Commission, 1989). The prices used to 'deflate' nominal exchange rates are GDP/GNP deflators. The results provided in Figure 4.4 are even more striking and fully support the conclusions reached using the Bank of Italy indicators based upon wholesale/producer prices of manufactures.

It can be concluded, then, that a rigorous exchange rate policy has been followed only by Italy and Denmark, each tolerating significant appreciation in real terms, notwithstanding the current account

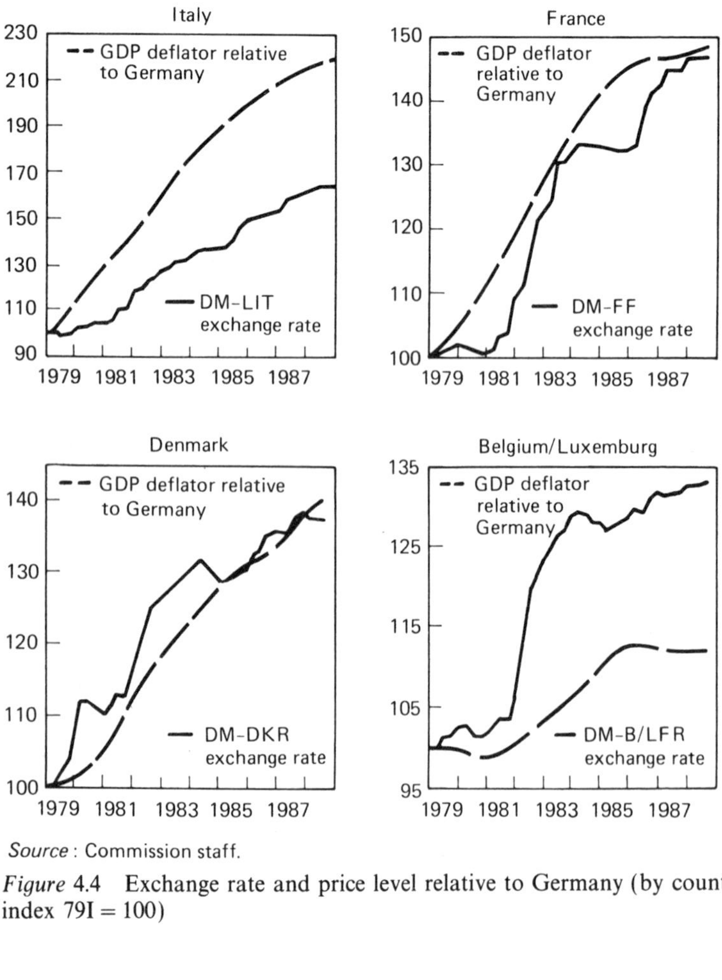

Source: Commission staff.

Figure 4.4 Exchange rate and price level relative to Germany (by country – index 79I = 100)

weakness that has been a characteristic of the 1980s for the two countries. Belgium and the Netherlands obtained quite substantial competitiveness gains vis-à-vis the other ERM countries. In particular, the former achieved this result through depreciation unwarranted by inflation differentials.

These are important developments, not sufficiently taken into account in the analysis of the EMS. They strongly suggest that the extent to which rigorous exchange rate policies, and thus severe monetary policies, have been followed has not been so much due to the rules and obligations of the System but rather the consequence of policy choices adopted domestically, by each member country, with a certain degree of autonomy.

In other words, in Italy, for instance, it was the determination to narrow inflation differentials vis-à-vis the other ERM countries that led to the adoption of a degree of monetary tightness implying, together with the relaxed fiscal policy followed during most of the EMS period, an appreciation of the lira in real terms. No written or unwritten rule of the System could have prevented the Italian monetary authorities from requesting larger depreciation, on the occasion of the realignments, so as to avoid the loss of price competitiveness that Italy sustained in the EMS period. Instead, this was rightly considered an acceptable price to be paid for decisive success on the inflation front.

In passing, it is worth noting that France's anti-inflation strategy, especially in the last few years, has relied more than Italy's on the control of domestic costs (see Section 8) rather than on the adoption of the 'strong currency option'.

The rationale for such a strategy necessarily rests on the anti-inflationary effects of a strong currency. Estimates of the impact of a depreciation show that in both France and Italy the inflationary cost of a trade balance adjustment via depreciation is high. Figure 4.5 reports the results of a simulation (Vona and Bini Smaghi, 1988) in which a joint depreciation of the ERM currencies vis-à-vis the other main currencies is considered. Even in this case, which is more favourable in terms of the inflationary impact than the depreciation of a single ERM currency, about half of the depreciation translates into higher domestic prices (p_i) and a larger proportion into higher prices of exports to the non-ERM countries (p^{NE}). This is especially because the two economies are highly dependent upon imports. The elasticity of domestic prices to the import prices of both raw materials and manufactures is 60–65 per cent in all three cases,[8] while elasticity to unit labour costs is approximately one third. The results concerning

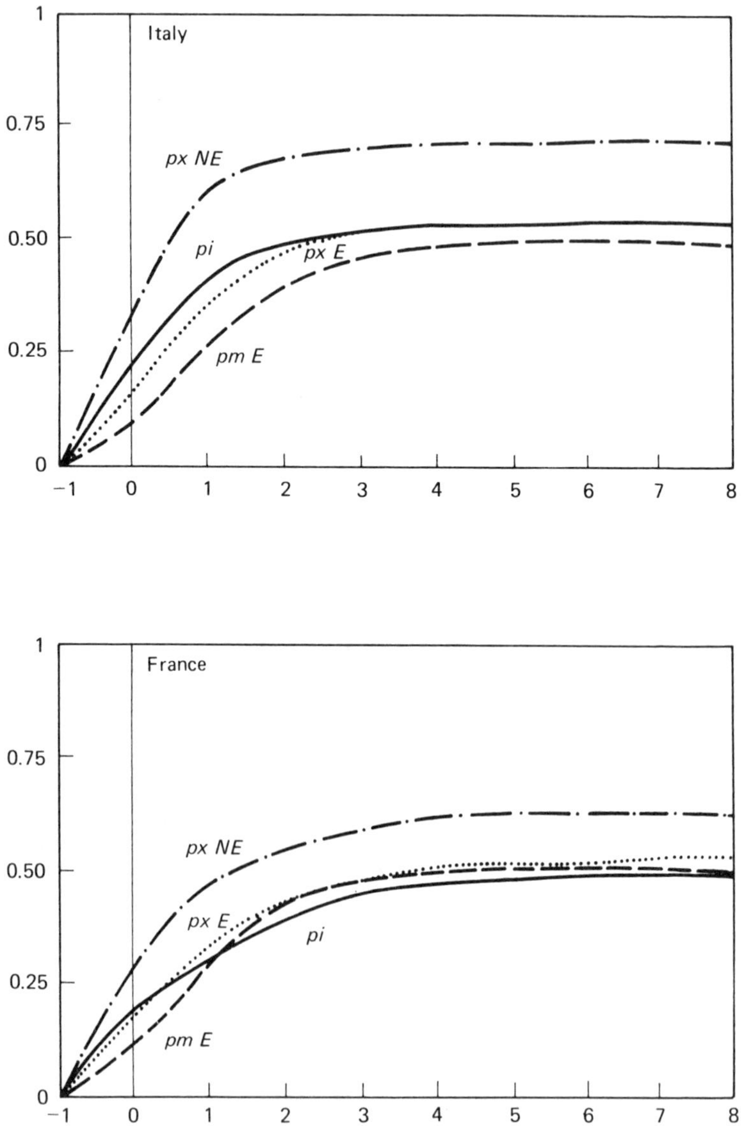

Key: *E* = ERM countries; *NE* = non-ERM countries;
px = export prices; *pm* = import prices; *pi* = domestic wholesale prices

Note: Devaluation with respect to all the currencies external to the ERM area.
Source: Vona and Bini Smaghi (1988)

Figure 4.5 Effects on prices of a joint devaluation of ERM currencies

the inflationary impact of a deterioration have been confirmed, in the case of Italy, by simulating the large macro-model of the Bank of Italy (see Gressani, Guiso and Visco, 1987).

However, the values of the parameters estimated for 1977–85 show that the French manufacturing sector suffers some structural weakness, revealed by an income elasticity of imports much higher than the Italian and the German ones (see Table 4.6). Preventing a French trade deficit thus requires slower growth in France than in the rest of the OECD area, for given price competitiveness.

The problems of French industry are confirmed by the recent development of the overall trade balance in manufactures, which deteriorated by $13 billion between 1984 and 1987 (see Table 4.7), and by the loss of export market shares and of competitiveness that are revealed by the Constant Market Share Analysis (see Table 4.8).

By both indicators the position of Italian industry appears much better. In particular, the CMSA shows that French industry lost market shares both in 1978–83 and in 1983–6 in all three commodity groups considered – high, medium and low levels of technology intensiveness

Table 4.7 USA, Japan and EEC countries: trade balances in manufactures (US $ billions)

	USA	*Japan*	*EEC*	*France*	*Germany*	*Italy*	*UK*
1973	0.2	23.3	38.5	2.3	28.4	5.0	4.2
1974	6.1	37.9	57.4	3.6	42.0	7.0	4.5
1975	17.2	41.7	68.7	9.4	38.2	12.4	8.4
1976	9.8	51.2	65.2	5.5	41.3	11.7	8.5
1977	3.1	63.9	80.6	9.0	46.9	16.3	10.3
1978	– 4.2	75.5	88.7	10.2	53.6	20.8	8.4
1979	6.9	74.2	89.8	11.5	58.9	22.1	6.2
1980	19.5	96.6	95.0	7.0	61.9	17.2	8.7
1981	8.9	118.3	99.8	8.9	62.0	22.9	4.1
1982	– 8.2	106.6	94.9	3.0	67.1	22.8	1.1
1983	– 33.4	112.8	88.3*	6.9	59.3	25.3	– 7.3
1984	– 83.2	131.1	89.9*	9.6	59.9	21.8	– 7.8
1985	– 108.3	137.1	97.3*	7.9	67.2	22.2	– 6.3
1986	– 141.0	161.5	101.6*	2.0	88.9	25.2	– 11.6
1987	– 153.0	170.1		– 3.5	104.5	21.5	– 14.4

Note: Exports fob, and imports cif.
* EEC with 12 countries.

Sources: GATT for the USA, Japan and the EEC; OECD for France, Germany, Italy and the United Kingdom.

Table 4.8 Results of the constant market share analysis (CMSA) at current prices (yearly average percentage changes)

	Exports % changes		*Effect*					
			Commodity		*Market*		*Residual*	
	Total (1)	*Difference with OECD* (2)	(3)	(4)	(3)	(4)	(3)	(4)
1978–83								
GERMANY								
Total manufactures	2.9	−2.2	0.1		0.0		−2.3	
High technology	4.4	−4.5	(0.6)	−0.1		0.0		−4.4
Medium technology	3.2	−2.5	(0.2)	−0.1		0.1		−2.5
Low technology	1.2	−0.7	(−0.7)	0.0		−0.1		−0.6
UNITED KINGDOM								
Total manufactures	0.4	−4.8	0.5		0.0		−5.2	
High technology	3.6	−5.3	(1.0)	0.1		−0.1		−5.3
Medium technology	2.0	−3.6	(0.4)	0.1		0.1		−3.9
Low technology	−4.6	−6.5	(−0.9)	0.0		0.0		−6.4
FRANCE								
Total manufactures	3.6	−1.6	0.3		−0.3		−1.6	
High technology	7.5	−1.3	(0.7)	0.0		0.0		−1.3
Medium technology	3.4	−2.3	(0.4)	0.1		−0.2		−2.2
Low technology	1.5	−0.4	(−0.9)	0.0		0.0		−0.4
ITALY								
Total manufactures	6.1	1.0	−0.5		0.2		1.3	
High technology	9.5	0.6	(0.5)	0.0		−0.1		0.7
Medium technology	6.1	0.4	(0.2)	−0.1		0.2		0.3
Low technology	5.3	3.4	(−1.1)	0.2		0.9		3.1
OECD								
Total manufactures	5.1							
High technology	8.8							
Medium technology	5.7							
Low technology	1.9							

1983–86								
GERMANY								
Total manufactures	16.3	4.3	0.4		2.0		1.9	
High technology	17.3	3.7	(0.2)	−0.1		1.5		2.3
Medium technology	16.8	3.8	(0.8)	0.4		1.8		1.6
Low technology	14.4	5.6	(−0.6)	0.4		2.8		2.4
UNITED KINGDOM								
Total manufactures	10.1	−2.0	−0.3		0.8		−2.5	
High technology	11.1	−2.5	(0.2)	−0.5		0.6		−2.6
Medium technology	10.5	−2.5	(—)	−0.9		0.8		−2.4
Low technology	8.2	−0.7	(−0.5)	0.8		0.9		−2.4
FRANCE								
Total manufactures	11.2	−0.9	−0.1		0.7		−1.5	
High technology	13.5	−0.1	(0.2)	−0.6		1.5		−1.0
Medium technology	11.3	−1.7	(0.4)	−0.2		0.1		−1.6
Low technology	9.1	0.2	(−0.7)	0.3		1.3		−1.4
ITALY								
Total manufactures	12.5	0.4	0.5		0.2		−0.3	
High technology	12.2	−1.4	(0.2)	−0.1		−0.1		−1.2
Medium technology	12.4	−0.6	(0.5)	0.2		−0.2		−0.6
Low technology	12.6	3.7	(−0.2)	2.9		0.5		0.3
OECD								
Total manufactures	12.1							
High technology	13.6							
Medium technology	13.0							
Low technology	8.9							

Notes:
(1) Yearly average percentage change of exports over the period. (2) Difference between the percentage change of the exports of the country considered and those of the OECD area. A (+) sign indicates an increase in the country's world market share. (3) Global effect measured on the basis of the whole exports matrix; in parenthesis the total commodity effect is broken down in the three technological sectors. (4) Effect measured within each technological sector; the sum by row corresponds to the differential with the OECD growth rate in (2).

Source: Rebecchini and Vona (1990).

– with the exception of the low-technology group in 1983–6. The residual, which, widely defined, takes in competitiveness, is clearly negative in all the cases considered, suggesting that this effect has hurt French industry's export performance. On the contrary, the loss of market shares has not been due to the sectoral or geographical pattern of specialisation, given that the commodity and market effects are generally positive in the periods under review.

The position of Italian industry appears somewhat stronger. Besides its sizeable trade surplus (see Table 4.7), it gained market shares over the entire period considered, although at a slower rate in the second sub-period. Its performance was also better than that of British industry and, in the first sub-period, of German industry too. As concerns the latter, it is worth noting that the considerable gains of export market shares in the 1983–6 period were more pronounced in the low technology industries and were largely caused by competitiveness, as revealed by the residual term of the CMSA decomposition.

The study cited (Vona and Bini Smaghi, 1988) also quantifies the effects of some of the external factors that made it possible to compensate for the growing trade imbalances within the ERM, namely the appreciation of the dollar and other non-ERM currencies in 1980–5 and the strong growth of domestic demand in the US between 1983 and 1985. These factors greatly alleviated the output cost to the high-inflation countries, where very restrictive monetary policies were being used to bring inflation down into line with the rest of the System. The low-inflation countries, in turn, were growing at very modest rates, providing no real stimulus and actually subtracting real growth from the others as a result of their very large trade surpluses.

7 CORRECTING THE IMBALANCES – WHAT POLICY?

Once the basic reasons for the growing intra-EMS imbalances have been singled out, the most suitable policy for correcting them must be identified. This is a question to which only tentative answers can be given. Rather than embarking on the analysis of the set of complicated theoretical issues which have to be considered in order to achieve reasonably well-founded solutions, I shall focus the following discussion upon the policy courses actually followed in the ERM countries and, more generally, the philosophy on which authorities currently base their policy choices.

In this respect, the Vona–Bini Smaghi model is of little help. Some insights might have been obtained by simulation of complex interlink macro-models such as the OECD's, which can allow a careful examination of both the effects of different policies and the interactions among different countries. Since such simulations are not available we relay perforce upon speculative arguments. These require the explicit consideration of fiscal policy and domestic cost trends in the ERM countries; the former is especially important in the determination of the development of real domestic demand, the latter in that of price competitiveness. Fiscal policy approaches are discussed below, while costs are treated only summarily in the conclusions.

It has often been noted that in the ERM area convergence has not progressed as much in fiscal policy as in the monetary sphere (see Boltho, 1986). However, since 1981–2 member countries have followed a restrictive fiscal policy (see Table 4.9). Italy has been the only exception in this sense, despite the desirability of such a policy having been unanimously recognised.

Judgment of this strategy, which is usually referred to as 'fiscal consolidation', requires the discussion of issues that are very complex theoretically and would be outside the scope of this chapter. I shall therefore confine my discussion to several considerations that are particularly relevant to the debate on the EMS, without exploring all their implications.

The basic tenet of fiscal consolidation is opposition to state intervention in the economy, grounded in the opinion that public expenditure is 'less productive' than private and that taxes are likely to distort the allocation of resources (Laffer's curve). These two free-market

Table 4.9 General government net lending (% GDP)

	1979	*1980*	*1981*	*1982*	*1983*	*1984*	*1985*	*1986*	*1987*	*1988**
Belgium	−7.1	−9.0	−12.7	−10.9	−11.2	−9.3	−8.3	−8.9	−7.2	−7.1
Denmark	−1.7	−3.3	−6.9	−9.1	−7.2	−4.1	−2.0	+3.1	+2.1	+0.9
Germany	−2.6	−2.9	−3.7	−3.3	−2.5	−1.9	−1.1	−1.3	−1.8	−2.3
France	−0.8	0.0	+1.9	−2.8	−3.2	−2.8	−2.8	−2.9	−2.5	−1.9
Ireland	−11.4	−12.7	−13.4	−13.7	−11.6	−9.6	−11.1	−11.0	−9.1	−6.5
Italy	−8.3	−8.5	−11.3	−11.3	−10.6	−11.5	−12.5	−11.4	−10.5	−10.0
Netherlands	−3.7	−3.9	−5.4	−7.0	−6.3	−6.2	−4.7	−6.0	−6.3	−5.2

* Commission forecast.

Source: *Lo SME: dieci anni di progressi nella cooperazione monetaria europea*, EEC Commission, 1989.

paradigms have been supplemented by other 'theoretical' considerations based on an 'accounting economics' which relies upon ex-post identities between the financial balances of the macro-sectors of the economy: the private sector (firms and households), the public sector and the foreign sector. Thus, depending on the economic situation of the country concerned, a reduction in public sector dissaving can be viewed as tantamount to either (i) and equivalent rise in private investment or (ii) an equal contraction in the external deficit. One scenario assumes full crowding-in, the other zero crowding-in of private expenditure.

The experience of the countries that have pursued this strategy most consistently shows that reality is much more complex than the simple 'identity' approach would lead one to suppose. In the UK, for instance, aggressive fiscal consolidation has been associated with a dramatic current account deterioration ($27 billion in three years); in Denmark, the achievement of a budget surplus has not led to any significant improvement of the persistent current account deficit; and even in the US the sizeable reduction of the federal deficit in 1987 has not been reflected in a comparable reduction of the current account deficit.

It would be improper, however (i) to conclude that demand restraint through fiscal policy is not effective in bringing about current account adjustment, and (ii) to extend this argument to the opposite situation to justify contractionary fiscal policy in countries running current account surpluses, such as Germany and the Netherlands in the 1980s (see Table 4.9). As a matter of fact, the adherence to fiscal consolidation, as against fiscal activism for demand management, has spread to those countries too. There is hardly any evidence that this policy has brought about a reduction of the excess of saving over investment, in those countries. On the contrary, the resources left free by reducing public sector dissaving have been exported in the form of larger capital outflows.

If the short-run impact of fiscal consolidation is controversial, what this general attitude in the budgetary policy means for the EMS is that the path of domestic demand growth in each member country tends to be increasingly determined by pure market forces, government interference being progressively reduced.

Smoothing out cyclical peaks is left to monetary policy but, being geared to the long-run objective of low or no inflation and to exchange rate stability, this cannot be used to stimulate domestic activity in periods of slack, unless a fully coordinated policy action is agreed by all member countries and the possibility of some inflationary effects is tolerated. With capital increasingly mobile among ERM countries, interest rate management by a single country is becoming more difficult. A policy inducing higher interest rates, for instance, also implies an undesired rise in the real exchange rate, as a consequence of capital inflows that are too large to be sterilised in full. This would worsen the trade balance before the real consequences on domestic demand (reduction), owing to the interest rate increase, actually materialise. As usual in these situations, the most affected component of domestic demand would be investment, impairing medium-term growth and also non-price competitiveness. In this setting it is difficult to smooth out the differential effects of real external shocks which, according to the textbooks, should be dealt with by fiscal policy.

Moreover, as noted above, differences in growth rates are increasingly due to the private sector growth potential. Harmonisation of actual growth rates thus cannot be achieved by macroeconomic policy, but only by movements of factors of production.

In sum, fiscal consolidation is one of the pillars of the medium-term financial strategy that was considered essential at the turn of the decade to foster the conditions for sustained non-inflationary growth capable of reducing unemployment, especially in Europe. As a matter of fact, the convergence of real growth rates in the EMS tends to be downwards, not upwards, and Europe still has a much higher unemployment rate than the US or Japan. The conceptual framework outlined in the previous section provides no way out of this impasse. Accordingly, each country has its own 'specific' potential output growth which cannot, in reality, be shifted upward by macroeconomic policy, because this would only imply higher inflation (vertical Phillips curve).

Only through the lengthy process of implementing 'structural reforms' aimed especially at enhancing supply and making the markets work properly can the rate of potential output growth be increased. I have argued elsewhere (Gomel, Saccomanni and Vona, 1989) that it is extremely difficult to assess the macroeconomic impact of the micro-economic measures that form the basis of the structural reforms. It is even more uncertain whether they could lead to the convergence of growth rate towards the highest possible rate or, in any event, could help reducing the differences which cause intra-ERM trade imbalances. To this end the only opportunity left, within the present institutional setting, is factor mobility, which however requires long lags to be effective.

In a shorter-term perspective and in the present policy setting, trade imbalances among member countries cannot be reduced either by real exchange rate adjustments or by fiscal stimulus aimed at an upward convergence of growth rates. The danger, then, is that, as in the past, unless favourable external factors such as the 1986 oil countershock provide some leeway for countries seeking faster growth, external constraints impose convergence on the lower growth rate chosen by the country at the centre of the System, i.e. Germany (Spaventa, 1988, p. 408). This could happen well before the growth promoting effects of structural policies may, eventually, materialise.

On these grounds the conclusion that can be drawn from the foregoing is that the ERM has a deflationary bias, not so much as a consequence of its intrinsic nature[9] as a fixed but adjustable exchange rate agreement, but rather because of three interrelated factors that have given rise to a state of affairs in which macroeconomic policy cannot be used to sustain growth: (i) the modest growth of the German economy, whether for objective or for policy reasons; (ii) the philosophy underlying economic policy in the area; and (iii) the internal organisation that came to prevail in the EMS. The dramatic events of 1989–90 suggest that no changes in the first two factors can be expected, and that the third is already in a phase of transformation, with the conditions that led to German leadership being gradually modified. At this stage, however, it is impossible to predict the final outcome of the process and whether it will be more conducive to growth and convergence.

All in all, I share the opinion (Padoan, 1988, p. 61) that the EMS has worked successfully as a defensive mechanism against external instability rather than as an endogenously dynamic system.

8 CONCLUSIONS

I have tried to explain in this chapter why intra-EMS trade imbalances are a systemic problem and which are their causes. It has also been shown that adjustment through nominal exchange rate changes is not advisable, especially because it could lead to widening inflation differentials. In any event, this strategy sharply contrasts with the current view of the authorities of member countries, which are increasingly reluctant to vary central rates in the EMS. The present attitude in favour of fiscal consolidation eliminates another policy instrument potentially useful to cope with the problem of intra-ERM trade imbalances.

Is, then, this problem (and related tensions) insoluble in a growth-promoting setting? I think not, provided that a decisive step towards monetary union is taken. Monetary union based on one single currency is the only feasible long-run solution. By abolishing balances of payments, it would allow the growth rate of the entire area to be determined as the average of the national growth rates. Without union, the cohesion of the system remains under threat. Moreover, there is the danger that latent protectionist pressures induced by the trade imbalances might jeopardise the goals of 1992.

In the meantime, if a too long and idle wait has to be avoided, what options are available? Unfortunately, there is no broad menu of alternatives. The most likely, and the least welcome, is that after France, Italy too will converge on the low growth rates of the 'core' countries.

However, one may posit an 'intermediate solution' whereby the System can strengthen its cohesion while moving gradually towards monetary union. This solution has to discount some lowering of the growth rates of those countries with higher growth potential, but it should also be based on a strategy aimed at improving their competitiveness, including non-price competitiveness, by a combination of faster productivity gains and slower wage increases. The French experience in the last few years provides an example of the way this policy can be implemented. Since 1985 French unit labour costs have risen considerably less than those of the other ERM countries (see Figure 4.6). Nonetheless, the full success of this strategy is impeded by the structural problems that have emerged in the French industrial sector over the last decade. Italy's industry may be better equipped to pursue this strategy, but it can only succeed if the enormous inefficiency of the public sector is reduced, an issue which is clearly stressed by Masera (1990).

Moreover, some leeway can be provided by the formation of the Single European Market, which should spur growth in the area as a whole and could also foster convergence towards the average.

Finally, another option would be a coordinated strategy to foster growth in a non-inflationary environment. This is not only difficult to outline, but very unlikely even to be considered, given the present attitude of policy-makers in the EMS. The complete lack of effectiveness of the 'Two-handed' approach is a discouraging example in this connection. However, if it expects to compete successfully with the US and the Japanese economies, Europe cannot afford to renounce growth. In a stagnating economy, the European single market would be not a fortress but a prison.

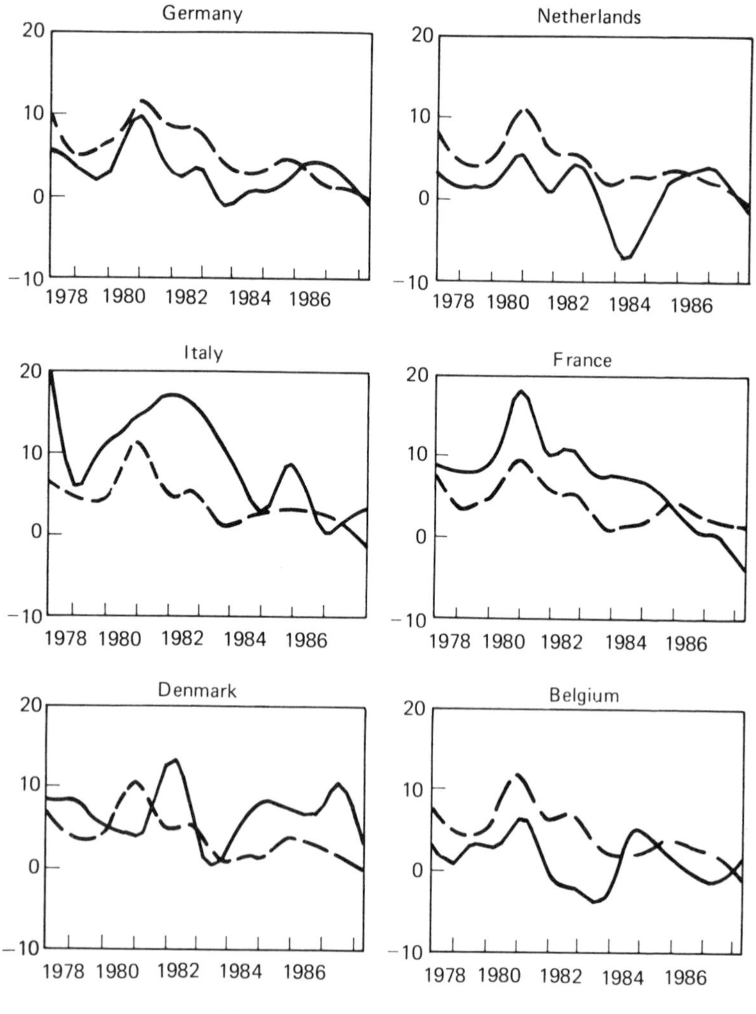

Key: domestic costs —— Other members' costs (weighted average) – –

Note: The data are interpolated with Henderson curves.

Source: Bank of Italy

Figure 4.6 Unit labour costs in the ERM countries (percentage changes over the same period of the previous year)

Notes

1. Comments by L. Bini Smaghi and C. Mastropasqua are gratefully acknowledged. The author is responsible for any remaining error. The views expressed do not necessarily coincide with those of the Bank of Italy.
2. Evidence of the bias of the literature towards monetary issues is provided in the excellent survey by M. Guitián (1988).
3. The issue of the lack of convergence has been frequently called upon by the opponents of progress in the monetary and exchange rate areas.
4. For a brief discussion of the 'rules versus discretion' issue in the EMS, see Padoa-Schioppa (1988a, p. 371).
5. In this respect it has been noted (De Cecco, 1988) that the large and increasing German surplus in the ERM area is a feature which distinguishes the EMS from both the gold standard and the Bretton Woods systems, and that the structural trade surplus of the leading country vis-à-vis its partners represents a weakness for the entire System.
6. In fact, for the three countries considered and in the case of trade with both ERM and non-ERM countries, the sum of export and import price elasticities is always above 1.
7. Hence, the idea that the ERM has been fostered by the reciprocal advantage of high inflation and low inflation countries, with the former gaining in terms of monetary stability, the latter obtaining competitiveness gains (Melitz, 1988), seems to be strictly valid for the LIT/DM relation only.
8. Italy is the country with the highest elasticity to import prices of raw materials (0.17), about twice that of France (0.08) and three times that of Germany (0.06).
9. On the contrary, Boltho (1986) argued that the EMS has played a deflationary role by itself.

References

Artis, M.J. and Taylor, M.P. (1988) 'Exchange Rates, Interest Rates, Capital Controls and the European Monetary System: Assessing the Track Record', in F. Giavazzi, S. Micossi and M. Miller (eds) *The European Monetary System* (Cambridge University Press).

Banca d'Italia (1989) *Economic Bulletin*, no. 8, February.

Basevi, G., Calzolari, M. and Colombo, C. (1983) 'Monetary Authorities' Reaction Functions and the European Monetary System', in D.R. Hodgman (ed.) *The Political Economy of Monetary Policy: National and International Aspects*, Proceedings of a Conference held in Perugia, Italy, July.

Bini Smaghi, L. (1988) 'Exchange Rate Variability, Trade and Capital Mobility', Ph.D. Dissertation, University of Chicago, February, unpublished.

Bini Smaghi, L. and Vona, S. (1989) 'The Effects of Economic Convergence and Competitiveness on Trade among the EMS Countries', in D.R. Hodgman and G.E. Wood (eds) *Macroeconomic Policy and Economic Interdependence* (London: Macmillan).

Bofinger, P. and Gerberding, C. (1988) 'EMS: A Model for a World Monetary Order?', *Intereconomics*, September/October.

Boltho, A. (1986) 'L'economia italiana a confronto 1973–1985', in Ente Einaudi (ed.) *Oltre la crisi* (Bologna: Il Mulino).

Collins, S.M. (1988) 'Inflation and the European Monetary System', in F. Giavazzi, S. Micossi and M. Miller (eds) *The European Monetary System* (Cambridge University Press).

Committee for the Study of Economic and Monetary Union (1989) *Report on the Economic and Monetary Union in the European Community*, April.

De Cecco, M. (1988) 'Il Sistema Monetario Europeo e gli interessi nazionali', in P. Guerrieri and P.C. Padoan (eds) *L'economia politica dell'integrazione europea* (Bologna: Il Mulino).

De Grauwe, P. (1987) 'International Trade and Economic Growth in the European Monetary System', *European Economic Review*, vol. 31, no. 1/2, February/March.

Dini, L. (1988) *The Liberalisation of Capital and the Strengthening of the EMS*, Hearing before the European Parliament, Brussels. Bank of Italy, Documenti, no. 221, July.

EC Commission (1989) *Lo SME- dieci anni di progressi nella cooperazione monetaria europea.*

Giavazzi, F. and Pagano, M. (1985) *Capital Controls and the European Monetary System*, Occasional Paper, Euromobiliare, June, Milan.

Gomel, G., Saccomanni, F. and Vona, S. (1989) 'Tripolar Economic Policy Coordination: Problems of a Multi-Country Pole', *International Spectator*, no. 3/4, July–December.

Gressani, D., Guiso, L. and Visco, I. (1987) 'Il rientro dell'inflazione: un'analisi con il modello econometrico della Banca d'Italia', Bank of Italy, *Temi di Discussione*, no. 90, July.

Guitián, M. (1988) 'The European Monetary System: A Balance Between Rules and Discretion', in *Policy Coordination in the European Monetary System*, IMF, Occasional Paper no. 61, Washington, D.C.

Kaufman, H. (1985) 'The Deutschemark between the Dollar and the European Monetary System', *Kredit und Kapital*, no. 1.

Masera, R.S. (1987) *L'unificazione monetaria e lo SME* (Bologna: Il Mulino).

Masera, R.S. (1990) 'The European Monetary System Ten Years On: Problems and Perspectives', ch. 10, present volume.

Melitz, J. (1988) 'Monetary Discipline and Cooperation in the European Monetary System: A Synthesis', in F. Giavazzi, S. Micossi and M. Miller (eds) *The European Monetary System* (Cambridge University Press).

Micossi, S. (1985) 'The Intervention and Financing Mechanisms of the EMS and the Role of the ECU', *Banca Nazionale del Lavoro Quarterly Review*, no. 155.

Micossi, S. and Padoa-Schioppa, T. (1984) *Can Europeans Control Their Interest Rates?*, CEPS Papers, no. 17.

Padoan, P.C. (1988) 'Il Sistema Monetario Europeo e le politiche nazionali', in P.C. Padoan (ed.) *Politiche monetarie e politiche di bilancio nella Comunità Europea* (Bologna: Il Mulino).

Padoa-Schioppa, T. (1988a) 'The European Monetary System: A Long-Term View', in F. Giavazzi, S. Micossi and M. Miller (eds) *The European Monetary System* (Cambridge University Press).

Padoa-Schioppa, T. (1988b) 'The International Monetary System: The Next Twenty-Five Years', Per Jacobson Lecture, Basle, June.

Rebecchini, S. and Vona, S. (1990) 'The Decline of the EEC in International Trade: A Search for Some Structural Causes', in A. Courakis, F. Moraroque and G. Iannopulos (eds) *Trade Patterns and Policies in Southern Europe* (forthcoming).

Rogoff, K. (1985) 'Can Exchange Rate Predictability be Achieved without Monetary Convergence? Evidence from the EMS', *European Economic Review*, vol. 28, no. 1.

Spaventa, L. (1988) 'Old Rules and a New Reality?', in F. Giavazzi, S. Micossi and M. Miller (eds) *The European Monetary System* (Cambridge University Press).

Ungerer, H. *et al.* (1986) *The European Monetary System: Recent Developments*, IMF, Occasional Paper no. 48, Washington, D.C.

Vona, S. and Bini Smaghi, L. (1988) 'Economic Growth and Exchange Rates in the European Monetary System: Their Trade Effects in a Changing External Environment', in F. Giavazzi, S. Micossi and M. Miller (eds) *The European Monetary System* (Cambridge University Press).

5 The EMS and International Transmission Mechanisms

Jean-Paul Fitoussi and Jacques Le Cacheux

INTRODUCTION

At first sight, the EMS appears (or is said) to be an island of stability in a choppy ocean. For sure, the waves affect the shores of the island. But by and large the degree of stability of the inside land is enhanced, thus favouring intra-European trade. The metaphor has flimsy empirical and ambiguous theoretical foundations. It is common sense but common sense is often wrong, especially when applied to new problems.

When evaluating the records, one has to recognise that it has not been the case that intra-European trade has been booming relatively to oversea trade; quite the contrary (De Grauwe and Verfaille, 1988). And it was not the case that the countries of the EMS enjoyed better macroeconomic performances than the other unprotected islands in the ocean. In defence, it can be argued that these poor records have nothing to do with the EMS. Europe had to cope with specific problems – the so called Eurosclerosis thesis – or adopted the wrong policy mix (Blanchard, 1987). And there is nothing of a puzzle in the fact that a restrictive policy lowers activity, including international trade. But what if these policies were induced by the will to keep the EMS functioning? And what would be the rationale for this will?

From a theoretical point of view, the advantages of tying one's hands in a fixed exchange rate system are not obvious. Is it beneficial to restrain the degree of autonomy of monetary policy at the very moment the world is experiencing large and unexpected shocks? We have to restrain ourselves from too quick an answer to this list of queries. Open macroeconomic theory is not so firmly established as to lead to definitive conclusions. Also, the EMS is not a constraint but the choice of an exchange rate policy to achieve other goals; and it has to be evaluated as such.

Two polar cases have to be distinguished if we want to understand the channels through which the shocks of the 1980s have affected the level of activity in the European countries, account being taken of the existence of the EMS. In both cases we consider the world to be composed of two countries of about equal size, 'Europe' (the home country) and the US (the foreign country). This is probably an acceptable simplification – which does not mean that it is innocuous – as the major 'macroeconomic' shocks of the 1980s originated in the US. (If we were also to take into account the structural shocks to which Europe was exposed, then the consideration of a third area, namely Japan and the New Industrialised Countries, would have been necessary).

In the first polar case we consider Europe as a monetary union between individual countries, each one being subject to the same constraints: to keep its currency at a fixed exchange rate in terms of a numeraire, the ECU, in order to try to manage its own exchange rate vis-à-vis the dollar. This way of assessing the first polar, symmetrical case is self-explanatory of the difficulties the individual countries are confronted with. Each single country has to follow the same monetary policy as the average of the other countries, a first uncertainty, without knowing how the other countries would react to a variation in the value of the dollar, a second uncertainty. Moreover each European country being too small in size, they follow the fate of the small, open economy case in the Mundell–Fleming model of not having the possibility of affecting the world interest rate. In this first case the world interest rate is determined by the US policy mix, although Europe as a whole is equal in size to the US. Hence perhaps an explanation of Europe's passivity.

In the second polar case, one European country, say Germany, takes the lead. The others agree to tie their currency to the DM, perhaps because as suggested by Rogoff (1985) a country may benefit from appointing a central banker with a stronger aversion than society to inflation. Perhaps also, as we have tried to document elsewhere (Fitoussi and Le Cacheux, 1988a), the preferences of the policy-maker in the typical European country have changed, ranking low inflation as the first objective of economic policy in a lexicographical utility function. The move towards a more conservative policy was judged politically innocuous, as it happened at a time when, for good or bad reasons, the typical voter was persuaded that no other options were available. Once the choice has been made, the lexicographical order imposes that another objective can be dealt with only when the first has been reached.

'Sound finance' becomes for a while the absolute criterion by which to evaluate a policy-maker.

In such a system only (*n*-1) European countries tie their currencies to the DM. The last country, Germany, enjoys complete autonomy of its monetary policy. Furthermore, although the German economy is of a comparatively limited size, German monetary policy may affect the world interest rate, as any decision of its central banker entails a similar move of the money supply (or credit policy) of the other countries pertaining to the EMS (empirical evidence to support this story is that the range of variation of the real interest rates has been much smaller in Germany than in any other country of the G-7, except perhaps Japan). The legacy of the 1970s at the outset of the EMS has been a positive real interest rate in Germany and an almost null or negative one elsewhere. We assume, as the latter stylised fact seems to imply, that German policy-makers care about the real interest rate, trying to stabilise it, rather than about the DM exchange rate vis-à-vis the US dollar. This is a very crude and *non sequitur* interpretation of the German–US interest rate differential and we admit that there are several alternative candidates, but it will serve our purpose of evaluating the role of the EMS in the propagation of external shocks inside Europe.

When emphasising the importance of financial factors in 'causing' European unemployment (cf. Wyplosz, 1988), we are not denying that other factors, especially 'structural' ones, have had a detrimental influence on the course of unemployment.[1] The incomplete adaptation of real wages is indeed part of our story. However these factors cannot explain why the course of events has been so different after the second oil shock, from what came after the first. Moreover, a recent study has shown that these factors are not as common to the European countries as one would have thought. An empirical examination of the main economic indicators of the European countries (including those relative to the labour markets) lead to the conclusion that only GDP and industrial production exhibit a common trend (Reichlin, 1989).

This leaves the main 'innovations' of the 1980s to account for the particularly poor performances of the European economy, i.e. the EMS, the huge fluctuations of the nominal exchange rate of the dollar vis-à-vis the ECU, and the worldwide increase in the rate of interest, nominal and real, to historical highs.

This chapter is divided into three parts, the first one briefly presenting a few stylised facts, the other two dealing respectively with each of the polar cases above.

1 STYLISED FACTS

The stylised facts of the 1980s are now well established and may be summarised in the following way:

1. In the first part of the 1980s, there was a desynchronisation of the business cycle between Europe and the US. The divergent evolution of the unemployment rate in these two areas is a testimony of this fact.
2. The second part of the 1980s seems to have exhibited more convergent evolutions. The recovery of European growth until now has not been accompanied by a slump in America. It has to be noticed, however, that the former is incomplete: European unemployment is still high, and although decreasing in some countries, the prospect is that it will stabilise at some level well above what it was in the 1970s.
3. The real exchange rates of all European currencies in terms of the US dollar fell by more than 40 per cent between the third quarter of 1980 and the first quarter of 1985 and have risen by some 30 per cent since that date. The real effective exchange rates of the various currencies under study varied widely, although to a lesser extent (see Figure 5.1).
4. Inside the EMS the variations of the real exchange rate of each European currency vis-à-vis the others have been moderate but for the lira, which has appreciated by 30 per cent; by contrast the DM has depreciated by some 7 per cent (see Figure 5.1).
5. Real rates of interest have been at historic highs from 1982 onwards. This is generally agreed upon, even if there is no satisfactory way of measuring the real interest rate and thus of charting its course. But whichever way is chosen, this assessment is barely affected. Contrary to what happened to the real exchange rate of the dollar, there does not seem to exist a tendency for real interest rates to decelerate in the second part of the 1980s (see Figure 5.2).
6. The high level of the long-term real interest rate is clearly a new phenomenon in the countries under study, except for Germany. In the 1970s it was always positive in the latter country around 3 per cent while it was zero or negative in the other countries. Thus the sluggishness of the German real interest rate appears striking, especially when compared to the volatility of other countries' interest rates.
7. From the beginning of the 1980s the share of wages in value added decreased almost everywhere – an exception being Italy – but much more in Europe than in the USA, where the decrease has been moderate (see Figure 5.3).

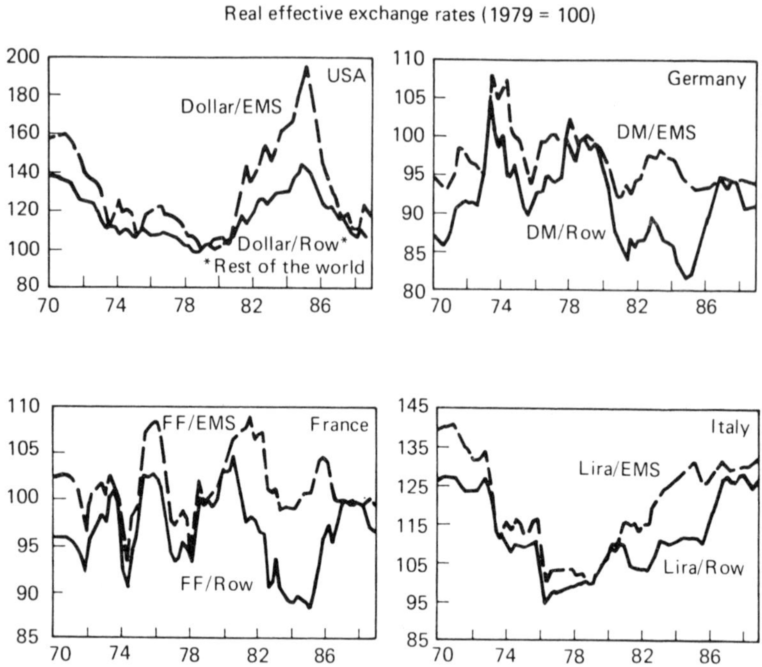

Source: OFCE

Figure 5.1 Real effective exchange rates (1979 = 100)

8. During the 1970s, when the dollar was depreciating against the European currencies and when real interest rates were low and decreasing, the mark-ups were typically characterised by an increasing trend in the USA and a decreasing trend in the three European countries under scrutiny (see Figure 5.4). During the 1980s real appreciation of the dollar and high levels of real interest rates combined in such a way that on average the mark-up in the USA was slightly above its 1970–80 trend (below the trend until the beginning of 1983 and well above after); while in Europe, in the first half of the 1980s, mark-ups were generally well above their 1970–80 trend, the departure in percentage of the trend's values being much greater than in the US. This statement has to be qualified for Germany where the picture is very similar to that of the US. In more recent years, mark-ups – at least as measured roughly by our simple index, which refers to the whole economy – have gone on increasing everywhere.

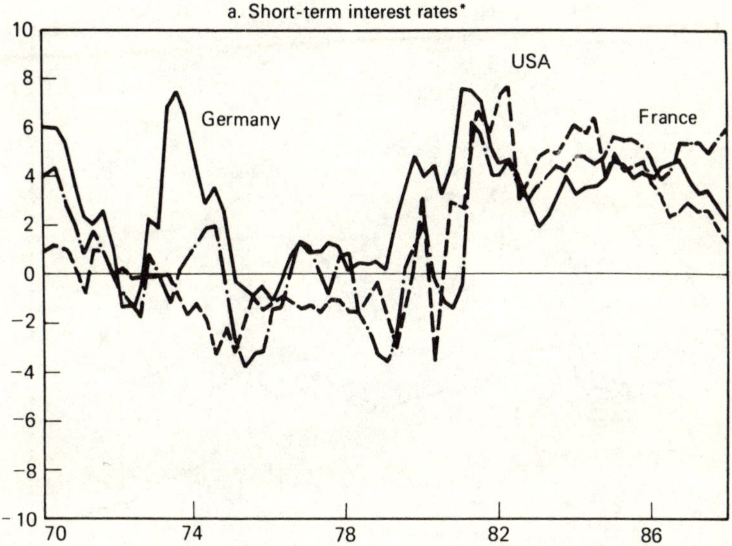

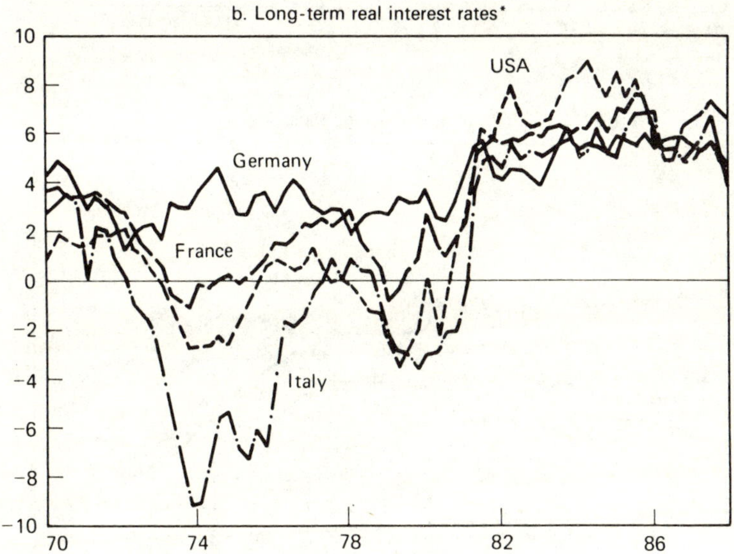

*End-of-quarter, nominal interest rates on overnight deposits, and end-of-quarter, nominal interest rates on long-term government bonds, deflated by a nine-quarter, centred moving average of the consumer price-index changes.

Sources: Authors' calculations from OECD data; OECD, *Main Economic Indicators*

Figure 5.2 a. Short-term real interest rates*. b. Long-term real interest rates*

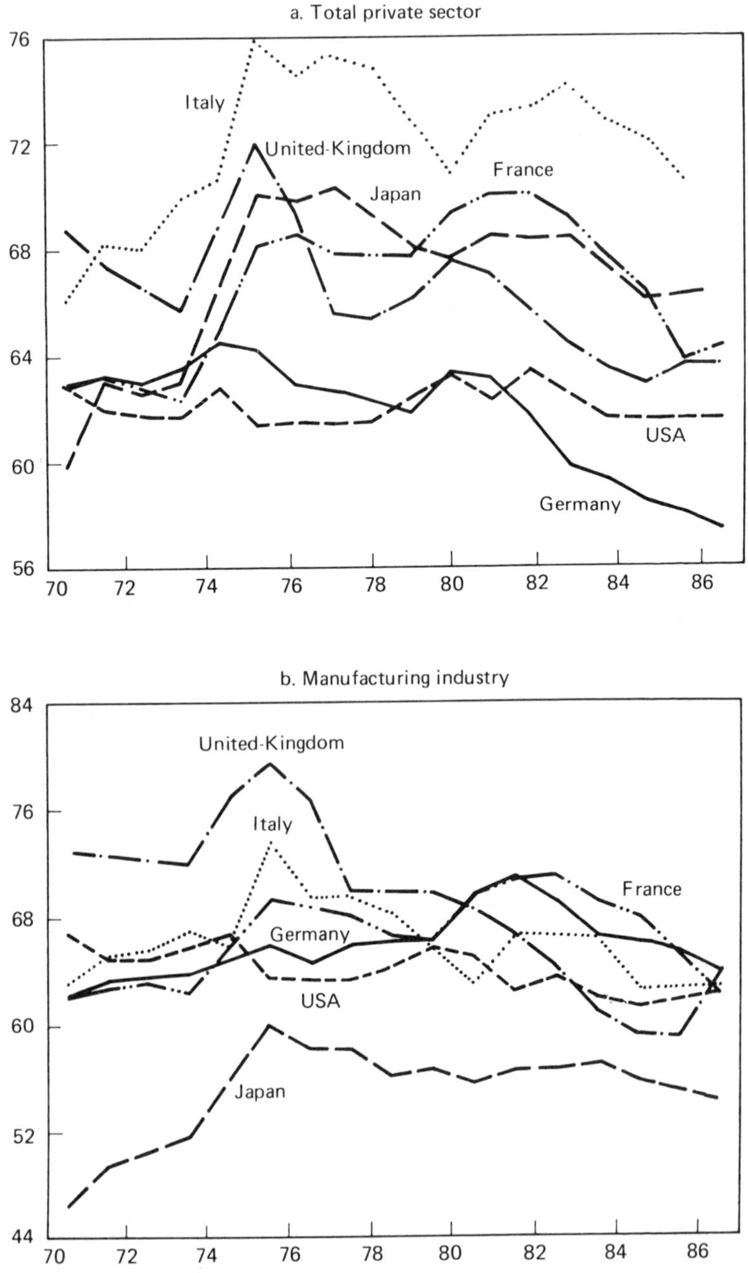

Figure 5.3 Wages share in value added

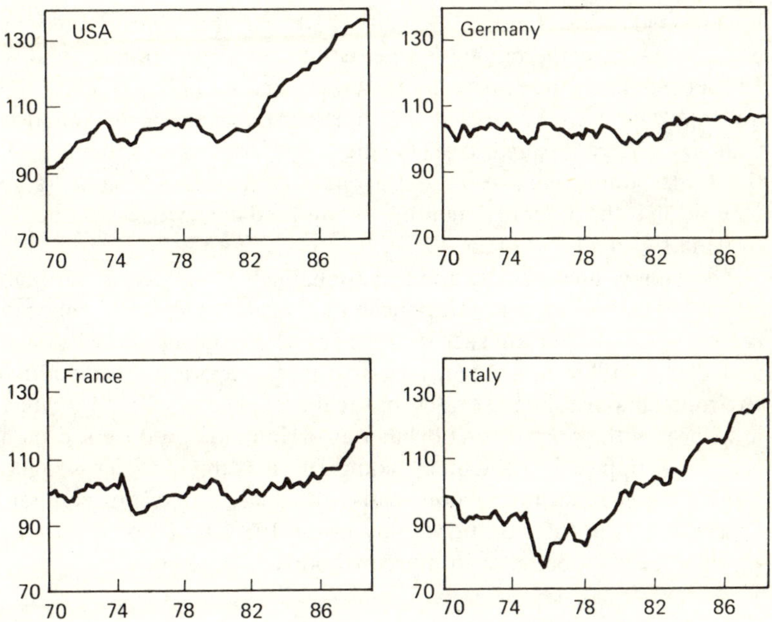

*Ratio of the GDP price deflator to the unit labour cost index.

Sources: Authors' calculations from OECD data (OECD, *Economic Perspectives* and *Main Economic Indicators*) and French price indicators (INSEE).

Figure 5.4 Mark-up indexes*

2 THE ROLE OF FINANCIAL VARIABLES IN INTERNATIONAL TRANSMISSION

It is often asserted that the peculiar policy mix adopted in the US during the first half of the 1980s, while producing a swift disinflation with little output loss in the American economy, had mainly detrimental consequences on the rest of the world, and primarily on Europe (see, for instance, Blanchard, 1987; Dornbusch, 1987). Yet according to the now-standard Mundell–Fleming analysis of the international transmission of macroeconomic policy disturbances, the overall effect of this shock on European economies ought to have been expansionary (see Fitoussi and Phelps, 1988). With unchanged macroeconomic policies in Europe, a rise in the world real rate of interest may have a negative effect on aggregate demand via its consequences on investment, but it also boosts money velocity and the total effect must be expansionary for the money market equilibrium condition to hold in Europe. Similarly the direct inflationary impact of a dollar appreciation on import prices may worsen the short-run unemployment–inflation trade-off and reduce real cash balances in European economies; but the trade connections between Europe and the US are actually so tenuous that the order of magnitude of this kind of negative effect ought to be fairly small (Wyplosz, 1988).

There may, however, be additional channels of influences through which foreign macroeconomic policies might get transmitted to an open economy. One important such channel has been emphasised by Fitoussi and Phelps (1988) in a recent monograph: in imperfectly competitive environments, real interest rates and real exchange rates exert a direct influence on the price setting behaviour of domestic producers, even if actual – as opposed to potential – competition by foreign firms is slight. Taking this channel into account leads to an analysis of macroeconomic developments in the world economy in the 1980s that would seem to fit observed data better than more orthodox explanations.

2.1 A simple aggregative model of a two-country world economy

In order to analyse the specific transmission process of real interest rates and real exchange rates onto producer prices, we use a simple aggregative model of a two-country world that departs as little as possible from standard open-economy analyses (see, for instance, Dornbusch, 1980). The major departure concerns price equations, which have been designed to capture mark-up behaviour of firms in imperfectly competitive markets. The model is a streamlined version[2] of the 'customer market' model proposed by Fitoussi and Phelps (1988); it has been linearised for convenience and all variables – except for interest rates – have been expressed as deviations with respect to trend.

The basic two-country model has the following set of equations:

$$z = -\alpha r + d \qquad (IS) \qquad (5.1)$$
$$z^* = -\alpha^* r^* + d^* \qquad (IS^*) \qquad (5.1^*)$$
$$m - q = z - \beta i \qquad (LM) \qquad (5.2)$$
$$m^* - q^* = z^* - \beta^* i^* \qquad (LM^*) \qquad (5.2^*)$$
$$c = w + \delta r + \gamma(z - k) \qquad (MC) \qquad (5.3)$$
$$c^* = w^* + \delta^* r^* + \gamma^*(z^* - k^*) \qquad (MC^*) \qquad (5.3^*)$$
$$p = \lambda c + (1 - \lambda)(p^* + e) \qquad (PS) \qquad (5.4)$$
$$p^* = \lambda^* c^* + (1 - \lambda^*)(p - e) \qquad (PS^*) \qquad (5.4^*)$$

w	$= \theta q$	(WI)	(5.5)
w^*	$= \theta^* q^*$	(WI^*)	(5.5*)
q	$= \varphi p + (1 - \varphi)(p^* + e)$	(CP)	(5.6)
q^*	$= \varphi^* p^* + (1 - \varphi^*)(p - e)$	(CP^*)	(5.6*)
r	$= r^* + x^e$	(IP)	(5.7)
x^e	$= e^e + p^{*e} - p^e$	(RE)	(5.8)
i	$= r + p^e$	(NR)	(5.9)
i^*	$= r^* + p^{*e}$	(NR^*)	(5.9*)

where all Greek letters are behavioural parameters, and lower case letters represent percentage changes in the corresponding variables. Non-starred variables refer to the 'home' country – EMS Europe – and starred ones to the 'foreign' country – the United States. All parameters are assumed to be positive.

Equations (5.1) and (5.1*) are standard aggregate demand equations, which capture the traditional negative effect of real interest rates on demand, mainly investment demand. d is a shift variable representing exogenous changes in fiscal policy or autonomous changes in consumption, or else in preferences for the foreign and the domestic goods. The absence of any relative price effect in the aggregate demand equations[3] may be justified either by supposing that, initially, domestic firms have only domestic customers and foreign firms only foreign customers – so that there is no trade in the initial situation (Fitoussi and Phelps, 1988) – or, more consistently with the rest of the model, by assuming some inertia in market shares, which is in broad agreement with the findings of recent studies of international trade in the context of imperfect competition (Krugman and Baldwin, 1987; Le Cacheux and Lecointe, 1987). Both assumptions are almost equally acceptable descriptions of US–EC trade relations, which represent a small fraction of total output in each country. Because we ignore this 'expenditure switching' effect of exchange rate changes, variations in domestic expenditure are equivalent to variations in domestic output.

Equations (5.2) and (5.2*) are also standard LM-type relations, in which the income elasticity of money demand has been constrained to unity for convenience, m and m^* are respectively the domestic and the foreign money supplies, assumed to be the monetary policy instrument in each country. q and q^* are consumer price indices, defined as geometric averages of foreign and domestic producer prices, with fixed weights (equations 5.6 and 5.6*).

The specifications of supply and pricing behaviour are less conventional and require some more explication.[4] In the spirit of imperfect competition, it is assumed that firms in each country have a desired mark-up over marginal cost. The latter is supposed to be mainly affected by the wage rate (w) and to be an increasing function of demand, in the short term – that is, given production capacity (k and k^*). Owing to the imperfectly competitive environment, which gives rise to a trade-off between present profits and market shares – or equivalently between present profits and future profits (Phelps and Winter, 1970; Fitoussi and Phelps, 1988; Froot and Klemperer, 1988) – desired mark-ups of individual firms in each country are assumed to be positively related to real interest rates. Actual price-setting behaviour is described by equations (5.4) and (5.4*), which state that firms take their (potential) foreign competitors' prices into account when posting their own sale prices, so that producer prices in each country may be represented by a weighted average of domestic, desired prices and foreign competitors' actual prices.[5]

Nominal wage rates in each country are assumed to be determined by a simple mechanism of contemporaneous indexation on consumer prices, with an indexation coefficient θ, $0 \leqslant \theta \leqslant 1$ (equations 5.5 and 5.5*). Thus we ignore possible endogenous influences of unemployment on wage-setting behaviour – there is no traditional Phillips relation in our model.

The evolutions of financial variables are described in the last four equations, with the simplest possible specifications. Equation (5.7) is an international financial arbitrage condition, imposing equality of expected real interest rates. Expected changes in the real exchange rate (x^e) are defined in equation (5.8), while nominal interest rates are determined by a Fisher equation in each country (equations 5.9 and 5.9*). In addition, we assume in this section that the US economy – the 'foreign' country – is large in world financial markets, so that it effectively determines the world real interest rate. This is equivalent to treating the 'home' country – Europe – as a collection of small countries linked together by fixed exchange rates, but with no common or coordinated monetary policy; the home country model may thus be regarded as a 'representative' small open economy.

Before turning to the comparative statics properties of this simple model, it will be convenient to rewrite the price equations in terms of changes in the real exchange rate, x, defined as:

$$x = e + p^* - p \tag{5.10}$$

In the present, imperfectly competitive environment, the law of one price does not hold, at least in the short run, so that the real exchange rate may change. (Here a positive x corresponds to a real appreciation of the foreign currency, namely the dollar.) In the home country, rewriting equations (5.4) and (5.6) yields:

$$p = c + \frac{1-\lambda}{\lambda} x \tag{5.4'}$$

$$q = p + (1-\varphi)x \tag{5.6'}$$

Using equations (5.3) and (5.5), and substituting, we get the change in domestic consumer prices:

$$q = \frac{\delta}{1-\theta} r + \frac{\gamma}{1-\theta}(z-k) + \frac{1-\lambda\varphi}{\lambda(1-\theta)} x \tag{5.11}$$

And similarly for the foreign country:

$$q^* = \frac{\delta^*}{1-\theta^*} r^* + \frac{\gamma^*}{1-\theta^*}(z^*-k^*) - \frac{(1-\lambda^*\varphi^*)}{\lambda^*(1-\theta^*)} x \tag{5.11*}$$

These equations summarise the influences of financial variables on the general price level in each country. Together with *LM* relations, they define a short-run output–inflation trade-off in each country. As expected, the indexation coefficients (θ and θ^*) play a central part in the transmission of changes in the real interest rates and in the real exchange rate: given the other parameters, the larger θ or θ^*, the larger the impact of these changes on the corresponding consumer prices. In addition, the larger the sensitivity of current mark-ups to real interest rates (δ and δ^*), the more inflationary an increase in real interest rates will be, given the indexation coefficients. Finally, the impact of the real exchange rate depends as much on the degree of openness of goods markets, as measured by φ and φ^*, as on the extent to which domestic pricing decisions are influenced by foreign producer prices (λ and λ^*).

2.2 The transmission of the US policy mix

The specific properties of this simple model may be illustrated by carrying out a graphic analysis for a policy experiment that may be judged broadly descriptive of the US policy mix in the first half of the 1980s (Sachs, 1985): thus, we consider the effects of a combination of monetary tightening and fiscal stimulus in the 'foreign' country.[6] Treating expectations as exogenous, the complete model may be solved for changes in domestic and foreign outputs (z and z^*), in the real interest rates and in the real exchange rate (see Appendix). Substituting

(5.11) and (5.11*) for (5.2) and (5.2*) respectively, and using (5.7), yields the following reduced form:

$$z = -\alpha(r^* + x^e) + d \tag{5.1}$$

$$z\left[\frac{1-\theta+\gamma}{1-\theta}\right] = m + \frac{\gamma}{1-\theta}k + \beta p^e + \left[\beta - \frac{\delta}{1-\theta}\right](r^* + x^e) - \left[\frac{1-\lambda\varphi}{\lambda(1-\theta)}\right]x \tag{5.2'}$$

$$z^* = -\alpha^* r^* + d^* \tag{5.1*}$$

$$z^*\left[\frac{1-\theta^*+\gamma^*}{1-\theta^*}\right] = m^* + \frac{\gamma^*}{1-\theta^*}k^* + \beta^* p^{*e} + \left[\beta^* - \frac{\delta^*}{1-\theta^*}\right]r^* + \left[\frac{1-\lambda^*\varphi^*}{\lambda^*(1-\theta^*)}\right]x \tag{5.2*'}$$

Solving (5.1) and (5.2) for the real exchange rate, x, and substituting into (5.2*′), we get the following pair of equilibrium equations for the foreign country in terms of foreign endogenous variables:

$$z^* = -\alpha^* r^* + d^* \qquad (IS^*) \tag{5.1*}$$

$$A^* z^* = m^* + B^* r^* + C^* \qquad (LM^{*\prime\prime}) \tag{5.2*''}$$

where $A^* > 0$ and B^* has an ambiguous sign, depending on the magnitude of the various parameters,[7] while C^* groups together all the variables treated as exogenous (see Appendix to this chapter). The corresponding equilibrium is depicted on the upper left-hand side of Figure 5.5. The US policy mix ($m^* < 0$ and $d^* > 0$) shifts both curves upwards, resulting in an expansion of foreign output and a rise in the real interest rate.

The consequences in the home country are shown on the upper right-hand side of Figure 5.5. The two curves have the following equations (see Appendix):

$$z = -\alpha r^* - \alpha x^e + d \qquad (IS) \tag{5.1}$$

$$Az = B(r^* + x^e) - H(A^* d^* - m^*) + C \qquad (LM'') \tag{5.2''}$$

where $A > 0$, B has again an ambiguous sign, $H > 0$ and C summarises all other exogenous factors (see Appendix). Foreign policies unambiguously shift the LM'' curve inwards, while leaving the IS curve unaffected. The result is a contraction of home output. What happens

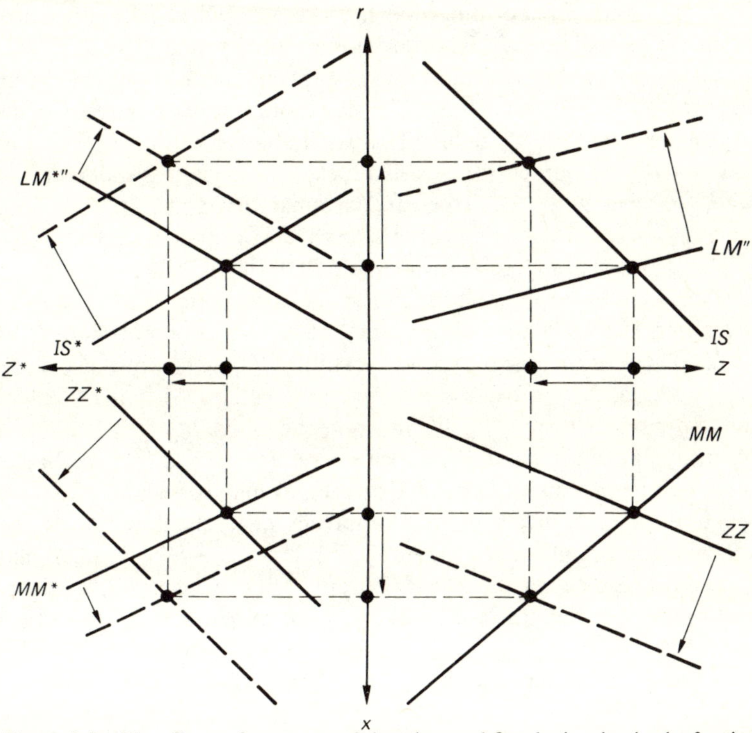

Figure 5.5 The effects of monetary tightening and fiscal stimulus in the foreign country

to the dollar real exchange rate in the process may be read on the two lower quadrants of Figure 5.5.

Clearly, with our assumptions, the US policy mix improves the inflation–output trade-off there, thanks to the dollar appreciation it induces. This is the consequence of the negative effect of real appreciation on US mark-ups, compensating the inflationary effect of the increase in the real interest rate. In European economies, both the real depreciation of local currencies and the real interest rate increase work to inflate mark-ups, so that the domestic trade-off worsens. Hence, US policies produce a recession *and* inflation in Europe, with an unchanged policy stance in the 'domestic' economy. European policies appear, *ex post*, to have been more restrictive though, since real balances shrink, the full-employment budget surpluses increase and real interest rates rise.

Even though these general patterns may seem to be in broad agreement with observed developments on both sides of the Atlantic, the conclusions may be somewhat less dramatic when taking account of expectational effects. The preceding formal analysis has been conducted with the assumption that changes in financial variables were regarded as being permanent. Clearly, though, policy developments in the US were not indefinitely sustainable, and this aspect was undoubtedly accounted for in private expectations. Our model is not suited to deal with the issues of sustainability and dynamics, but something may be said about the consequences of such expectational effects. If the real appreciation of the dollar was actually expected to be reversed in the future, the rise in European real rates of interest must have been less than that in US real rates. With our notations, this means that x^e turned negative, which shifts *IS* upwards, but also shifts *LM″* and *LM*″* upwards on Figure 5.5. This implies that r^* has to increase more than previously, and that the US policy mix has a less expansionary effect on the American economy, and a less restrictive impact on European economies. However, as may be seen in the lower part of Figure 5.5, the current real appreciation of the dollar has to be sufficient for expansion to materialise in the US, which implies that there must still be a recession in Europe. Thus, expectational factors tend to mitigate the previous results without reversing their direction.[8]

2.3 The dollar decline and the European recovery

With the afore-mentioned qualifications concerning expectations, the foregoing analysis implies that the adoption of a more accommodating monetary policy in the US will tend to improve the situation in both regions, by pulling down real interest rates and the dollar real exchange rate. In terms of our model, increasing the US money supply, with an unchanged fiscal stance, will shift the *LM*″* and *LM″* curves back down in Figure 5.5, *IS** and *IS* being unaffected. These moves tend to boost domestic and foreign output, while decreasing the world real interest rate. In the bottom half of Figure 5.5, *MM** shifts outwards and *MM* inwards, producing a decline in the real value of the dollar. On the whole, output and inflation are increased in the US, whereas Europe enjoys a recovery together with disinflation, which broadly fits the patterns observed in the post-1985 period of falling dollar and falling real interest rates in the US. Again, these developments take place with European policies unchanged, but appearing less restrictive.

However, this comparative statics experiment ignores at least two factors which prevent a symmetric working of the model and may produce some persistence in the European stagflation problem of the first phase. With our specifications, capacity output enters exogenously in the price determination process. Owing to the length of the period characterised by real high interest rates and a high real value of the dollar, it would seem reasonable to assume that the capital stock in both regions has had time to vary. In the US, the real interest rate increase ought to have penalised investment; but a large part of the fiscal stimulus during the 1981–5 period was in the form of corporate tax relief and investment incentives, which mitigated the negative consequences of high real interest rates on investment demand (see Gubian, Guillaumat-Tailliet and Le Cacheux, 1986; Fitoussi and Phelps, 1988; Feldstein and Elmendorf, 1989). On the whole, the American recovery was actually characterised by an exceptionally strong investment growth. While this development tended to lessen inflationary pressures in the US, Europe, where no such fiscal stimulus to investment was injected, only felt the negative consequences of high real interest rates on investment, implying a decline in the capital stock – with respect to trend. Entering the second phase with reduced capacity, European economies may have benefited less from the US policy reversal than suggested in our second comparative statics experiment, in so far as the output–inflation trade-off has deteriorated through this channel.

Another factor hindering the favourable evolutions of the second period relates to fiscal policies. High real interest rates in the world economy tend to lead to a build-up in public debts, a phenomenon that is ignored in our model. In the US, this necessarily arises as a result of the expansionary fiscal stance; but European countries also face the consequences of high real interest rates on outstanding public debts, which, if prolonged, adds up to the existing stocks, with unchanged fiscal policies.[9] The higher level of public debts carries over to the second phase and may encourage the adoption of a restrictive fiscal policy stance in Europe, which might also hinder recovery.[10]

These two long-lasting consequences of high real interest rates – via 'memorised' effects on the stocks of productive capital and of public debt – suggest that variations in real interest rates induce major hysteretic effects on the economy.

3 ASYMMETRY WITHIN EUROPE?

Most existing analyses of the functioning of the European monetary system have focused on the consequences of nominal shocks occurring within the system (see, for instance, Giavazzi, Micossi and Miller, eds,

1988). For that purpose, representing the EMS as a two-country, closed system with fixed exchange rates is appropriate. Our contention, however, is that the major shocks affecting Europe in the 1980s were real disturbances, originating from outside the system, as illustrated in the previous section. Clearly, if this was indeed the case, unless European economies are perfectly identical in all respect, what is required is real adjustment within Europe. Depending on the institutional arrangements, the European exchange rate mechanism will interfere with the transmission of external shocks by amplifying or dampening their effects on the various economies, thus affecting the sharing of the burden of adjustment in Europe.

3.1 Transmission in a three-country model

In order to analyse the transmission of external real shocks, a three-country version of the previous model is needed. As in the foregoing, the US and Europe are treated as relatively closed economies, with major links operating through real interest rate and real exchange rate variations. This model is therefore similar to the one presented in Section 2, except that European countries are now assumed – realistically – to have extensive trade relations with each other, so that the intra-EMS real exchange rate has a direct effect on the demand for domestic goods in each European country.

So long as the world repercussions of European policies are ignored, the US economy may be represented by a single, reduced-form equation, derived from (5.1) and (5.2′), and relating the world real interest rate and the dollar–EMS real exchange rate[11] to domestic policies in the US:

$$(\alpha^* A^* + B^*)r^* = A^* d^* - m^* - C^{*\prime} x \tag{5.12*}$$

Given the definitions of parameters in equation (5.12*), $C^{*\prime}$ is always positive, so that imposing $(\alpha^* A^* + B^*) > 0$ implies an inverse relationship between changes in the US real interest rate and the dollar real appreciation rate, given US policies. This restriction is also a necessary condition for negative transmission of the US policy mix implemented in the first half of the 1980s, so that it will be assumed to hold in the following.

The two European economies are represented by a system of equations which is almost identical to that developed in the previous section, notation being the same.

$$z_1 = -\alpha_1 r_1 - \varepsilon_1 \pi + \mu_1 z_2 + d_1 \tag{5.1.1}$$

$$z_2 = -\alpha_2 r_2 - \varepsilon_2 \pi + \mu_2 z_1 + d_2 \tag{5.1.2}$$

$$m_1 - q_1 = \xi_1 z_1 - \beta_1 (r_1 + q_1^e) \tag{5.2.1}$$

$$m_2 - q_2 = \xi_2 z_2 - \beta_2 (r_2 + q_2^e) \tag{5.2.2}$$

$$c_1 = w_1 + \delta_1 r_1 + \gamma_1 (z_1 - k_1) \tag{5.3.1}$$

$$c_2 = w_2 + \delta_2 r_2 + \gamma_2 (z_2 - k_2) \tag{5.3.2}$$

$$p_1 = \lambda_1 c_1 + (1 - \lambda_1)[\eta_1 (p^* + e) + (1 - \eta_1) p_2] \tag{5.4.1}$$

$$p_2 = \lambda_2 c_2 + (1 - \lambda_2)[\eta_2 (p^* + e) + (1 - \eta_2) p_1] \tag{5.4.2}$$

$$w_1 = \theta_1 q_1 \tag{5.5.1}$$

$$w_2 = \theta_2 q_2 \tag{5.5.2}$$

$$q_1 = \varphi_1 p_1 + (1 - \varphi_1) p_2 \tag{5.6.1}$$

$$q_2 = \varphi_2 p_2 + (1 - \varphi_2) p_1 \tag{5.6.2}$$

$$r_1 = r^* + x^e \tag{5.7.1}$$

$$r_2 = r^* + x^e + \pi^e \tag{5.7.2}$$

$$x = e + p^* - p_1 \tag{5.8.1}$$

$$\pi = p_1 - p_2 \tag{5.9.1}$$

Equations (5.1.1) and (5.1.2) simply state that the demand for domestic output in each European country is negatively related to its bilateral, real exchange rate (π), and positively related to the level of activity in the partner's economy. Equations (5.2.1) and (5.2.2) are the usual money-market equilibrium conditions; but z now represents changes in the demand for domestic output, which, with bilateral trade, is no longer equivalent to changes in domestic expenditure.

The rest of the model is formally identical to the previous one, except that domestic producers in each country are now assumed to compete with both US producers and producers from the other European country. In the definition of price changes and of changes in the intra-EMS, real exchange rate (equation 5.9.1), we have imposed the condition of a fixed nominal exchange rate between the two European countries. (A rise in π is a real appreciation of country 1's currency vis-à-vis country 2's.)

By expressing price changes in terms of real exchange rates and rearranging the wage–price subsystems, we get the general price level equations for each country:

$$(1-\theta_1)q_1 = \delta_1 r_1 + \gamma_1(z_1 - k_1) + \frac{\eta_1(1-\lambda_1)}{\lambda_1} x - \frac{\lambda_1(1-\varphi_1) + (1-\lambda_1)(1-\eta_1)}{\lambda_1} \pi \quad (5.11.1)$$

$$(1-\theta_2)q_2 = \delta_2 r_2 + \gamma_2(z_2 - k_1) + \frac{\eta_2(1-\lambda_2)}{\lambda_2} x + \frac{1-\lambda_2\varphi_2}{\lambda_2} \pi \quad (5.11.2)$$

Their properties are similar to those obtained in Section 2 (equations 5.11 and 5.11*). In particular, increases in the real interest rates or in the dollar real exchange rate tend to shift these relations upwards, to an extent which depends on the degree of wage-indexation. This results in a worsening of the inflation–output trade-off in both countries. Conversely, a real appreciation of the domestic currency tends to improve the domestic trade-off by shifting the corresponding equation downwards.

In order to investigate the real consequences of US policies on the two European countries, this set of relations may be reduced to a five-equation system determining the changes in five endogenous variables – the world real rate of interest, domestic outputs in country 1 and country 2, and two real exchange rates (x and π) – just as previously (see Appendix):

$$z_1 = -F_1 r_1 - G_1 \pi + (d_1 + \mu_1 d_2) \quad (5.1.1')$$

$$z_2 = -F_2 r_2 + G_2 \pi + (d_2 + \mu_2 d_1) \quad (5.1.2')$$

$$A_1 z_1 = m_1 + B_1 r_1 - C_1 x + D_1 \pi + H_1 \quad (5.2.1')$$

$$A_2 z_2 = m_2 + B_2 r_2 - C_2 x + D_2 \pi + H_2 \quad (5.2.2')$$

$$(\alpha^* A^* + B^*) r^* = A^* d^* - m^* - C^{*\prime} x \quad (5.12^*)$$

with $r_1 = r^* + x^e$

$$r_2 = r_1 + \pi^e = r^* + x^e + \pi^e$$

All parameters are assumed positive. In particular G_1, $G_2 > 0$, which states that in each country a real depreciation has a globally positive effect on the demand for domestic output.[12]

Solving again, with exogenous expectations, for the consequences of the US policy mix considered in the first part of the previous section – monetary contraction cum fiscal stimulus, producing a real interest hike and a real appreciation of the dollar – the outcome in each country hinges on the values of the whole set of structural parameters. Clearly, with passive policies in European countries, the intra-EMS real exchange rate (π) will be unaffected if and only if the two European countries are identical in every respect. This may be illustrated with the help of Figure 5.6, where the two curves represent the relations between the real interest rate and the intra-EMS real exchange rate corresponding to reduced forms of each country model:

$$(RR_1) \quad K_1 r^* + L_1 \pi - (C_1/C^{*\prime})(A^* d^* - m^*) + m_1 = 0$$

$$(RR_2) \quad K_2 r^* - L_2 \pi - (C_2/C^{*\prime})(A^* d^* - m^*) + m_2 + (A_2 F_2 + B_2)\pi^e = 0$$

With our usual assumptions, the slopes are as depicted and the US policy mix shifts both RR_1 and RR_2 outwards. Only when the horizontal magnitude of both shifts is the same – that is, when European economies are identical in all respects – will there be no change in π. In general, however, the intra-EMS real exchange rate will be affected in the process; but according to the parameter constellation, it may increase or decrease (see Appendix).

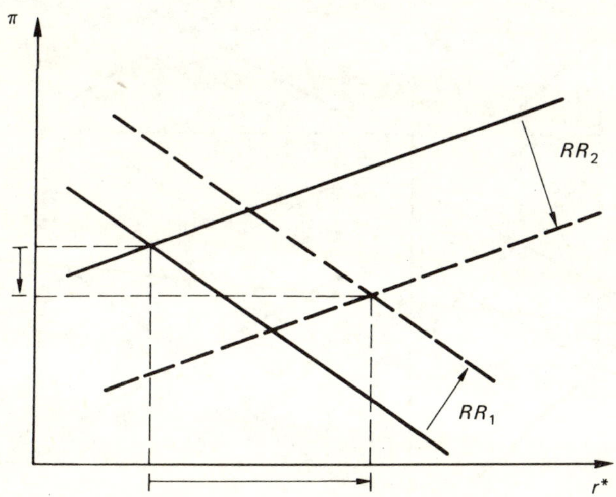

Figure 5.6 The relation between the real interest rate and the intra-EMS real exchange rate

The complexity of adjustmenets to the external disturbance in the two European economies may be grasped on Figure 5.7, where the curves correspond to the following reduced form relations:

$$(IS_1')\quad z_1 = -\Delta_1 r^* + (G_1 C_2/C^{*\prime})(A^* d^* - m^*) + \ldots$$

$$(LM_1')\quad z_1 = M_1 r^* - \left(\frac{D_1 C_2 + C_1}{C^{*\prime}}\right)(A^* d^* - m^*) + \ldots$$

$$(IS_2')\quad z_2 = -\Delta_2 r^* + (G_2 C_1/C^{*\prime})(A^* d^* - m^*) + \ldots$$

$$(LM_2')\quad z_2 = M_2 r^* - \left(\frac{D_2 C_1 + C_2}{C^{*\prime}}\right)(A^* d^* - m^*) + \ldots$$

$$(ZZ_1)\quad z_1 = -\phi_1 \pi - (F_1 C_2/C^{*\prime})(A^* d^* - m^*) + \ldots$$

$$(MM_1)\quad z_1 = \chi_1 \pi + N_1 (A^* d^* - m^*) + \ldots$$

$$(ZZ_2)\quad z_2 = \phi_2 \pi - (F_2 C_1/C^{*\prime})(A^* d^* - m^*) + \ldots$$

$$(MM_2)\quad z_2 = -\chi_2 \pi + N_2 (A^* d^* - m^*) + \ldots$$

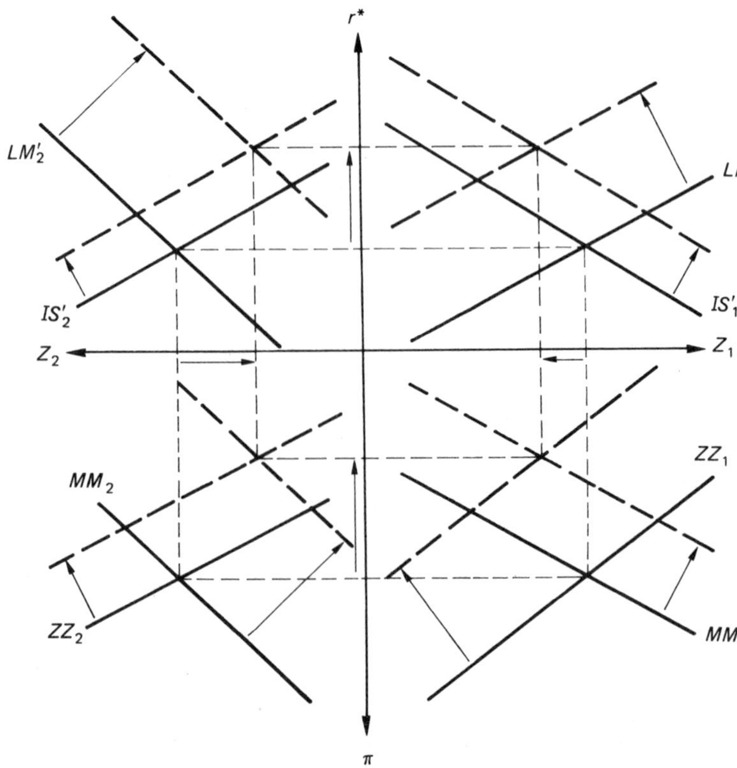

Figure 5.7 Adjustments to extensive disturbances in a three-country model

Given our initial assumptions, the signs of the various slopes are unambiguously as depicted on Figure 5.7; but all curves are shifted by the external shock considered. In the upper part of Figure 5.7, the directions of the moves are necessarily as shown, since there must be an increase in the world real interest rate and a contraction of output in Europe, according to our results of the previous section. However, things are less clear-cut in the bottom half of Figure 5.7: indeed, N_1 and N_2 in MM_1 and MM_2 have an ambiguous sign, so that these curves may shift in either direction, meaning that, as already emphasised, π might increase or decrease, but also that the contractionary impact may be felt more in one country than in the other. In addition, although there are conditions on parameter values associated with each case, there is no general relationship between the direction of the intra-EMS real exchange rate adjustment and the sharing of the burden of output loss amongst European economies. In the special case of Figure 5.7, a real depreciation of country 1's currency vis-à-vis country 2's is associated with a larger (in percentage) contraction of output in country 2.

3.2 Asymmetric reactions

So far, no explicit account has been taken of the specific European exchange rate mechanism. There are, at least, two ways in which an EMS-type, fixed exchange rate system in Europe will interfere with the adjustment processes just analysed: private exchange-rate expectations and monetary policy reactions. As it stands, our model is ill-equipped to deal properly with endogenous adjustments in these variables, but we may trace the major consequences of plausible, exogenously specified reactions.

Insofar as variations in the intra-EMS real exchange rate reflect divergences in inflation rates, they may trigger devaluation expectations. According to the previous analysis, this will happen when the combined effect of a rise in the world real interest rate and of a dollar real appreciation worsens the output–inflation trade-off more in one country than in the other. Let us assume this to be the case in country 2, so that, ignoring expectational changes, the outcome corresponds to that of Figure 5.7. If the real appreciation of country 2's currency induces expectations of a devaluation, $\pi^e > 0$[13]. This drives a wedge between the real interest rates in country 1 and in country 2, the latter becoming superior to the former. Output contraction will thus necessarily be more pronounced in country 2. In graphic terms on Figure 5.7, IS_1' is shifted further up, and LM_1' back down, while IS_2' is shifted back in and LM_2' further up. This allows r^* to remain constant, whereas country 2's output is decreased by more than before, and country 1's by less.

The other major influence of a fixed exchange rate system on the transmission mechanism has to do with money supply processes. This aspect may be illustrated by introducing an – admittedly rather crude – characterisation of asymmetric intervention practices in the EMS. In agreement with numerous recent analyses of the European exchange rate mechanism (see, for instance: Giavazzi and Giovannini, 1987), we assume that country 1 – Germany – being the nth country, provides the nominal anchor of the system by refraining from interventions in the exchange markets and by completely sterilising foreign interventions, thus perfectly controlling her domestic money supply ($m_1 = 0$, in formal terms). Country 2 – say France or Italy – bears the burden of resisting incipient pressures on the intra-EMS nominal exchange rate by intervening without sterilising. Invoking again the small-country assumption, possible effects of changes in country 2's money supply on the world real interest rate may be ignored. If, as seems reasonable, country 2's currency is expected to devalue when the inflation differential with country 1 widens – that is, when it appreciates in real terms – then a fall in π will induce a contraction of country 2's money supply. In the adjustment process just analysed, this tends to shift some additional burden onto this country's output.

4 CONCLUDING REMARKS

The models discussed in this chapter were designed to emphasise some rather unorthodox channels of international transmission policy disturbances inducing real shocks that affect open economies through supply responses. Rock-bottom as they may be regarded, they appear to give a fair account of major developments in the international economy during the 1980s. When plausible asymmetries in the policies of European countries are introduced, unbalanced consequences of external real shocks are the likely outcome, although the exact conditions for this to happen, and the proper specification of monetary policies in an exchange union where parity alterations are allowed, remain to be worked out.

What about the consequences in the EMS of the US policy shift to a more accommodating monetary policy, inducing a reduction in the

US real interest rate and a dollar decline? The case in which European authorities remain passive has been shown to yield a recovery with disinflation in Europe, with a slowdown – though not a recession – with some inflation in the US. However, if Germany is effectively in a position to control her own money supply and, via the exchange rate mechanism, the whole European money supply, this country is also in a position to set the standard for European real interest rates and to influence the world level of real interest rates. The dollar decline, being the result of capital outflows, part of which at least are inflows into Germany, tends to inflate the German money supply and to reduce real interest rates there, as well as in the rest of the EMS. But, if those capital inflows are sterilised by the Bundesbank, in the pursuit of a money supply target, real interest rates will be prevented from declining in Europe, at least to some extent. This strategy, which may be self-defeating insofar as maintaining high real interest rates tends to reinforce capital inflows, may well force the US authorities into a more restrictive monetary policy than they intended, in order to prevent a further depreciation of the dollar. The outcome could then be a ratchet effect on world real interest rates, which may hinder the recovery in Europe and keep inflation from declining.

Notes

1. The hysteresis hypothesis is also appealing (Blanchard and Summers, 1987). Note that this hypothesis is needed to explain persistence, whatever the origin of the shock. In *The Slump in Europe* (Fitoussi and Phelps, 1988), persistence is mainly due to the effect on capital stock of a long period of a high real rate of interest.
2. The present version is formally similar to that proposed by Sachs (1986) in his comment on Fitoussi and Phelps (1986).
3. In the Mundell–Fleming model the expansionary consequence of a foreign fiscal stimulus or of a tight monetary policy abroad on home country output is due to the fact that the competitive effect of a real depreciation dominates the restrictive effect of the increase in the real rate of interest. In writing equations (5.1) and (5.1*) this way, we are conscious that we rule out from the outset the first expansionary effect, leaving only the restrictive effect at work. In a way we are assuming what we would like to demonstrate. But in a way only. What we are assuming in fact, for reasons which will appear

later in the chapter, is that the interest rate effect dominates. Thus $(-\alpha)$ may be considered as measuring the combined two effects; it could be small but we constrain it to be negative. We will leave for further research the task of establishing the exact conditions for this assumption to hold. The results of econometric studies of the relevant elasticities are, to say the least, ambiguous. Moreover, in the model of section 2, we will explicitly take into account the demand effect of changes in the real exchange rate in European economies.

4. For more detailed justifications, see Fitoussi and Phelps (1988).
5. Here we neglect the fact, consistent with imperfect competition, that staggered price-setting by individual firms will normally produce inertia in aggregate producer prices (Fitoussi and Le Cacheux, 1988b).
6. This is clearly a very simplified description of the actual US policy mix. In fact, it may be argued that there was first a monetary squeeze, then a sustained fiscal stimulus with monetary expansion. See, for instance, Feldstein and Elmendorf (1989).
7. We rule out the cases in which $B^* < 0$, since they can be shown to prevent a simultaneous increase in r^* and z^* to be associated with the policy mix considered here.
8. Exchange rate expectations also ought to influence pricing decisions (equations 5.6 and 5.6*), as suggested in Fitoussi and Le Cacheux (1988b) and in Froot and Klemperer (1988). However, with a sustained dollar rise and a real interest rate increase, the effect on current price-setting is ambiguous.
9. This aspect may be regarded as an open-economy illustration of the famous 'unpleasant monetarist arithmetics' (Sargent and Wallace, 1981). See also Dornbusch (1988).
10. Here, we again appeal to the assumption that each European country is small in the world economy. Otherwise fiscal policy has an effect on the world real interest rate. As to the US, it may easily be seen that, in our world, a more restrictive fiscal policy produces a recession, but improves the situation in European economies, only to the extent that it decreases real interest rates and the dollar real exchange rate.
11. It will be convenient to assume that prices in the US are influenced only by German (country 1) prices. Alternatively, x would have to be treated as the change in the dollar real effective exchange rate, hence as a combination of the two real exchange rates vis-à-vis each European currency. The choice made here does not greatly affect the results of our analysis for European countries as long as US prices influence price-setting in both countries.
12. This is equivalent to assuming that a devaluation improves the trade balance, which involves the Marshall–Lerner conditions on trade elasticities and the 'critical elasticities theorem'.
13. Here we ignore any repercussion of this expectational shift on the third country – the US – and possibly on the world real interest rate. Thus, r^* is assumed not to be affected.

References

Blanchard, O.E. (1987) 'Reaganomics', *Economic Policy*, no. 5, October.

Blanchard, O. and Summers, L.H. (1987) 'Hysteresis in Unemployment', *European Economic Review, Papers and Proceedings of the First Annual Congress of the European Economic Association*, 31, no. 1/2, February/March.

De Grauwe, P. and Verfaille, G. (1988) 'Exchange Rate Variability, Misalignment, and the European Monetary System', in R. Marston (ed.) *Misalignment of Exchange Rates: Effects on Trade and Industry* (Chicago, Ill., and London: University of Chicago Press).

Dornbusch, R. (1980), *Open Economy Macroeconomics* (New York: Basic Books).

Dornbusch, R. (1988), 'The EMS, the Dollar and the Yen', in F. Giavazzi, S. Micossi and M. Miller (eds) *The European Monetary System* (Cambridge University Press).

Feldstein, M. and Elmendorf, D. (1989) 'Budget Deficits, Tax Incentives, and Inflation: A Surprising Lesson from the 1983–4 Recovery', NBER WP no. 2819, March.

Fitoussi, J.-P. and Le Cacheux, J. (1988a) 'Ruptures et continuités dans l'orientation des politiques macroéconomiques des pays de l'OCDE', *Revue de l'OFCE*, no. 22, January.

Fitoussi, J.-P. and Le Cacheux, J. (1988b) 'On Macroeconomic Implications of Price Setting in the Open Economy', *AEA Papers & Proceedings, American Economic Review*, 78, no. 2, May.

Fitoussi, J.-P. and Phelps, E.S. (1986) 'Causes of the 1980s Slump in Europe', *Brookings Papers on Economic Activity*, no. 2.

Fitoussi, J.-P. and Phelps, E.S. (1988) *The Slump in Europe* (Oxford: Blackwell).

Froot, K.A. and Klemperer, P. (1988) 'Exchange Rate Pass-Through when Market Share Matters', NBER WP no. 2542, March.

Giavazzi, F. and Giovannini, A. (1987) 'Models of the EMS: Is Europe a Greater Deutschmark Area?', in R. Bryant and R. Portes (eds) *Global Macroeconomics* (London: Macmillan for the IEA and the CEPR).

Giavazzi, F., Micossi, S. and Miller, M. (eds) (1988) *The European Monetary System* (Cambridge University Press).

Gubian, A., Guillaumat-Tailliet, F. and Le Cacheux, J. (1986) 'Fiscalité des entreprises et décision d'investissement. Eléments de comparaison internationale, France, Etats-Unis, RFA', *Revue de l'OFCE*, no. 16, July.

Krugman, P. and Baldwin, R.E. (1987) 'The Persistence of the US Trade Deficit', *Brookings Papers on Economic Activity*, no. 1.

Le Cacheux, J. and Lecointe, F. (1987) 'Changes réels et compétitivité de la France, l'Italie, la RFA et les Etats-Unis', *Revue de l'OFCE*, no. 20, July.

Phelps, E.S. and Winter, S.G. (1970) 'Optimal Price Policy under Atomistic Competition', in E. Phelps *et al.*, *Microeconomic Foundations of Employment and Inflation Theory* (New York: Norton).

Reichlin, L. (1989) 'Fluctations et croissance en Europe: une analyse empirique', *Revue de l'OFCE*, no. 26, January.

Rogoff, K. (1985) 'The Optimal Degree of Commitment to an Intermediate Monetary Target', *Quarterly Journal of Economics*, 100, no. 1, February.

Sachs, J.D. (1985) 'The Dollar and the Policy Mix: 1985', *Brookings Papers on Economic Activity*, no. 1.

Sachs, J.D. (1986) Comment on Fitoussi and Phelps' 'Causes of the 1980s Slump in Europe', *Brookings Papers on Economic Activity*, no. 2.

Sargent, T.J. and Wallace, N. (1981) 'Some Unpleasant Monetarist Arithmetics', *Federal Reserve Bank of Minneapolis Quarterly Review*, no. 5, Autumn.

Wyplosz, C. (1988) 'The Swinging Dollar: Is Europe out of Step?', CEPR WP no. 241, June.

APPENDIX

A.1 Two-country model

The starting point for solving the model is (5.1)–(5.2′)–(5.1*)–(5.2*′). Solving (5.1) and (5.2′) for the real exchange rate yields:

$$-\alpha\left(\frac{1-\theta'+\gamma}{1-\theta}\right)(r^*+x^e)+d\left(\frac{1-\theta+\gamma}{1-\theta}\right)=m+\frac{\gamma}{1-\theta}k+\beta p^e$$
$$+\left(\beta-\frac{\delta}{1-\theta}\right)(r^*+x^e)-\left(\frac{1-\lambda\varphi}{\lambda(1-\theta)}\right)x$$

Hence:

$$x\left[\frac{1-\lambda\varphi}{\lambda(1-\varphi}\right]=\left[\left(\beta-\frac{\delta}{1-\theta}\right)+\alpha\left(\frac{1-\varphi+\gamma}{1-\theta}\right)\right](r^*+x^e)$$
$$-d\left(\frac{1-\theta+\gamma}{1-\theta}\right)+m+\frac{\gamma}{1-\theta}k+\beta p^e$$

Substituting into (5.2*′):

$$(5.2^{*\prime\prime})\qquad A^*z^*=m^*+B^*r^*+C^*$$

with

$$A^*=\frac{1-\theta^*+\gamma^*}{1-\theta^*}>0$$

$$B^*=\left(\beta^*-\frac{\delta^*}{1-\theta^*}\right)+H^*\left[\left(\beta-\frac{\delta}{1-\theta}\right)+\alpha\left(\frac{1-\theta+\gamma}{1-\theta}\right)\right]$$

$$C^* = m^* + \frac{\gamma^*}{1-\theta^*} k^* + \beta^* p^{*e}$$

$$+ H^* \left\{ \left[\left(\beta - \frac{\delta}{1-\theta} \right) + \alpha \left(\frac{1-\theta+\gamma}{1-\theta} \right) \right] x^e - d \left(\frac{1-\theta+\gamma}{1-\theta} \right) \right.$$

$$\left. + m + \frac{\gamma}{1-\theta} k + \beta p^e \right\}$$

$$H^* = \frac{\lambda(1-\theta)(1-\lambda^* \varphi^*)}{\lambda^*(1-\theta^*)(1-\lambda\varphi)} > 0$$

Similarly, solving (5.1*) and (5.2*′) for x, then substituting into (5.2′) yields:

$$(5.2'') \qquad Az = B(r^* + x^e) - H(A^* d^* - m^*) + C$$

with

$$A = \frac{1-\theta+\gamma}{1-\theta} > 0$$

$$B = \left(\beta - \frac{\delta}{1-\theta} \right) + H \left[\left(\beta^* - \frac{\delta^*}{1-\theta^*} \right) - \alpha^* \left(\frac{1-\theta^*+\gamma^*}{1-\theta^*} \right) \right]$$

$$C = m + \frac{\gamma}{1-\theta} k + \beta p^e - H \left[\frac{\gamma^*}{1-\theta^*} k^* + \beta^* p^{*e} \right]$$

$$H = \frac{\lambda^*(1-\theta^*)(1-\lambda\varphi)}{\lambda(1-\theta)(1-\lambda^* \varphi^*)} > 0$$

We assume $B^* > 0$ and $B > 0$. Clearly, sufficient conditions for that to hold are:

$$\beta \geqslant \frac{\delta}{1-\theta} \qquad \text{and } \beta^* \geqslant \frac{\delta^*}{1-\theta^*}$$

In order to obtain the equations of the curves shown in the bottom part of Figure 5.5, r^* is eliminated from (5.1), (5.2′), (5.1*) and (5.2*′), using the same procedure as above.

A.2 Three-country model

Eliminating z^* from (5.1*) and (5.2*′) yields the reduced-form equation for the foreign country:

$$(\alpha^* A^* + B^{*\prime}) r^* = A^* d^* - m^* - C^{*\prime} x \qquad (5.12^*)$$

with

$$B^{*\prime} = \beta^* - \frac{\delta^*}{1-\theta^*}$$

$$C^{*\prime} = \frac{1-\lambda^*\varphi^*}{\lambda^*(1-\theta^*)} > 0$$

We assumc:

$$(\alpha^* A^* + B^*) > 0$$

The complete three-country system may be reduced to the following:

$$z_1 = -F_1 r_1 - G_1 \pi + (d_1 + \mu_1 d_2) \tag{5.1.1'}$$

$$z_2 = -F_2 r_2 + G_2 \pi + (d_2 + \mu_2 d_1) \tag{5.1.2'}$$

$$A_1 z_1 = m_1 + B_1 r_1 - C_1 x + D_1 \pi + H_1 \tag{5.2.1'}$$

$$A_2 z_2 = m_2 + B_2 r_2 - C_2 x - D_2 \pi + H_2 \tag{5.2.2'}$$

$$(\alpha^* A^* + B^*) r^* = A^* d^* - m^* - C^{*\prime} x \tag{5.12*}$$

with

$$F_1 = \frac{\alpha_1 + \mu_1 \alpha_2}{1 - \mu_1 \mu_2} > 0$$

$$G_1 = \frac{\varepsilon_1 - \mu_1 \varepsilon_2}{1 - \mu_1 \mu_2} > 0$$

$$F_2 = \frac{\alpha_2 + \mu_2 \alpha_1}{1 - \mu_1 \mu_2} > 0$$

$$G_2 = \frac{\varepsilon_2 - \mu_2 \varepsilon_1}{1 - \mu_1 \mu_2} > 0$$

$$A_1 = \left(\xi_1 + \frac{\gamma_1}{1-\theta_1}\right) > 0$$

$$A_2 = \left(\xi_2 + \frac{\gamma_2}{1-\theta_2}\right) > 0$$

$$B_1 = \left(\beta_1 - \frac{\delta_1}{1-\theta_1}\right)$$

$$B_2 = \left(\beta_2 - \frac{\delta_2}{1-\theta_2}\right)$$

$$C_1 = \frac{\eta_1(1-\lambda_1)}{\lambda_1(1-\theta_1)} > 0$$

$$C_2 = \frac{\eta_2(1-\lambda_2)}{\lambda_2(1-\theta_2)} > 0$$

$$D_1 = \frac{\lambda_1(\eta_1-\varphi_1)-\eta_1+1}{\lambda_1(1-\theta_1)} > 0$$

$$D_2 = \frac{1-\lambda_2\varphi_2}{\lambda_2(1-\theta_2)} > 0$$

The (RR) equations are similar to equation (5.12*):

$$(RR_1) \qquad K_1 r^* + L_1\pi - (C_1/C^{*\prime})(A^*d^* - m^*) + m_1 = 0$$

$$(RR_2) \qquad K_2 r^* - L_2\pi - (C_2/C^{*\prime})(A^*d^* - m^*) + m_2 + (A_2F_2 + B_2)\pi^e = 0$$

with

$$K_1 = A_1F_1 + B_1 + \frac{C_1(\alpha^*A^* + B^*)}{C^{*\prime}} > 0$$

$$K_2 = A_2F_2 + B_2 + \frac{C_2(\alpha^*A^* + B^*)}{C^{*\prime}} > 0$$

$$L_1 = A_1G_1 + D_1 > 0$$

$$L_2 = A_2G_2 + D_2 > 0$$

The reduced-form equations corresponding to the curves on Figure 5.7 are the following:

$$(IS_1') \qquad z_1 = -\Delta_1 r^* + (G_1C_2/C^{*\prime})(A^*d^* - m^*) + \dots$$

$$(LM_1') \qquad z_1 = M_1 r^* - \left(\frac{D_1C_2 + C_1}{C^{*\prime}}\right)(A^*d^* - m^*) + \dots$$

$$(IS_2') \qquad z_2 = -\Delta_2 r^* + (G_2C_1/C^{*\prime})(A^*d^* - m^*) + \dots$$

$$(LM_2') \qquad z_2 = M_2 r^* - \left(\frac{D_2C_1 + C_2}{C^{*\prime}}\right)(A^*d^* - m^*) + \dots$$

$$(ZZ_1) \qquad z_1 = -\phi_1\pi - (F_1C_2/C^{*\prime})(A^*d^* - m^*) + \dots$$

$$(MM_1) \qquad z_1 = \chi_1\pi + N_1(A^*d^* - m^*) + \dots$$

$$(ZZ_2) \qquad z_2 = \phi_2\pi - (F_2C_1/C^{*\prime})(A^*d^* - m^*) + \dots$$

$$(MM_2) \qquad z_2 = -\chi_2\pi + N_2(A^*d^* - m^*) + \dots$$

with

$$A_1' = A_2 G_2 + D_2$$

$$A_2' = A_1 G_1 + D_1$$

$$\Delta_1 = F_1 A_1' + G_1 \left[A_2 F_2 + B_2 + \frac{C_2 \Delta^*}{C^{*\prime}} \right]$$

$$\Delta^* = \alpha^* A^* + B^*$$

$$\Delta_2 = F_2 A_2' + G_2 \left[A_1 F_1 + B_1 + \frac{C_1 \Delta^*}{C^{*\prime}} \right]$$

$$M_1 = A_2 F_2 + B_2 + D_1 A_1' + \frac{C_2 \Delta^*}{C^{*\prime}}$$

$$M_2 = A_1 F_1 + B_1 + D_2 A_2' + \frac{C_1 \Delta^*}{C^{*\prime}}$$

$$\Phi_1 = F_1 A_1' + \Delta_2 G_1$$

$$\Phi_2 = F_2 A_2' + \Delta_1 G_2$$

$$\chi_1 = A_1' \left(B_1 + \frac{C_1 \Delta^*}{C^{*\prime}} \right) + D_1 \Delta_2$$

$$\chi_2 = A_2' \left(B_2 + \frac{C_2 \Delta^*}{C^{*\prime}} \right) + D_2 \Delta_1$$

Part III
The EMS and the Impact of the Single Market

6 The EMS and the Completion of the Internal Market

Pippo Ranci

6.1 THE STRATEGY OF DYNAMIC DISEQUILIBRIUM

Both the EMS and the Single European Internal Market (IM) rely on a strategy of 'dynamic disequilibria' in order to overcome the difficulty of achieving strong political agreement on the institutional issue (Micossi, 1988). This is not a novelty, since the whole Common Market experience since the 1950s can be seen as a grand experiment in unleashing economic processes that will produce enough welfare gains and enough economic benefit for the politically influential interest groups, so that in due time there will be the necessary consensus for the construction of the political institutions, which in turn are necessary to maintain the mentioned benefits.

The interesting novelty is the parallel development of two distinct initiatives, one related to money and the other to trade and capital movements. A specific question arises on the interactions between the two processes: are these interactions mainly positive, i.e. such as to reinforce the two processes, or is there a serious case for expecting negative interactions? The purpose of this chapter is to examine some of the arguments that can help answer these questions.

While recognising that political processes have their own very important linkages, I shall concentrate on economic interactions.

6.2 IS EXCHANGE RATE STABILITY GOOD FOR COMMERCIAL INTEGRATION?

The question is almost rhetorical. One of the basic assumptions behind the launching of the EMS was that greater exchange rate stability would be beneficial to trade. Yet it is worth devoting some attention to it since the discovery of a 'hysteresis' effect has shaken the faith in the general validity of the statement that exchange rate stability is good for trade.

The great swing in the value of the dollar between 1979 and 1986 has apparently resulted in a permanent shift in the relationship between exchange rate and trade balance. The possibility that this could happen was first based on the observation that 'some of the inroads made by foreign firms in the US market during the overvaluation will remain even after the dollar returns to its old purchasing power parity level' (the *New York Times* quoted by Baldwin, 1986). The search for solid theoretical foundations that could also allow a generalisation of the statement led to the formulation of a number of models.

A convincing explanation for the phenomenon of hysteresis is provided by the existence of fixed selling costs that are sunk and durable in an imperfectly competitive world: costs such as the setting up of a distribution and service network, including the shaping of firm-specific human capital with market-specific training (Baldwin, 1986). The case of European luxury cars sold in the US market can be taken as an example.

Other models could support the same hysteresis effect. Sunk selling costs are important in some sectors, not in all. Sectors characterised by large-scale economies may present multiple equilibria, where an exchange rate shock could knock the economy from one equilibrium to another (ibid.). This model could apply to the semiconductor industry.

Lastly, hysteresis can result from demand-side dynamics, in the case of 'experience' goods, where consumers are uncertain about the quality of goods they have never tried and are therefore ready to pay more for the known brand. A temporary cost advantage, created by the dollar overvaluation, eased the entry of foreign producers. Once the advantage has disappeared, the product is known (ibid.).

A generalisation of the models leads to the following conclusion. The extension of trade is normally limited by the existence of a number of obstacles, such as fixed and sunk selling costs, multiple equilibria in imperfect competition, and imperfect information on the consumer side in experience-goods markets. As a consequence, comparative advantage in production is not sufficient to determine trade. A temporary cost advantage, induced by an exchange rate fluctuation, creates an opportunity for overcoming the obstacles and hence permanently increasing trade. All hysteresis models point to a once-for-all incentive to exploit some comparative advantage that was already there but was not exploited; given a large enough incentive, the effect will be permanent.

A regime of stable exchange rates within the EEC rules out the possibility of such temporary opportunities emerging, and therefore constrains trade within limits which are narrower than those defined by comparative advantage in production. Fluctuating exchange rates would present at least one advantage in the pursuit of trade growth.

The advantage should of course be set against the well-known disadvantage of greater uncertainty, and the higher costs required to cover the exchange rate risk. Then the standard conclusion that the EMS exchange rate discipline is good for trade could still hold: its acceptability could be seen to depend on the relative weight of the two arguments.[1]

6.3 THE IMPACT OF THE SINGLE INTERNAL MARKET

Although it could be held on a theoretical basis, the hysteresis argument in favour of exchange rate instability is in practice weak in the present European situation, because the completion of the Single Internal Market already provides a substantial shock to firms.

The effect of the IM program is twofold. First, in the sectors where important non-tariff barriers are being eliminated, the extent of trade is obviously being increased. Second, it seems that an expectation of increasing interchange and competition has rapidly spread through the whole economy. There is evidence that operators are wary of being caught unprepared by 1992, and are devoting much effort to setting themselves into a strong European position before their competitors. Actions are being taken even in sectors such as textiles and clothing where little direct impact from the IM programme can be expected.

It looks plausible that, in the present climate of Euro-activism by firms, the reassuring function of stable exchange rates is more beneficial than a temporary incentive to exploit cost advantage in the other European markets would be. After all, hysteresis does not mean that all the effect is permanent; and temporary adjustment crises are not needed when the process of creating the single IM already provides a great need for adjustment.

I have discussed how good exchange rate stability is for commercial integration, overlooking the fact that the IM deals not only with trade but also with capital movements. 'For a given degree of freedom in capital movements, too little exchange rate stability makes that freedom useless and dangerous. Useless, because the exchange rate risk tends to freeze financial transactions, even if allowed. Dangerous, because it can feed speculative bubbles, so contributing to accentuate the same exchange rate instability' (Bruni and Monti, 1988, p. 92).

6.4 IS THE SINGLE INTERNAL MARKET GOOD FOR MAINTAINING FIXED EXCHANGE RATES?

Let us first consider the transition period. I shall not deal, though, with short-run exchange rate stability, which is largely dependent on interest rates and on the coordination of macroeconomic policies; I shall focus on the medium-term determinants of the exchange rate, i.e. the balances of current account and of long-term capital movements.

There is little doubt that the implementation of the IM programme will have effects on those balances which will differ in sign and size according to the degree of protection that each country presently enjoys (or suffers).

Let us recall the debate that took place at the time of the Rome Treaty. Writing in 1958, Tibor Scitovsky noted that 'most Europeans believe that integration would and should always lead to a reallocation of production from less to more efficient producers' and answered with the classical comparative advantage argument:

> Even if every German industry should be more efficient than its French counterpart, it need not follow that a general shift of industrial production from France to Germany would be desirable. Except in the unlikely case of perfect international labour mobility, such a shift would lead to underemployment of France's labour force and the resulting loss would far outweigh any gain from the higher average productivity of the employed labour force. Reallocation between countries therefore is subject to the limitation that it must not increase unemployment. To render this and no greater amount of reallocation profitable, exchange rates (or relative price levels) would have to be different from what they are at present and such that the amount and direction of trade that result lead to approximate balance-of-payments equilibrium (Scitovsky, 1984, p. 40–1).

The present outlook could be described similarly, putting the Community enlargement and the 1992 liberalisation programme in place of the original tariff removal. Today again the fear of economic growth concentrating in the 'strong' areas of the Community denotes neglect of the old comparative advantage principle; but the working of that principle requires that exchange rates be left free to adjust during a transitory phase. Policy coordination and structural polic:·s play an important role in reducing instability and disequilibria, and will play a particularly decisive one in the following stage, when the transition is over; but they cannot be more than partial substitutes for exchange rate flexibility during the transition period.

As an example, from the point of view of the Italian economy there are two reasons for expecting a further worsening of the present current account deficit: (a) the new member economies of Spain and Portugal and the possible new commercial agreements with other Mediterranean countries bring competitive pressures on the typical Italian productions; (b) the removal of external protection is going to produce asymmetrical effects, damaging Italy's trading position in the EEC (the Multifibre Agreement is a shield for Italy's large textile-clothing sector; Italy has the strictest national quota on imports of Japanese cars).[2] It is difficult to imagine that realignments will not be necessary in the next few years.

Similar considerations probably apply to other Community members with weak currencies. Structural weaknesses and weak currencies go together. The implementation of the IM programme will not leave the 'equilibrium' exchange rates unaffected, and weakening is likely for already weak currencies and vice versa.

6.5 THE PROBLEMS OF TRANSITION

Consideration of inflation rates leads to the same conclusion. The convergence of inflation rates to the Community average is slow and even if successful will require more realignments: 'Since the disinflation process is only a gradual one, the countries with low inflation at the outset obtain a certain advantage in terms of competitiveness' (Padoa-Schioppa, 1987, para. 8.1).

> A European monetary union with irreversibly fixed exchange rates would pose difficult problems for those countries whose international competitiveness in the past has depended upon periodic devaluations of their currencies. The transition cannot be simply taken for granted, and this is, indeed, the main economic reason why we do not envisage an easy move to fix parities irrevocably (ibid., para. 12.1.5).

Notice that the countries with a tendency to inflation and devaluation are probably the same countries showing the structural weakness noted above (see also note 4 below). This is sufficient to exclude that the necessary adjustment may take place via price levels rather than via exchange rates.

Transition to the single IM should then be accompanied by exchange rate adjustments. Establishment of fixed exchange rates should come, if ever, after full trade and capital liberalisation have produced their effects and allowed the new equilibrium exchange rates to emerge. This is broadly consistent with the timetable set by the Delors Committee.

That exchange rate fixing should come last is also a result of the literature on the 'order of liberalisation' between trade and capital movements (see Kahn and Zahler, 1983; Gandolfo and Padoan, 1988, pp. 8–9, with an extensive survey). The two liberalisations appear to be complementary, and capital movements should not be freed too fast, while trade liberalisation should not be too slow. It seems that these prescriptions are not being followed, since a definite timetable has been set for capital liberalisation, while many important actions in the areas of public procurement, external non-tariff barriers, tax harmonisation and other issues affecting trade are slow in taking shape.

6.6 LONG-RUN PROBLEMS

In the long run, exchange rate stability can be maintained if the sources of divergent behaviour by the current account and by capital flows are either sufficiently reduced or adequately compensated. That sources of divergence will subsist is hardly debatable.

Differences in macroeconomic policies should be brought under control, yet if we remain faithful to the original choice of letting the economic forces set the stage for political action we cannot rely on policy coordination too much. Although this is ground for political rather than economic talk, it seems to me that assuming a perfect policy coordination is inconsistent with giving up political and even complete monetary unification on the grounds of national pride and cultural differences. If these obstacles cannot be overcome, then even policy coordination will be possible only up to a certain point.

Even assuming policy coordination, inflation rates may diverge until monetary union is completed and prices are set in a unique currency. The idea that policy coordination can ensure a unique rate of inflation is extreme, although strongly-backed by academic support it implies that there are no sources of price change other than money creation. If we accept a more pragmatic view we must be worried, as the authors of the Padoa-Schioppa Report are, by the variety of industrial relations habits and institutions, which will long persist.[3]

In any case, divergences in inflationary pressures and in trade flows are inevitably created by structural dynamics. There is no reason to believe that productivity will grow at the same rate in the different European economies, that industrial structures and specialisation patterns will follow the same evolutionary path; it does not even happen among regions in the same country.

Assuming similar growth rates of income, the present expenditure elasticities of imports and exports of the European countries do not always warrant the maintainability of the current account barriers for any fixed level of price competitiveness (Vona and Bini Smaghi, 1988, pp. 151–3).

Will the single IM, once established, significantly reduce the sources of divergence? It is likely that union behaviour will gradually become more homogeneous, as an effect both of the greater consideration given by unions to European matters and of the increase in the transnational organisation of firms that leads to a parallel transnational union activity.

Less clear, as yet, is the impact of the IM on the tendencies of industrial structures. There are good arguments in favour of a divergence hypothesis, such as the cumulative dynamics of the existing comparative advantage; and equally appealing arguments in favour of convergence, such as the experience of the first tariff removal in the 1960s, and the likely effect of territorial expansion by firms.

Optimistic as we can be on the reduction of divergence sources, the example of regional divergences within economies is decisive in coming to the conclusion that divergence will always arise and that fixed exchange rates must rely on adequate compensation mechanisms.

6.7 COMPENSATION MECHANISMS

Compensation can take three forms (i) variation of the growth rate of income, (ii) private capital flows spontaneously matching the current account balance, (iii) public or government-induced transfers and capital flows. So the question becomes: will the IM make compensation easier? Through which one of the three forms?

(i) *Growth rates of income.* The very idea of compensating divergent balance-of-payments trends through a slowing down of the deficit countries' growth is contrary to the commonly held tenet that 'the (European) Exchange-Rate Mechanism countries should now try to progress toward the harmonisation of their growth patterns' (Vona and Bini Smaghi, 1988, p. 167), not to mention the simple (but powerful among non-economists) idea that equal growth is better that unequal growth.

Moreover, since the likely candidates to current account deficits are the weak currency countries, whose per capita income is lower,[4] the price for exchange rate stability may be a widening of the income differentials. This is a possible outcome of the EMS, independent of the possible deflationary bias that would slow down the growth rate of Community income as a whole.

On the other side, the IM should provide faster growth through better allocation, scale economies, and stronger incentives (Catinat, Donni and Italianer, 1988); thus balancing a possible deflationary bias in the EMS. But what about differentials? The Padoa-Schioppa Report is moderately pessimistic, and points to the risk of regional differences being increased by divergent processes activated by market integration.

It is then worrying if both the EMS and the IM are likely to produce such differences in growth rates as to increase income differentials within the Community. It will be difficult to rely on systematically slowing down the growth rates of deficit countries in order to maintain stable exchange rates. There are political limits to the acceptability of increasing income differentials. Even if accepted, differences in growth rates could be counterproductive in the medium term: in fact, the economic rationale of such a strategy is based on the coexistence of strong neoclassical adjustment effects, such as the response of prices to capacity utilisation and of wages to unemployment, and weak cumulative chains such as the one linking production growth, investment, innovation and competitiveness. If cumulative chains are strong relative to neoclassical price effects, slow growth may result in an actual worsening of the current account performance.[5]

(ii) *Private capital flows.* Neglecting short-term movements and interest-rate differentials, we can expect intra-EEC capital movements to assume the same character as inter-regional capital movements in an economic system, once a unified capital market is established.[6] Liberalisation of capital movements, which is part of the IM programme, should then facilitate the solution to the problem of exchange rate stability created by the EMS.

After an initial phase in which portfolio adjustments induced by liberalisation prevail, capital should flow from the high-income and current-account surplus countries to their European partners. A virtuous circle model could be envisaged for the low-income countries of Europe, with capital inflow sustaining industrial development according to the historical experience of the late starters in economic development.

Even if the potential for growth is not any greater in the deficit countries, capital flows can assume a compensating character if the capital market is unified. A complete monetary union is not strictly necessary for this to happen. It is sufficient that the expectation of fixed exchange rates is strongly rooted, so that capital does not respond to expected variations in the exchange rates. Clearly the surest way of achieving this is for a large ECU capital market to develop.

(iii) *Public transfers and capitals.* The weaker one's confidence in the above recalled equilibrating mechanisms, the greater the need for intervention. Intervention takes the twin shape of structural and regional policies, which are strongly advocated by both the Padoa-Schioppa and the Delors reports. A stronger Community policy in the direction of stabilisation and distribution is necessary 'not so much to enlarge the competence of the Community for its own sake, but to ensure the success of the "allocation programme" implicit in the decision to enlarge the membership of the Community to Spain and Portugal and to create a market without internal frontiers by 1992. Indeed, if no action is taken in these areas, even the *acquis* in other fields would be at stake' (Padoa Schioppa, 1987, ch. 10).

The Delors Report defines the Economic union as made of four basic elements, one of which is the single market proper; the second is the specific policy necessary to create a competitive single market, i.e. competition policy; the other two are common structural and regional policies, and macroeconomic coordination. If macroeconomic coordination takes care of the short run, the long-run sustainability of fixed exchange rates is the job of structural and regional policies.

These policies have a double face. By promoting structural change and regional development, they should reduce the sources of divergence. By channelling funds towards the lagging areas, they should help in compensating the balance-of-payments disequilibria that would still appear in the presence of divergent trends and fixed exchange rates. The former function is declared, but not always achieved; the latter is seen with lesser enthusiasm, for fear of misuse.[7]

Scepticism may be justified, but the compensating nature of transfer policies can be easily misunderstood. Of course, transfer payments can be a source of waste and of perverse incentives, yet each modern state, even the most friendly to the market and most inimical to welfare policies, manages a very large system of taxes and payments just to perform its basic functions. It is relevant that 'the mere existence of national taxation and national Government expenditures is likely to stabilise the balance of inter-regional payments .... These are sometimes referred to as built-in stabilisers of income and activity; let us remember that they are built stabilisers also of the balance of inter-regional payments' (Scitovsky, 1984, pp. 93–4).

Nation states have always been reluctant to accept Community taxation and expenditure. When they accepted that the Community should have its 'own resources', they kept calculating the give and take of each national economy, setting strict limits to inter-state redistribution by the Community budget (redistribution has taken to following complex and sometimes irrational paths; an even more complex but consistent proposal is in Padoa-Schioppa, 1987, Appendix D).

In principle, the Community budget, based on own resources and charged with well-defined policy objectives covering the whole Community economy, should not be limited by national quotas. The introduction of such national constraints, whether explicit or implicit, obviously reduces its ability to act as a built-in stabiliser of the balances of payments of member states. Redistribution has then to be obtained through specific transfer or loan programmes, which would be less necessary if the same goal were left to the automatic working of even a small 'federal' budget.

In any case, some fiscal compensation will be permanently necessary. Again we can recall Scitosvky's early attention to the problems of currency union: 'The analysis suggests that a common all-European capital market and a common all-European employment policy would be prime requisites of a common currency' (Scitovsky, 1984, p. 95). Of course a contemporary economist would put monetary policy in place of employment policy; yet, outside a doctrinaire monetarism, it may be wise to think twice before giving up the use of fiscal instruments, and particularly of fiscal stabilisers of the current account.

Notes

1. The same literature on hysteresis provides a counterargument, supporting the standard conclusion. Baldwin (1988) shows that 'in a simple industrial organisation model, large exchange rate shocks can have persistent real effects, while small shocks cannot'. The question becomes: is the EMS preventing large, potentially hysteresis-inducing, exchange rate fluctuations or only small ones? On the other side the benefit of exchange rate stability, which is connected with the reduction of uncertainty, will be minimal when uncertainty is about small exchange rate variations.
2. There could be a third reason: Italy's relative weakness in the industries facing public procurement and in the finance and insurance, transport and communications industries, where the IM effect is going to be most severe;

but it can be observed that weakness of Italian firms in services should result more in an inflow of capital by competitors setting up their Italian subsidiaries than in a worsening of the current account balance, at least for a number of years.

3. The sentences reported above on the difficulty of transition are in the paragraph of the Padoa-Schioppa Report dealing with industrial relations. The Report stresses that the strategies of voluntary-based organisations such as the unions cannot change rapidly and that they depend on historically-experienced inflation rates. As long as unions remain national, even a common inflation experience does not guarantee perfectly consistent behaviour.
4. A simple cross-country regression of the average 1977–86 inflation rates of the twelve (INFL) on their per capita net national income levels (PCNNI) yields the following result:

$$\text{INFL} = 20.8 - \underset{(-4.35)}{1.09}\ \text{PCNNI} \qquad \text{adj.R2} = .62$$

5. This is of course a Kaldorian view of the relation between competitiveness and growth (Kaldor, 1981; Targetti, 1989, pp. 422–8).
6. 'Indeed, equilibrating capital flows among regions of the same country are probably the main reason why one never hears of balance-of-payments difficulties in inter-regional relations.... On the international plane, the operation of the London capital market during the few decades before World War I provides perhaps the only example of an international flow of capital ... able ... to exert an equilibrating influence on the balance of payments' (Scitovsky, 1984, p. 88–91). Noting that the only alternative equilibrating factors 'exert their equilibrating influence by changing incomes ... and are bound to be hamstrung by a domestic economic policy aimed at keeping incomes stable', Scitovsky goes on: 'we conclude that in international relations among countries in which domestic stability is an important aim of economic policy, the only fully effective factor that tends automatically to maintain balance-of-payments equilibrium is the international flow of capital prompted by international differences in yields. No wonder, then, if balance-of-payments difficulties loom so large today, when domestic stability is a prime requirement everywhere and international capital movements are either restricted or governed by political rather than economic considerations' (p. 92).

   That was indeed a distant world from the one we live in today. Yet, if we try to think of an area of monetary cooperation and stable exchange rates, Scitovsky's approach resumes relevance.
7. 'Excessive reliance on financial assistance through regional and structural policies could cause tensions. The principal objective of regional policies should not be to subsidise incomes and simply offset inequalities in standards of living' (Delors, 1989).

References

Baffi, P. (1989) 'Il negoziato sullo SME', *Bancaria*, 1.

Baldwin, R. (1986) 'Hysteresis in Trade', mimeo, NBER.

Baldwin, R. (1988) 'Hysteresis in Import Prices: the Beach-head Effect', NBER WP no. 2545.

Bruni, F. and Monti, M. (1986) 'Protezionismo valutario e integrazione internazionale', in T. Padoa Schioppa (ed.) *Il sistema dei cambi, oggi* (Bologna: Il Mulino).

Catinat, M., Donni, E. and Italianer, A. (1988) 'The Completion of the Internal Market: Results of Macroeconomic Model Simulations', *EEC Economic Papers*, 65.

Delors, J. *et al.* (1989) 'Report on the Economic and Monetary Union in the European Community'.

Gandolfo, G. and Padoan, P.C. (1988) 'Conseguenze della liberalizzazione dei movimenti di capitali: un'analisi sistemica', *Note Economiche*, 2.

Kahn, M. and Zahler, R. (1983) 'The Macroeconomic Effects of Changes in Barriers to Trade and Capital Flows: A Simulation Analysis', *IMF Staff Papers*, 2.

Kaldor, N. (1981) 'The Role of Increasing Returns, Technical Progress and Cumulative Causation in the Theory of International Trade', *Economie Appliquée*, 4.

Micossi, S. (1988) 'The Single European Market: Finance', *Banca Nazionale del Lavoro Quarterly Review*.

Padoa-Schioppa, T. *et al.* (1987) *Efficienza stabilita' ed equita'* (Bologna: Il Mulino).

Scitovsky, T. (1984) *Economic Theory and Western European Integration* (Stanford, Cal.: Stanford University Press, 1958; repr. Westport, Conn.: Greenwood Press, 1984).

Targetti, F. (1989) *Nicholas Kaldor. Teoria e politica economica di un capitalismo in mutamento* (Bologna: Il Mulino).

Vona, S. and Bini Smaghi, L. (1988) 'Economic Growth and Exchange Rates in the European Monetary System: Their Trade Effects in a Changing External Environment', in F. Giavazzi, S. Micossi and M. Miller (eds) *The European Monetary System* (Cambridge University Press).

7 Divergent European Labour Markets

David Metcalf

1 EMPLOYMENT PATTERNS AND LABOUR MARKET INSTITUTIONS IN THE EC

1.1 Employment patterns

There are both similarities and differences in the pattern of employment among EC countries. Some evidence for the five largest countries is given in Table 7.1. Male labour force participation rates (the percentage

Table 7.1 Labour market information for selected EC countries

	France	*Germany*	*Italy*	*Spain*	*UK*
Total employment 1987, millions					
Males	12.7	16.1	13.8	8.3	14.0
Females	9.0	10.0	7.0	3.5	10.8
% part-time in total	12	13	5	—	22
Labour force participation rate (age 15–64) 1987 %					
Males	76	80	79	80	88
Females	56	52	43	38	62
Annual hours full-time employees 1984					
Manufacturing	1679	1701	1727	—	1876
Insurance	1688	1756	1766	—	1675
Growth in employment, annual average %					
1980–83	−0.1	−0.7	0.6	−1.8	−1.7
1984–89	−0.2	0.5	0.6	1.1	1.1
Standardised unemployment rate % 1987					
Total	10.9	10.6	11.8	20.1	10.3
Youth (age 15–24)	23.0	7.9	35.5	38.9	17.4
Labour market programmes, public spending as a % of GDP					
Employment promotion	0.74	0.99	0.46	0.76	0.89
Income maintenance	2.33	1.35	0.81	2.54	1.68

Sources: OECD (1988) tables 1.2, 1.3, 1.4, 1.6, 1.10, 3.1, H; TUC (1988b).

of a given age/sex population in the workforce) are similar, but female participation rates are substantially higher in France, Germany and the UK than they are in Italy and Spain. Consequently women account for a much larger fraction of the total labour force in the former set of countries than in the latter two. There is also great variation in the proportion of jobs that are part-time: Italy has only a quarter the number of part-time jobs that the UK has.

Another dimension of the labour supply is annual hours. The norm for all EC countries for full-time workers was around 1750 hours of work per year in 1984. Most European countries have fairly similar annual hours in the production and service sectors. In Britain, by contrast, manufacturing employees work some 200 hours a year more than their counterparts in services. Some common themes are emerging on working time even though systems of collective bargaining are very different in the EC (TUC 1988b). There is considerable interest in reducing weekly hours from the union side. But employers and governments are increasingly pushing for greater flexibility in working time, including Sunday working (e.g. Belgium) and extended daily and weekly hours (e.g. Greece, Netherlands). Many countries are extending workers' rights to paid leave for education (e.g. Germany) or childcare (e.g. Luxembourg). Flexible retirement schemes to allow older workers to mix part-time work with pension income have been set up in Denmark, France and Spain.

Most EC countries experienced a fall in jobs in the early 1980s, but growth in employment in the latter part of the decade. Spain and the UK both had greater amplitude in employment fluctuations than the other large EC economies. In all EC labour markets females are projected to boost their relative share in employment by year 2000.

Unemployment rates in four of the 'big-five' labour markets were very similar in 1987, a remarkable convergence from the position at the beginning of the decade. But youth unemployment rates, while falling in most countries, vary enormously: Spain and Italy face the biggest youth unemployment problem. In Britain youth unemployment is projected to evaporate in the 1990s because demographic changes imply a substantial cut in the number of teenagers available for work.

There is a real spread in public spending on employment programmes as a percentage of GDP among EC economies. Spain and France spend well over double the amount spent by Italy. Active employment promotion consists of spending on employment services, training, special youth measures, direct job creation and employment subsidies and special measures for the disabled. Income maintenance consists of unemployment compensation and early retirement programmes. All EC countries except Greece and Portugal spend more on income maintenance than they do on active employment promotion.

1.2 Labour market institutions

Labour market institutions are truly heterogeneous among EC countries. Such institutional information has recently been admirably surveyed by Boyer (1988) and his summary is reproduced in Table 7.2. Boyer states that the main impact of trade unions in the process of collective bargaining is at firm or workplace level in Italy, Britain and Ireland, at sector level in Germany and at national level in Denmark. Not only does the focal point of union activity vary among EC countries, but density levels are also very different. This topic is analysed in Section 2.

Employers' associations also show considerable diversity. In Britain and Ireland they have no central power or financial resources whereas in Germany they are highly structured, representing an entire industry thereby guaranteeing the application of the agreements reached. France and Italy are cited as intermediate cases where employers' organisations take part in national agreements but have little power over individual firms. Table 7.2 also shows great variation across countries in the role of the state in wage formation.

2 UNION DENSITY: DIVERGENCE AND FUTURE UNCERTAINTY

2.1 Evidence

A quarter of a century ago some distinguished US commentators predicted that industrial relations systems would converge among advanced western countries (Kerr, Dunlop, Harbison and Myers, 1964). The evidence in Section 1 (Boyer, 1988) suggests the contrary. Even leaving countries like Japan, Sweden and the US out of consideration and concentrating solely on the EC, we find considerable divergence in union density (the percentage of the workforce that is unionised). Clearly, if union density varies substantially among EC countries, then so must their industrial relations systems.

The evidence is set out in Table 7.3. All countries experienced a rise in density in the 1970s. But in the 1980s changes in density have been

Table 7.2 A summary comparison of methods of organising wage/labour relations in seven European countries

	France	*UK*	*Ireland*	*Belgium*	*Spain*	*Italy*	*W. Germany*
Trade union movement	Very low unionisation; competition between rival unions; fairly loose organisation	Very high unionisation of blue- and, to a lesser extent, white-collar workers; proliferation of trades and industrial unions	Very high unionisation; claims generally wage-related; labour disputes extensive	High rate of unionisation; pluralist, competing unions	Workers operate under corporatist system; unions illegal until 1977	Periods of union strength and unity alternate with others of division and decline	Average rate of unionisation; well structured; unions extremely united
Employers' organisations	Split into various trends and bodies; not much structure or power	Fairly weakly organised	Significance of 'small' multinationals	Relative unified	Obligation under Franco to belong to vertical sectoral unions	Frequent oppositions; public holdings/private companies	Powerful, well organised, with certain binding powers
Government intervention	Massive intervention; almost all national accords tripartite; historically, change initiated by the law or public settlements	Principle of voluntary negotiations between firms and unions; from 1960s periodic tripartite agreements negotiated and wage norms fixed	Legislative system similar to UK: principle of non-intervention by government, but growing involvement in the 1970s	Significant government mediation in labour relations and especially wage formation; sophisticated network of social consultations at all levels	Heavy involvement in management of labour relations before and after 1977; less so in the 1980s	Major legislative interventions in response to worker struggles (*Statuto dei lavoratori*, 1970)	Government excluded from contractual relations between social partners
Types of collective agreement							
Level of negotiations	Dominant role of agreements within or between sectors; little bargaining in firms until Auroux laws	Originally mainly between firms, or even plants, but trend towards centralisation since 1960s	Centralised until 1970s and additional local negotiations	Minimum conditions set at sectoral level, then negotiations to improve them within firms	Quite heavily centralised despite recent changes	Centralisation at confederal level in 1950s, then an upsurge in decentralised contracts after 1969	Sector or large firms
Frequency of agreements	Usually annual	Annual	Annual	Annual/pluri-annual	Annual	Annual	Annual

Role in wage formation of:							
Productivity	Government announced principle of distributing 'dividends of progress' in 1961; consequently, minimum wage and public sector pay policy	General principle of distribution accepted; various examples of efficiency bonuses; generally no explicit clauses	Agreement with a view to boosting productivity; productivity clauses in some wage agreements	Distribution principle accepted since 1954, but few explicit agreements	Few implicit references to any distribution	Not explicitly provided for, either by government policy or in collective agreements	Exists implicitly at national level
Cost of living	Indexation illegal but practised increasingly from late 1960	No indexation clause as such, but increases often backdated	Explicit clauses fixed in 1970 and 1972; proportional in 1974 and 1975	Explicit indexation procedures	Revision clauses based on inflation, past and predicted	Indexation clauses have become wide spread and comprehensive	In theory, all indexation prohibited
Labour market	Little direct effect on average wages, but some effect in certain sectors (e.g. public works)	Little influence until early 1970s	Major role of migration in adjustment of job market	Significant in the past and for certain competitive sectors	Initially, political pressure, after 1980, suspension clauses where firms might go out of business	Particularly sensitive during boom periods and when job market is tight	General economic situation, especially abroad, taken into account
Social security							
Extent	In line with EEC average	Significantly lower than EEC average	Initially poor, but growth in the 1960s	Widespread	Patchy	Initially poor and regressive	Widespread
Level of benefits	In line with EEC average	Significantly lower than EEC average	Lower than in UK, but higher than in comparable countries	Close to EEC average	Well below that of other European countries	Always below EEC average	About EEC average, except for unemployment benefit
Finance	Mainly by employers, but also the insured and the state	Predominantly financed from national budget; small contribution by employers and insured	Social welfare by government; social insurance by employers and employees	Employers and government; small contributions by the insured	Overwhelmingly by employers	Mainly by employers, the state, and marginally, the insured	Especially by employers, plus roughly equal contributions from the insured and public funds

Source: Boyer (1988, Table 1.1).

Table 7.3 Level of and changes in union membership as a percentage of non-agricultural wage and salary employees across countries

	1970	*1979*	*1986*	*70–79*	*79–86*	*70–86*
Countries with rising density						
Denmark	66	86	95	+20	+9	+29
Belgium	55	69	74	+14	+5	+19
Countries with moderate increase in density						
Italy	39	51	45	+12	−6	+6
Germany	37	42	43	+5	+1	+6
France	22	28	26	+6	−2	−4
Ireland	44	49	51	+5	+2	+7
Countries with stable or declining density						
UK	51	58	51	+7	−7	0
Netherlands	39	43	35	+4	−8	−4

Note: Evidence on unionisation and employment comes from different sources, therefore cross-country comparisons must be treated cautiously. For example, in some countries but not others, union members might include the self-employed, the unemployed and pensioners. But time series comparisons for one country are valid.

Source: Freeman (1989)

more varied. Where unionisation was well entrenched (e.g. Denmark, Belgium) density has continued to rise. But in Italy, France, UK and Netherlands the gains made by unions in the 1970s have been partially or completely reversed in the 1980s. The reasons for these different episodes among countries are discussed in Section 2. It must be emphasised that density figures do not, by themselves, adequately indicate the influence of labour. In Germany employees are represented by Works Councils and in France by enterprise committees and a big majority of the members of such organisations are also union members. Further, in France, pay rates set by collective bargaining are imposed on non-union workplaces.

Although the level of union density and movements in density vary by country, there are some consistent points of convergence. Union density is tending to decline among men and manual workers and in the private sector, and to increase among women and non-manual workers and in the public sector. In each country where separate evidence exists on unionisation in the public and private sectors, the share of unionisation is declining among blue-collar manufacturing workers and is rising for public sector workers (Table 7.4). In some countries the

Table 7.4 Private sector blue-collar share and public sector share of union membership (%)

	Private sector blue collar share			*Public sector share*		
	1970	*1980s*	*Change*	*1970*	*1980s*	*Change*
United Kingdom	55	45	– 10	34	39	+ 5
Germany	54	48	– 6	33	35	+ 2
Italy	65	55	– 10	18	24	+ 6
Netherlands	51	39	– 12	37	46	+ 9

Source: Freeman (1989)

very survival of unions as a force in the private sector is being questioned. The future of private sector unionism is therefore examined in Section 3.

2.2 Reasons for the divergence in union density

Freeman (1989) has analysed the following potential reasons for the divergence in density experience:

differential changes in the composition of employment
public opinion towards unions differs among countries
differences in workers' need for unionisation
differences in real pay levels and changes
differences in business cycle variables
effectiveness of management opposition to unions
whether or not unions operate in a corporatist environment
union responses to economic changes.

He rejects the first four explanations of divergent density experience among countries but accepts the latter four.

First, shifts in the composition of employment are quite similar so cannot explain divergences in density levels and changes. Second, there is no real evidence that public opinion is more favourably disposed to unions in high/rising density countries than it is where density is low or falling. Third, if anything density has declined where the state has reined back worker protection, and has grown in those countries with highly regulated labour markets. Therefore, the underlying idea that union regulations substitute for lack of employment protection legislation appears to be wrong. Similarly, fourth, changes in union density are not associated with the level of, or changes in, real wages across countries – contrary to what is predicted if high or improving pay reduces the desire for unions.

The remaining factors do contribute to an explanation of divergent density experience. Fifth, macroeconomic factors play some part. In particular, rapid inflation is associated with union growth, perhaps because workers need union coverage to protect real pay. Rising density is also weakly associated with declining employment and growing unemployment (where the union delivers the social security benefits).

Sixth, density is influenced by changes in the level and effectiveness of management opposition to unions. Employer policy is itself influenced by the attitude of the state towards unions. Although the best examples of changes in employer policy causing a reduction in density are to be found in the US and Japan, the change in the balance of power between labour and capital is an ingredient in explaining divergent British experience in the 1970s and 1980s.

Seventh, unions have tended to fare well in neo-corporatist countries like Denmark and Germany, where unions and management bargain nationally. The employers' federation establishes a national going-wage rate and encourages union recognition.

Finally, union responses to economic change are themselves important. In Britain, for example, until very recently unions have behaved defensively. Their response to moving away from an adversarial style to the more cooperative industrial relations style now required by employers in the 1980s has been, at best, sluggish.

2.3 The future of private sector unionisation

In most, if not all, EC countries blue-collar private sector workers now account for a substantially smaller fraction of total union membership than they did two decades ago. Evidence for selected countries is given in Table 7.4. In Britain, for example, the fraction of private sector employees who are union members has fallen from 44 per cent ten years ago to around 30 per cent at present and the future of collective bargaining in the private sector is under scrutiny. Marsden (1989a) shows that the future role of private sector unions is uncertain in most EC countries. He cites a number of reasons for this hesitancy.

First, employment is declining in former strongholds of union membership – heavy industry, manufacturing, and large plants. Second, internationalisation of production makes it harder for union bargainers to get the information they need and to find the most suitable part of management for bargaining purposes. Third, new financial groupings (e.g. GEC-Siemens) may conduct their employee relations differently from the old order. Further, collective bargaining traditionally rests on congruence between the legal entity of a company and its economic reality. The new groupings may drive a wedge between the legal definition and the economic performance of the company which will make collective bargaining more difficult.

Fourth, new technology has caused major changes in organisation of skilled work. This, in turn, upsets traditional notions of craft-based skills in Germany and Britain, and internal labour markets with their traditional job classifications and hierarchies in France and Italy. Finally, the growth of 'non-standard' employment like part-time, temporary and agency jobs represents a real challenge to union recruitment.

Healthy private sector unionisation requires, among other things:

continuing concern about productivity
coming to terms with changes in payments systems
monitoring of unions' own structures.

Such issues are quite independent of 1992. But, in addition, industrial relations developments connected with 1992 *may* also provide private sector unions with positive opportunities (Marsden, 1989a). There are two key potential developments:

- a union role in the mutual recognition of skills, i.e. the regulation of vocational training via collective bargaining
- development of a European industrial relations system including advances in industrial democracy and a chance to build on a European-wide floor of rights.

Unfortunately we do not yet know for sure whether such opportunities will emerge. To the extent that European governments are reluctant to enhance the collective strength of unions, the main opening for unions probably concerns training. The scope for future vigour founded on procedural developments in industrial democracy and substantive changes in the floor of rights is discussed in Section 4 and looks more limited.

Union voice and cooperation are key elements in sustaining *productivity growth* and firms' performance. They are complementary. Voice without cooperation prolongs old-fashioned industrial relations.

Cooperation without voice reduces the union to be the employer's poodle. The voice element for European unions might include, for example, the same array of factors dealt with by German Works Councils: working time, monitoring the application of collective agreements and legislation, social planning for redundancies, and training. In Britain the controversial electricians' single union deals are the best-known example of blending voice and cooperation, but many other unions are engaged in such exercises. In Germany the recent agreement in the metal-working sector shows how union voice and cooperation can be combined to benefit all parties.

One key outcome in this productivity area is enhanced flexibility in the use of labour. Such flexibility can come via changes in work rules or by management altering working arrangements not covered by rules. In the UK craft demarcations have been the main focus of such negotiations, while in France the thrust has been to alter patterns of working time.

Payments systems are changing rapidly and unions must come to terms with such developments in order that they do not get left behind. Unions have considerable scope and reason to influence these innovations. The changes are typically introduced to enhance the performance of the firm, sometimes via human resource management (see Marsden, 1989b). They all undermine or modify collective approaches which have traditionally emphasised the rate for the job. The developments include:

individual contracts
merit components to pay, where rules and criteria can still be collectively negotiated
workplace or firm-based profit sharing schemes of ESOPs which emphasise company performance
local bargaining at the expense of national, what German unions call *Betriebsegoismus* (plant selfishness).

It must be recognised that these developments are very likely to undermine unions' attempts to foster solidarity and will temper the equality-enhancing effects of unions.

There is not much evidence on how *union structure and organisation* influence company and national performance, but it is worth raising some questions concerning union mergers. Such mergers are presumably desirable for the parties because they bring scale economies and protection for smaller groups. But mergers do not, by themselves, boost aggregate union membership. They also raise some difficult issues.

First, from the viewpoint of the firm and the economy (rather than from that of the union) which mergers are more welcome? For example, are mergers which reduce multi-unionism at workplace level best for the health of the firm, the workers in the firm and the economy? The predicted spate of conglomerate union mergers in Britain will do little to reduce multi-unionism. Second, are such large agglomerations helpful to membership drives? In the UK the most successful union in recent years has been the Royal College of Nursing which has a specific professional and craft identity.

Skill formation rests on cooperation between unions, employers and sometimes the state. The prospect of market failure is ever present in connection with vocational training. Imperfect capital markets inhibit employees from borrowing against future earnings; poaching and too high youth pay discourages firms from providing and financing training. Such market failures require a collective response. This, coupled with the whole question of skill recognition, provides unions with a real foothold in the occupational and industrial restructuring which will accompany 1992.

3 LABOUR MARKET FLEXIBILITY

Two main interrelated themes run through the diffuse, ubiquitous 1980s concern with reducing labour market rigidities in Europe. First, which labour market institutions produce the best pay and jobs outcomes? Corporatism, wage centralisation and associated macroeconomic performance are discussed in Section 3.1. Second, given the macroeconomic and national institutional environment, is there sufficient flexibility at sector and workplace level? In Section 3.2 we examine flexibility in the industrial pay structure and the extent of internal and external workplace job mobility.

Discussions of labour market flexibility often suggest commentators are searching for the holy grail. In fact, it is quite plausible that in Europe centralised institutions permit a superior pay–jobs trade-off, while decentralised collective bargaining is superior for labour productivity growth.

3.1 Corporatism, consensus, centralisation and macroeconomic performance

The association between corporatism and consensus and macroeconomic performance has been systematically investigated across and within a number of countries (e.g. Metcalf, 1987; Paloheimo, 1989). The evidence suggests that corporatism and consensus go hand-in-hand with superior macroeconomic performance on the jobs front. However, there are three important caveats. First, any such associations beg the causal mechanism which may run from good performance to consensus rather than vice versa. Second, while corporatist economies may deliver the employment goods they may fail on the productivity front (Minford, 1989). Third, if we focus on the much narrower indicator of wage centralisation, it has recently been argued that a U-shaped association exists between the degree of such wage centralisation and macroeconomic performance, countries with very centralised and very decentralised wage setting performing better than intermediate countries (Calmfors and Driffill, 1988).

Corporatism is defined by Bruno and Sachs (1985) as a 'model of social organisation in which groups rather than individuals wield power and transact affairs'. Their indicators of corporatism are:

whether negotiations take place at national or local level
the power of national vis-à-vis local labour organisations
the extent of employer coordination
the power of local union stewards.

A country is defined as corporatist if: wage bargaining is highly centralised; wage agreements do not have to be ratified at local level; employers are organised; and local union officials have limited influence. The ranking of countries which emerges from these criteria seems sensible. The most corporatist countries are Austria, Germany, Netherlands and Scandinavia and the least corporatist are the USA and Canada. Japan and the rest of Europe rank in the middle.

Bruno and Sachs themselves suggest that corporatism is an important influence in economic performance. This is confirmed in thorough recent analyses (Bean, Layard and Nickell, 1986; Newell and Symons, 1987) which show that:

- more corporatist economics display a greater response of wage changes to unemployment in both the short run and the long run, i.e. a smaller increase in unemployment is required to get a given reduction in money wage inflation in corporatist economics;
- the impact of tax changes and import prices is lower in corporatist economics, i.e. it is easier to adjust to (e.g.) oil shocks because there is less real wage resistance in corporatist economies;

- the unemployment consequences of an increase in union militancy or a rise in real interest rates are lower in corporatist economies;
- the increase in unemployment in the last two decades and the level of unemployment in the 1980s is lower in the more corporatist economies.

The consensus–performance connection has also been investigated by an OECD working party (Soskice, 1983). They compared, for 16 countries, the Okun 'misery index' with the extent of consensus. The misery index is defined as the sum of the inflation and unemployment rates. The degree of consensus was based on three characteristics: the degree of centralisation of collective bargaining; trade union and employer willingness to concert action with the government; and the reliability of dispute settlement procedures. The evidence – for three separate time periods – shows an inverse association between consensus and misery. In each time period high consensus countries like Austria and Germany show up as low misery countries, while low consensus countries like the UK and Italy suffer more misery (though perhaps this has been compensated more recently by a superior labour productivity growth performance).

The weight of the evidence suggests that the pay–jobs trade-off is better in corporatist/consensus labour markets than ones with opposite characteristics. But Calmfors and Driffill (1988) have argued that concepts like 'corporatism' and 'consensus' are too vague. They state the key labour market variable influencing macroeconomic performance is much narrower – wage centralisation – defined as the extent of inter-union and inter-employer cooperation in wage bargaining with the other side. Their focus is more on the behavioural than on the procedural content in wage setting, in particular the extent to which coalitions are formed among unions and employers respectively. They argue that there is a hump-shaped relationship between the degree of centralisation in wage setting and the aggregate real wage and, therefore, a U-shaped relationship between job performance and wage centralisation. They advocate pursuing either complete centralisation (cf. Austria) or complete decentralisation of wage bargaining (cf. the USA, Japan, Switzerland). If they are right this is a bit worrying for EC countries, which are mostly in the intermediate group. The authors single out Belgium, the Netherlands and Germany as countries whose system of collective bargaining at the industry level will contribute the least to wage restraint.

3.2 Flexibility at the sector and enterprise level

(a) Industrial pay structure

Evidence on movements in the pay structure by industry in France, Italy, Germany and the UK is given in Figure 7.1. There are two important questions. First, what determines the observed changes in industrial pay structures? Second, does the flexibility in the industrial pay structure augment or hinder employment?

Marsden (1989b) shows that the pay rankings by industry are stable in each of the four countries, but as Figure 7.1 shows, there is considerable movement in the time series of industrial wage differentials. In Italy the trend decline is explained by the egalitarian wage policies pursued by unions to accommodate the influx of semi-skilled and

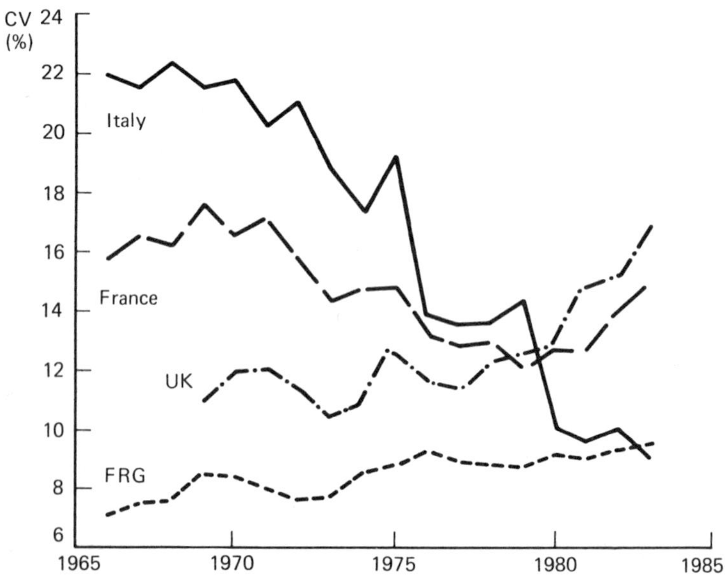

* Unweighted coefficient of variation over about 30 industries in mining, manufacturing, and construction.

Sources: Eurostat, Hourly earnings and hours of work; and Department of Employment, Earnings of manual workers in October, from Marsden (1989).

Figure 7.1 Industry Differentials in France, Italy, West Germany and the United Kingdom, October 1966–October 1983: Manual Men Average Gross Hourly Earnings*

unskilled workers in the 1960s and 1970s. This downward trend in differentials was compounded by changes in the indexation system in 1975 which resulted in equal cash payments for all workers for given percentage price rises. In Britain and in Germany pay differentials are contra-cyclical, rising when unemployment rises and falling in boom times.

Movements in industrial wage differentials can reflect either an allocation mechanism or a prosperity mechanism. The allocation mechanism requires a positive correlation between short-run movements in pay and employment across industries. There is no evidence of such a mechanism in recent years (OECD, 1986). Instead, there is some evidence that pay changes by industry have been positively correlated with movements in value productivity – thus employees have shared in the prosperity of their respective industries. Whether or not this prosperity mechanism augments employment is a rather complicated matter (Metcalf, 1987) but it seems to have done, or at least been neutral, in each of the countries analysed by the OECD except Japan.

(*b*) *Enterprise level*

There is considerable concern in EC countries to enhance labour flexibility at the workplace level. There are a number of strands to this concern. First, it is sometimes asserted that employment security laws lead to sclerotic labour markets. However, Emerson (1986) shows that there is no apparent association between the importance of obstacles to the termination of employment contracts and performance at the macroeconomic level.

Second, the EC is sometimes compared unfavourably with the USA and Japan. The OECD reports on labour market flexibility (OECD, 1986; Dahrendorf *et al.*, 1986) distinguished between external and internal mobility. External mobility involves a change of employer or enterprise; internal mobility takes place within one enterprise or with one employer. The *Financial Times* recently (30 May 1986) stated that Europe has high unemployment because it lacks either sort of mobility.

Some evidence on external job mobility is given in Table 7.5. Job tenure durations are the outcome of the process of external job mobility (in this context a 'job' refers to an individual's uninterrupted tenure with a particular employer). In the EC countries nearly one third of employees or more have held their current jobs for over 10 years. The EC lies between the USA and Japan. In the USA only a quarter of

Table 7.5 Distribution of on-going jobs by current tenures

Country	Year data refer to	Under 2 years, %	10+ years %	Average job tenure (years) Male	Female	All
Belgium	1978	18	36	8.7	5.6	8.0
France	1978	18	35	9.7	7.2	8.8
Germany	1978	19	38	8.9	5.7	8.5
Italy	1978	13	37	7.4	6.6	7.1
Netherlands	1979	28	31	8.9	3.7	8.2
United Kingdom	1979	24	31	9.6	6.4	8.6
Japan	1982	21	48	13.5	8.8	11.7
United States	1983	39	27	8.4	5.6	7.2

Notes: There are 3 distinct concepts of average employment duration: (i) the average (uncompleted) duration of jobs currently in progress; (ii) the expected duration of employment for someone beginning a new job; (iii) the expected completed duration of a job currently in progress. The information above refers to (i). Under certain circumstances (iii) is equal to twice (i). Concept (ii) produces shorter durations than (i).

Sources: OECD (1984, table 31); OECD (1985); OECD (1986, table II–1).

employees have held their current jobs for over 10 years while in Japan the corresponding fraction is one half.

Alternatively, any mobility problems in Europe might concern the use of labour inside the firm. But there is now evidence of increasing adaptability in the use of labour in the internal labour market in many EC countries. For example:

- the nature of the employment contract is changing. Many firms are reducing the number of their full-time core staff and accommodating fluctuations in demand or peripheral tasks by increasing the number of part-timers, temporary workers and sub-contractors;
- changes in the development and use of skilled labour are taking place. In some sectors skilled workers are becoming partially competent in a number of crafts and some barriers to mobility between semi-skilled, skilled and technician jobs are being eroded;
- work patterns are changing: collective agreements are now being struck which get away from the traditional basic workweek and instead encourage shift work, night work, weekend work and part-time work.

While Europe does not have either the external mobility of the USA or the internal mobility of Japan, its labour market is by no means as obdurate as it is sometimes painted. Certainly, the role of (insufficient) external and internal mobility in explaining European performance on productivity and jobs remains an open question.

4 1992 EMPLOYMENT CONSEQUENCES AND SOCIAL DIMENSION

The economic and financial integration in Europe raises two main labour market issues. First, what are the consequences for jobs? Second, will the economic integration be accompanied by social harmonisation? These will be considered in turn.

4.1 Employment consequences of 1992

The EC Commission (1988) has produced detailed forecasts of the medium-term macroeconomic consequences of market integration. It states that the EC will have to do more than demolish its internal trade barriers if it is to realise the full economic benefits of a single market.

The report warns that transition to a single market will involve a difficult adjustment process. Some job losses will be inevitable in the short term as industries are rationalised and restructured in the face of stiffer international competition.

It estimates that, without any accompanying change in macroeconomic policies, completion of the single market could enlarge the EC's total gross domestic product (GDP) by some 4.5 per cent and increase employment by 1.75 million over the medium term. The source of the extra jobs is as follows:

	million jobs
Supply-side effects, e.g. scale economies	.85
Jobs in financial services	.40
Jobs in public procurement sectors	.35
Jobs generated by axeing customs formalities	.20
	1.80

But if EC governments took advantage of the improved efficiency simultaneously to adopt more expansionary policies GDP could rise by 7 per cent and employment by 5 million.

The report indicates that the impact of the single market will vary widely between both countries and sectors. It will have the biggest impact in technologically advanced sectors such as electronics where the community's international competitive performance has been relatively poor. The effects are likely to be least in more traditional industries such as footwear, textiles and clothing where internal market barriers do not impose a severe competitive handicap.

4.2 The social dimension

Some EC countries, and the President of the EC, wish to complement economic harmonisation with both technical standardisation and upward harmonisation of workers' rights. By contrast, the UK government mainly emphasises the prospects for flexibility and deregulation in both economic and social affairs. This tension between harmonisation and deregulation has caused a stalemate on social issues. The distinguished labour lawyer Hepple (1987) recently went so far as to state: 'the prospects for a revival of the social action programme of the 1970s are nil.'

Two strands of social policy enjoy a wide measure of agreement. First, all countries support the use of the European Social Fund to increase the amount of training and to promote job generation schemes, particularly for the long term unemployed. Second, policy concertation on matters like education qualifications and, to some extent, social security is supported. The disagreement comes over the third strand – the use of EC-sponsored legislation and directives to harmonise employment practices.

There are two areas where such EC directives and recommendations have stalled in the 1980s. These are (i) reorganisation of working time coupled with enhanced rights for non-core workers; (ii) information, consultation and industrial democracy. However, there has been some strengthening of (iii) health and safety regulations and (iv) equal treatment for men and women. Unless some progress is made soon on (i) and (ii) there will be no real 'social dimension' to 1992.

Reorganisation of working time was accorded top priority by the EC in the 1980s, but progress has been minimal, limited to a recommendation concerning flexible retirement. In the face of rising unemployment the Commission suggested both a reduction in annual hours per worker and a stricter limitation on systematic overtime. This proposal was vetoed by the UK because of doubts over its potential for generating extra jobs. Hand-in-hand with reduced hours for full-time employees the Commission wished to strengthen the position of flexible workers such as part-timers, and those on temporary work and fixed duration employment contracts. For part-time workers it was proposed to implement the principle of equal rights with full-time workers. This included proportional rights on pay, holidays, redundancy and retirement payments, and a written contract of employment. This suggestion was opposed by the UK government because it conflicted with their aim of reining back all such employment protection legislation.

Company organisation and employee involvement have long been key areas of European social policy. The Fifth Directive has been discussed on and off since 1972 but is currently on ice. It lays out various forms of employee participation at board level in companies with 1000-plus workers. The complementary Vredling Directive recommended that every six months companies give their employees information on: company economic and financial position; company organisation; employment structure; production and investment programmes; rationalisation plans; and working methods. Employers' organisations and some governments have not been prepared to endorse either of these proposals for fear that they will undermine traditional managerial prerogatives.

The failure to advance and enlarge EC social policy in the 1980s, and the remote prospect of progress between now and 1992, raises two central issues. First, can there ever be a European-wide approach to social policy on the 'harmonisation upwards' lines normally advanced by the EC? The Commission typically scans member countries for best practice on a particular issue and then uses this as the benchmark for Draft Directives and recommendations. In practice it is very difficult to implement such proposals because of political differences among member countries and wide variation in their industrial relations practices.

Second, what is the role of the social partners? In particular, the British government is, presently, strongly anti-corporatist. This means that consensus on most EC social policy proposals is almost impossible to achieve inside Britain. Ironically it is now the TUC (1988) – which historically has been antagonistic or only lukewarm to the EC – which is the main proponent of the social dimension to accompany economic integration. But the TUC faces real difficulty in translating its aspirations on things like union recognition, employment protection and employee involvement into reality via the legislative route. The veto power of the government (tempered a little by qualified majority voting on some industrial relations issues) can be used to stymy progress on social matters. European-wide collective bargaining may turn out to be more fruitful than European legislation which falls on stony ground.

References

Bean, C., Layard, R. and Nickell, S. (1986) 'The Rise in Unemployment: A Multi-country Study', *Economica*, suppl., 53, 1–22.

Boyer, R. (ed.) (1988) *The Search for Labour Market Flexibility: The European Economies in Transition* (Oxford: Clarendon Press).

Brunetta, R. and Dell'Aringa, C. (eds) (1989) *Labour Relations and Economic Performance*, IEA Conference Proceedings (London: Macmillan).

Bruno, M. and Sachs, J. (1985) *The Economics of Worldwide Stagflation* (Oxford: Blackwell).

Callaghan, W. and Philpott, J. (eds) (1989) *Trade Unions and the Economy: Into the 1990s*, Employment Institute.

Calmfors, L. and Driffill, J. (1988) 'Bargaining Structure, Corporatism and Macroeconomic Performance', *Economic Policy*, vol. 6, April.

Dahrendorf, R. *et al.* (1986) *Labour Market Flexibility*, Paris, OECD, June.

Emerson, M. (1986) 'Regulation or Deregulation of the Labour Market: Policy Regimes for the Recruitment and Dismissal of Employees in Industrial Countries', Harvard University, mimeo, June.

European Commission (1988) 'The Economics of 1992', *European Economy*, no. 35.

Freeman, R. (1989) 'On the Divergence in Unionism among Developed Countries', in R. Brunetta and C. dell'Aringa (eds) *Markets, Institutions and Cooperation: Labour Relations and Economic Performance* (London: Macmillan).

Hepple, R. (1987) 'The Crisis in EC Labour Law', *Industrial Law Journal*, 16(2), June.

Kerr, C., Dunlop, J., Harbison, F. and Myers, C. (1964) *Industrialism and Industrial Man* (Oxford University Press).

Marsden, D. (1988) 'Short Run Wage Flexibility and Labour Market Adaption in Western Europe', *Labour*, 2(1).

Marsden, D. (1989a) 'Can European Trade Unions Survive 1992?', mimeo, LSE Industrial Relations Department.

Marsden, D. (1989b) 'Developments of Pay Level Patterns and Flexibility in Western Europe', Eighth World Congress of the International Industries Relations Association, Brussels.

Metcalf, D. (1987) 'Labour Market Flexibility and Jobs – A Survey of Evidence from OECD Countries with Special Reference to Great Britain and Europe' in R. Layard and L. Calmfors (eds) *The Fight Against Unemployment*, Macroeconomic Papers from CEPS (Cambridge: MIT Press).

Metcalf, D. (1989) 'Can Unions Survive in the Private Sector?', in W. Callaghan and J. Philpott (eds) (1989) *Trade Unions and the Economy: Into the 1990s*, Employment Institute.

Minford, P. (1989) 'Corporatism, the Natural Rate and Productivity', in W. Callaghan and J. Philpott (eds) (1989) *Trade Unions and the Economy: Into the 1990s*, Employment Institute.

Newell, A. and Symons, J. (1987) 'Corporatism, Laissez-faire and the Rise in Unemployment', *European Economic Review*.

OECD (1984) *Employment Outlook*, Paris.

OECD (1985) 'Job Turnover and Tenure in Selected OECD Countries', mimeo.

OECD (1986) *Flexibility in the Labour Market*, Paris.

OECD (1988) *Employment Outlook*, Paris, September.

Paloheimo, H. (1989) 'The Economic Effects of Trade Unions and Governments on Economic Performance', in R. Brunetta and C. Dell'Aringa (eds) *Labour Relations and Economic Performance*, IEA Conference Proceedings (London: Macmillan).

Soskice, D. (1983) 'Collective Bargaining and Economic Policies', Manpower and Social Affairs Committee, OECD.

Trades Union Congress (1988a) *Maximising the Benefits and Minimising the Costs*, Report on Europe 1992, July.

Trades Union Congress (1988b) *Review of Working Times in Britain and Western Europe*, Congress House, December.

Part IV
The EMS and Liberalisation of Capital Movements

8 The Liberalisation of Capital Movements and the EMS

Paul De Grauwe

1 INTRODUCTION

Major EMS countries like France and Italy have begun to liberalise capital movements. This process should lead to complete freedom of capital movements within the EMS by 1990. It is clear that this will have profound effects on the functioning of the EMS. Some observers worry that free capital mobility may lead to more fragility of the EMS, others that capital market integration in the EMS is the next and necessary step towards full monetary integration.

In this chapter some of the implications of a new environment of free capital movements for the EMS are analysed. More specifically we analyse two questions. First, we study the issue of the timing of the liberalisation. Does it come too soon, as some have claimed, or will it, on the contrary, strengthen the integration process? This issue is analysed in Sections 2 and 3. Second, how will the liberalisation of capital movements affect the monetary interactions in the EMS? Will it strengthen the position of Germany, or will it rather make the system more symmetric? We take up this question in Section 4.

2 'MONETARISTS' AND 'ECONOMISTS' ONCE AGAIN

Few will dispute that the free movement of capital constitutes an essential part of a full monetary union. Thus, ultimately, countries who wish to form such a union must completely liberalise capital movements. The issue which is at stake here concerns the timing of the liberalisation of capital movements. Should such a liberalisation be introduced as the final step to full union, i.e. when sufficient monetary cooperation among the candidate union-members exists? Or can it be used as a strategic device to force more monetary cooperation?

The issue resembles the old discussion between the 'monetarists' and the 'economists'. The former argued in the early 1970s that fixing the exchange rates would force the member countries in the union to coordinate their policies. The latter contended that exchange rate fixity could only be introduced when a sufficient level of cooperation existed. During the 1970s the 'economists' carried the day. It was widely believed that fixing the exchange rates without prior explicit agreements on how to coordinate national monetary policies would lead to failure. The experience with the EMS has made the 'monetarist' position respectable again. It appears that the EMS exchange rate agreement has forced its members to gradually increase their monetary cooperation, thereby vindicating the 'monetarists'.

Today there is a similar split between 'economists' and 'monetarists' about the role of capital mobility in the integration process. The 'monetarists' are optimistic about the role capital mobility can play in forcing the EMS-member countries to cooperate, the 'economists' are pessimistic.

Let us analyse the pessimistic view of the 'economists' first. In this view, capital controls are a defensive device which allows countries to maintain some monetary independence, and which make it possible to shield the domestic money market from speculative crises. Some authors have claimed that the success of the EMS in maintaining relatively stable exchange rates is to a large extent due to the existence of capital controls (see Giavazzi and Pagano, 1985).

According to these 'economists', the abolition of capital controls may jeopardise the success which the EMS has had in stabilising exchange rates. When speculative movements occur, the authorities will have no defence. They will be forced to change the exchange rate. These speculative movements are likely to arise because economic cooperation among the member states is not yet intense enough. In this view, the move towards capital market liberalisation within the EMS comes too soon, as the willingness to cooperate is not yet strong enough.

The 'monetarist' view about the role of capital mobility in the monetary integration process is optimistic. It can be phrased as follows. Every fixed exchange rate agreement faces a credibility problem. Economic agents are aware that conflicts may arise between the fixed exchange rate commitment of the authorities and their domestic policy objectives, such as employment and inflation. They suspect that when such conflicts arise the authorities may be tempted to renege on their commitment to maintain the exchange rate unchanged. Thus, the authorities who are serious about their commitment face the problem of how to convince a sceptical public. One possibility is to completely liberalise capital movements. This has the effect of making the stock of international reserves of the country hostage to the speculators. The cost for the authorities of following a policy which is not in tune with policies in the rest of the system increases, thereby reducing the incentive to follow such policies. Put differently, by liberalising capital movements, the commitment towards fixed exchange rates becomes more credible because the authorities have tied their own hands.

One can also turn around this argument. A country that maintains capital controls gives information to the market about its intentions. By segmenting the domestic money market, capital controls increase the incentives for the authorities to follow relatively independent policies and to increase the weight given to domestic policy objectives. As a result, credibility of the fixed exchange rate arrangement will be low, and speculative attacks will be frequent. Thus, in the 'monetarist' view the existence of capital controls itself is conducive to speculative crises.

In this 'monetarist' view of the world, the existence of capital controls has very little to do with the success of the EMS. There is another feature of the EMS which carries more weight. This is the existence of a relatively large band of free fluctuation of the exchange rate coupled with an implicit commitment to change the parities in amounts that do not exceed the width of the band significantly. More than 90 per cent of all realignments were smaller than the 4.5 per cent band of free fluctuation (12 per cent in the case of Italy until January 1990). This has led to a situation where after a realignment, the market exchange rates have been barely affected. Contrary to the situation in the Bretton Woods system, speculators know that there are no sure profits to be made by taking speculative positions prior to realignments.

In a nutshell the 'monetarist' position can be phrased as follows. The successful functioning of the EMS is not dependent on the existence of capital controls. In addition, eliminating these controls will strengthen the credibility of the system, because it disciplines national authorities. It is, therefore, an essential step in the strategy towards full monetary integration.[1]

How can these two opposing views about the role of capital mobility in the monetary integration process be evaluated? One way to do this is to analyse the past and present operation of the EMS. Within the present EMS we have a group of countries which have allowed complete freedom of capital movements (Germany and the Netherlands), and a group of other countries which have used some form of capital controls. A comparison of the interdependencies within these two groups can shed some light on the role of capital mobility.

3 THE TWO REGIMES IN THE EMS

In this section we present data on interest rates, money stocks and inflation in the EMS-countries. Figure 8.1 shows the evolution of the interest rates (short-term) in selected EMS-countries. It can be seen that the Dutch and German interest rates move very close to each other. This cannot be said for the French and Italian interest rates. Relatively large differences with the German interest rate are observed over the whole EMS-period, although recently these have narrowed somewhat. These differentials are to be interpreted as a premium for latent expectations of future devaluations of the French and Italian currencies vis-à-vis the German mark.

Figure 8.2 presents data on the growth rates of the money stock (M1). Again one observes a very close co-movement of the Dutch and German money stock growth rates. This is much less the case with France and Italy. Since 1986, however, a stronger convergence of the money stock data is observed between France, Italy and Germany.

Finally, Figure 8.3 shows the evolution of the inflation rates. The Dutch and German inflation rates move in close unison. As a result, the cumulative inflation differential between the Netherlands and Germany during 1979–88 is barely 3 per cent. This differential between France and Germany (and between Italy and Germany) is much larger, reaching 50 per cent in the case of France versus Germany. In the last few years, however, a strong convergence of the French and Italian inflation rates with the German one is observed.

The previous empirical evidence leads to the following interpretation. The EMS is characterised by the existence of two regimes. There is a first regime consisting of the Netherlands and Germany. These two countries allow complete mobility of capital. Their monetary policies are almost exact copies of each other. As a result, there are almost no differences in inflation rates. This has also allowed the guilder/DM rate to remain practically unchanged throughout the whole EMS-period.[2] The confidence in the fixity of the guilder/DM rate is so strong that the market exchange rate has moved within a band of less than 1 per cent around the parity during the last few years.

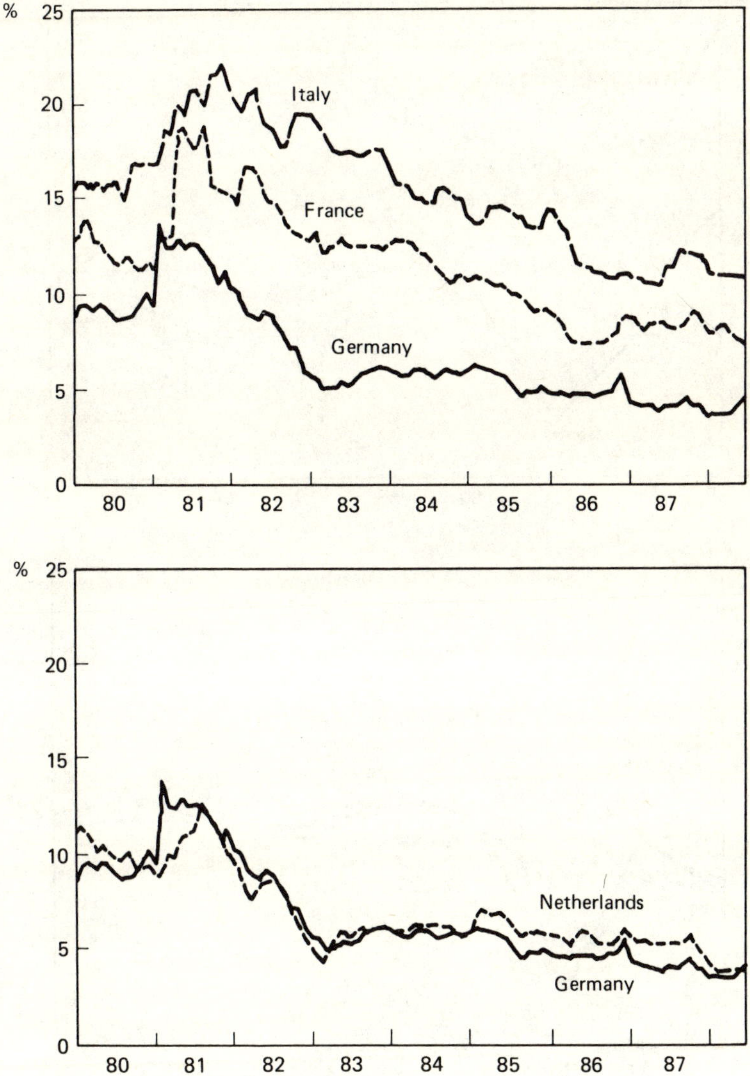

Source: IMF, *International Financial Statistics.*

Figure 8.1 Short-term interest rates (bank deposits)

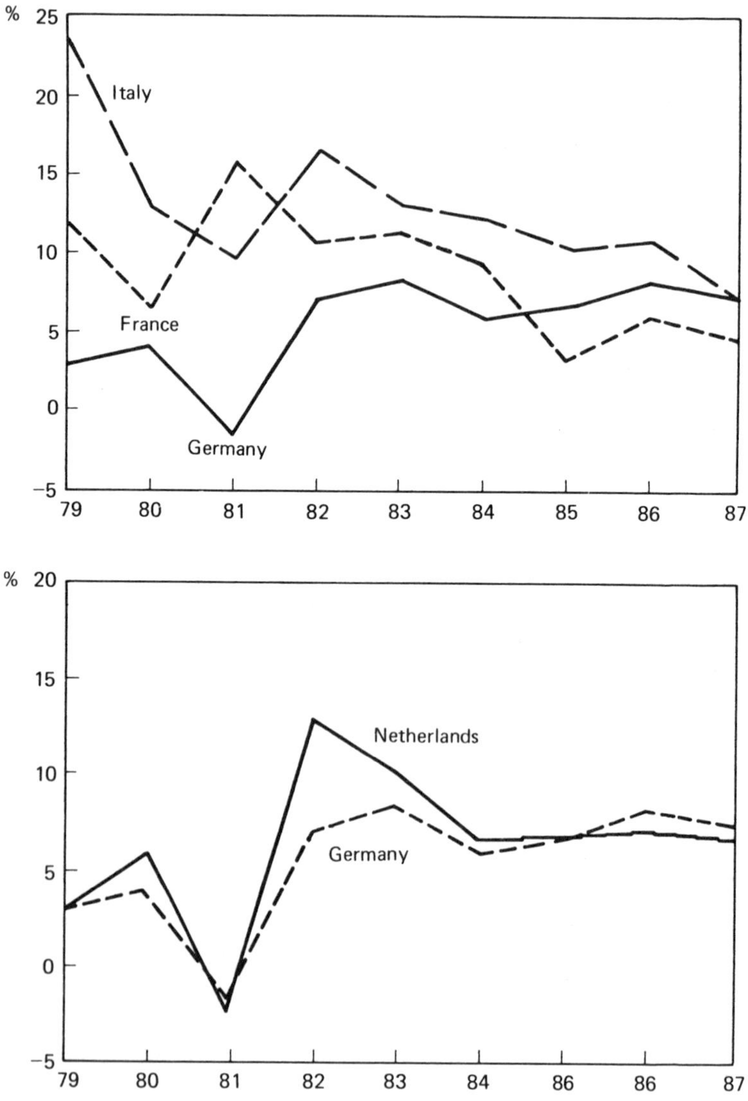

Source: IMF, *International Financial Statistics.*

Figure 8.2 Growth rate of the money stock

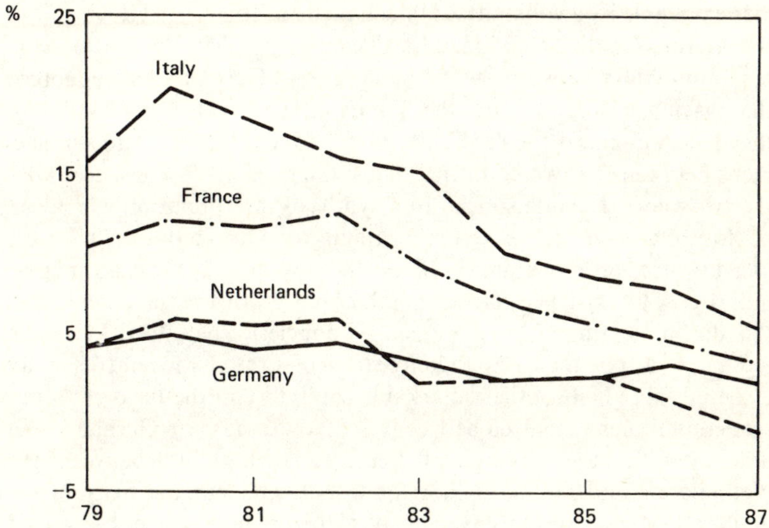

Source: OECD, *Main Economic Indicators*.

Figure 8.3 Inflation rates (CPI) in selected EMS countries

The second regime within the EMS comprises the other countries. These have used capital controls to shield their domestic money markets from the effects of speculative crises. We also observe substantial divergences of monetary policies among these countries, and compared to Germany. This has also led to relatively large divergences in price trends, and a need to realign the exchange rate regularly. For a few years, however, monetary policies, and inflation rates have become more convergent in this second group. The continuing existence of an interest rate premium on French and Italian assets compared to German assets, however, indicates that the market is not yet fully convinced of the fixity of the FF/DM and lira/DM rates.

What can we learn from this comparison between the two exchange rate regimes within the EMS? We observe that the countries in the EMS with open financial markets (the Netherlands and Germany) also experience a strong convergence of their monetary policies. Countries that have used capital controls have much less convergence of their monetary policies. This evidence is consistent with both the 'economist' and the 'monetarist' hypotheses. 'Economists' will claim that the free mobility of capital between the Netherlands and Germany has been made possible by a willingness of the Dutch authorities to closely follow the German policies. 'Monetarists' can argue that the existence of capital mobility between the Netherlands and Germany has reinforced the discipline imposed on the Dutch monetary policies, and has, therefore, enhanced the credibility of the fixed exchange rate arrangement between the two countries. Thus, the evidence is consistent with the two views. It can also lead to a synthesis interpretation which can be formulated as follows. Free capital mobility requires a strong convergence of monetary policies, as the Dutch–German regime indicates. The existence of free capital mobility, however, also reinforces the discipline on national monetary policies. The Dutch–German regime certainly indicates that freedom of capital movements is an essential ingredient of the remarkable credibility in the fixed exchange rate commitment achieved between the Netherlands and Germany. Put differently, in the absence of free capital mobility between the Netherlands and Germany, it is quite unlikely that the fixity of the guilder/DM rate would have achieved the credibility it has obtained today.

The recent convergence of monetary policies in the second group of countries adds additional power to this interpretation. This convergence has coincided with the start of the liberalisation of capital movements in these countries, and with a period of a remarkable absence of major speculative disturbances. Although the decision to liberalise has certainly been made possible by the convergence of policies, it is also likely that the increasing capital mobility between France and Germany, for example, has contributed towards forcing these countries to conform their monetary policies to each other. Thus, there may be a subtle interaction between capital mobility and monetary cooperation. The latter is necessary to allow capital to move freely. At the same time, the free movement of capital gives a strong incentive to national authorities to align their policies to the policies in the rest of the system.

This interpretation should lead to optimism about the prospects for further liberalisation of capital movements. The degree of monetary policy convergence achieved in 1989 in the second group of countries is substantial enough to make further liberalisation possible without upsetting the system. The existence of a relatively wide band of fluctuation, and the implicit commitment to keep the realignments small should be a sufficient defence against speculative crises, when they occur. In addition, by strengthening the credibility of the exchange rate commitment, the free movement of capital may help to reduce the likelihood of speculative crises.

4 CAPITAL MOBILITY AND ASYMMETRY IN THE EMS

We have identified two exchange rate regimes in the EMS. In the Dutch–German regime, where capital flows freely, the coordination of monetary policies is almost perfect. This coordination, however, is far from symmetrical. The Dutch monetary authorities abstain from any attempt to set their monetary policies in an independent way. Instead they almost automatically follow the monetary policy lead of the German authorities. The question that arises here is the following. If the Dutch–German regime can be considered as the forerunner of the future exchange rate regime in the whole of the EMS, does that imply that the EMS will also be run in an asymmetric way, with Germany in a dominant position? In other words, is capital market integration within the EMS going to reinforce the position of Germany, and make the EMS more of a DM-zone than it already is today?

In order to analyse this question it is useful to study the past and the present operations of the EMS. To what extent can it be said that the EMS has worked as a DM-zone? When we have answered this question we can return to the issue whether liberalisation will strengthen or diminish the asymmetric tendencies in the system.

It has been claimed by many observers that the EMS works in an asymmetric way. In this asymmetric interpretation of the workings of the EMS, Germany is seen as the centre country which determines its monetary policy more or less independently from what happens in the rest of the EMS. The other countries peg their currencies to the DM and, in so doing, subordinate their monetary policies to German policies. This interpretation of the EMS has led to the widespread view that the system is *de facto* a DM-zone. It is no exaggeration to state that this interpretation of the workings of the EMS has become the conventional wisdom.[3]

Recently, this view has been challenged by Fratianni and von Hagen.[4] These authors analysed the behaviour of the monetary aggregates in the EMS, and concluded that there is little evidence for the asymmetric hypothesis. In this section we study the behavior of interest rates, and we analyse in what sense, if any, it can be said that Germany has dominated the behaviour of interest rates in the EMS.

It is useful to start from the (closed) interest parity condition, which can be written as follows:

$$r_F = r_G + fp \tag{8.1}$$

where r_F and r_G are the interest rates in country F (France) and G (Germany); fp is the forward premium of the German mark relative to the French franc.

In efficient markets and in the absence of risk premia, the forward premium (fp) reflects prevailing expectations about the rate at which the DM will be revalued against the French franc in the future. We then obtain the open interest parity condition:

$$r_F = r_G + \mu \tag{8.2}$$

where μ is the rate at which the mark is expected to be revalued in the future. In a later paragraph, risk premia produced by capital controls are introduced.

We now consider what happens when, for some exogenous reason, agents expect a future revaluation of the DM relative to the French franc. Such an expectation will increase the forward premium of the DM (μ). It is then immediately clear from equation (8.2) that this must lead to an increase in the French interest rate (r_F) and/or a decline in the German interest rate (r_G). There are infinitely many combinations of French interest rate increases and German interest rate declines which can sustain this change in expectations.

The precise manner in which this speculative shock is absorbed by interest rate changes then depends on the way the two countries conduct their monetary policies. Consider, first, an *asymmetric* situation in which Germany sets its money stock independently from what happens in the DM/FF exchange market. The adjustment mechanism can then be described as follows. The expected revaluation of the DM leads to purchases of DM (sales of FF). In order to keep the DM/FF rate within the margins, the Banque de France will sell DM (buy FF). The sale of DM tends to increase the money stock in Germany. This effect, however, is automatically sterilised by the German authorities (who are assumed not to change their money targets). As a result, the German money market will be unaffected by the speculative disturbance. It also follows that the whole adjustment will have to come from France by an increase in the French interest rate.

A second adjustment mechanism is *symmetric*. This one implies that Germany allows the domestic money market to be affected by the speculative disturbance. This adjustment mechanism then also implies that the German interest rate declines, and that the French interest rate increases. It follows that the degree of deflation imposed on France is reduced compared to the asymmetric system.

In the previous discussion, it was assumed that open interest parity holds perfectly. If one or more countries use capital controls, however, there will be deviations from interest parity. This also allows for the adjustment following the expected realignment to be different than the one discussed in the previous paragraphs.

One can formalise the capital controls as follows.[5] Capital controls have the effect of introducing a wedge in the interest parity condition, i.e.

$$r_F - (r_G + \mu) = \pi \tag{8.3}$$

where π reflects the wedge in the interest parity condition introduced by capital controls in France.

The implications for the adjustment mechanism following a speculative disturbance can be described as follows. The expected devaluation of the franc leads to a positive μ in equation (8.3). The French capital controls, if fully effective, lead to an offsetting movement in π. As a result, the French interest rate does not change. In this case, both the domestic French money market and the German money market are insulated from the speculative disturbance. Thus, even in an asymmetric system (in which Germany pursues its independent domestic policy), the existence of capital controls allows the French authorities to keep the domestic money stock and interest rate unchanged, at least if capital controls can be made to work perfectly. In that case, the adjustment to the speculative disturbance becomes symmetric, even though Germany sets its money stock independently.

In practice, it will often be difficult to implement tight capital controls. The adjustment in π will then be less than the change in μ, so that France must allow a partial adjustment in its money market. Asymmetry will reappear, because capital controls cannot completely segment the two markets.

The previous theoretical discussion has set the stage for measuring the degree of asymmetry in the workings of the EMS. During periods of speculative crises, the forward premia (discounts) increase. This necessitates a combination of an interest rate increase in the weak-currency country and an interest rate decline in the strong-currency country. If the system works symmetrically, the upward and downward movements in the interest rate should be (approximately) equal in absolute value. In an asymmetric adjustment system, this will not be the case.

The time series of the interest rates in the EMS are presented in Figure 8.4, which shows the French and German *offshore* interest rates together with the forward premium of the German mark relative to the French franc. It can be seen that during periods of speculative pressure, when the forward premium increased, most of the interest rate

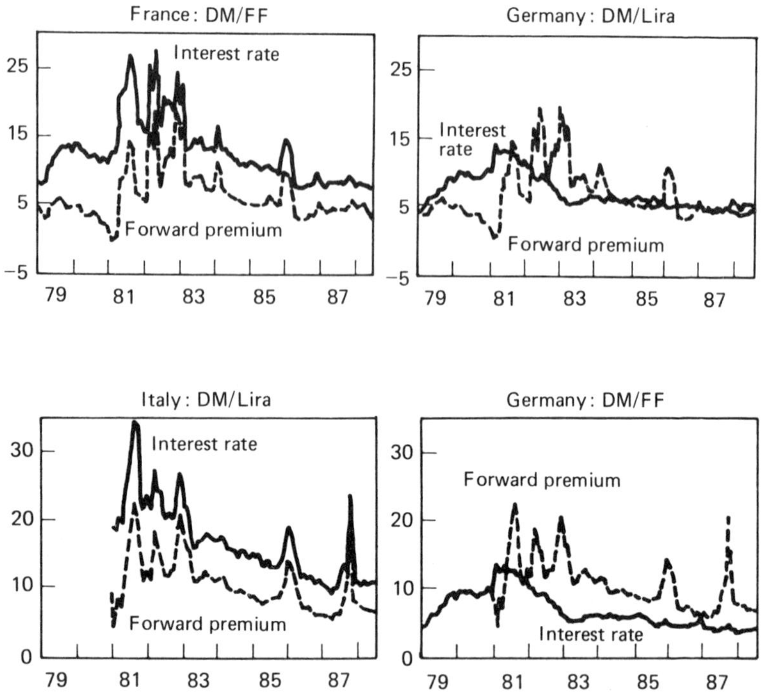

Source: Wharton Econometrics

Figure 8.4 Offshore three-month interest rates and forward premia

adjustments took the form of increases in the French interest rate. The same conclusion can be drawn from when the Italian interest rate is compared to the German one.

From this visual evidence, one may be tempted to conclude that the EMS has worked in an asymmetric way, forcing the weak currency countries to do all the monetary adjustment, and allowing the German authorities to insulate their domestic money markets from these speculative disturbances.[6]

This conclusion, however, is not warranted. In Figure 8.4, we have compared the *offshore* interest rates. In countries where capital controls exist, the *domestic* interest rates may deviate significantly from the offshore interest rates during periods of speculative crises. This can also be seen from equations (8.2) and (8.3). The former equation determines the French offshore interest rate, whereas equation (8.3) determines the French domestic interest rate. The difference between the two interest rates then will be equal to π. During periods of speculative crises, π will tend to increase so as to shield the domestic interest rate from speculative movements.

This is confirmed by Figure 8.5. It can be seen that especially during periods of speculative disturbance, the differential between the domestic and the offshore interest rates of the same currencies increased in countries like France and Italy.

In Figure 8.6 therefore, we compare the French and Italian *domestic* interest rates with their German counterpart and with the forward premium of the mark. It is now less obvious that the system has worked in an asymmetric way. We observe that during the periods of speculative crises (high forward premia), the French and Italian domestic interest rates do not seem to be affected very much. There is one interesting exception during the period 1981–2 in France. From 1983 on, however, little movement in the French domestic interest rate is observed during similar periods of speculative crises.

The visual evidence of Figures 8.4 and 8.6 also makes clear that the variability of the offshore interest rates has been much higher than the variability of the domestic interest rates in the weak currency countries. This is confirmed by Table 8.1 which presents the conditional and the unconditional standard deviations of the monthly changes in the EMS interest rates. It can be seen that in the offshore markets, the variability of the French, Italian and Belgian interest rates has been substantially higher than the German (and Dutch) interest rates. This difference in the variability of the interest rates, however, disappears completely in the domestic money markets. Thus, despite large variabilities of the offshore interest rates, which are associated with speculative disturbances, France, Italy and Belgium seem to have been able to almost completely insulate their domestic interest rates from these speculative shocks.

The previous evidence was descriptive. One can test more formally for the degree of asymmetry in the EMS using econometric techniques. This was done in De Grauwe (1988), and it confirmed the previous analysis. In addition, Granger causality tests performed on the interest rates revealed that although Germany is the most important country, there are also significant two-way interdependencies, involving for example the French and German money markets. Thus, it appears that there is more symmetry in interest rate behaviour than is recognized by those who consider the EMS to be a DM-zone. The idea that the EMS has operated like a DM-zone does not do justice to the rather subtle interest rate interdependencies within the system.

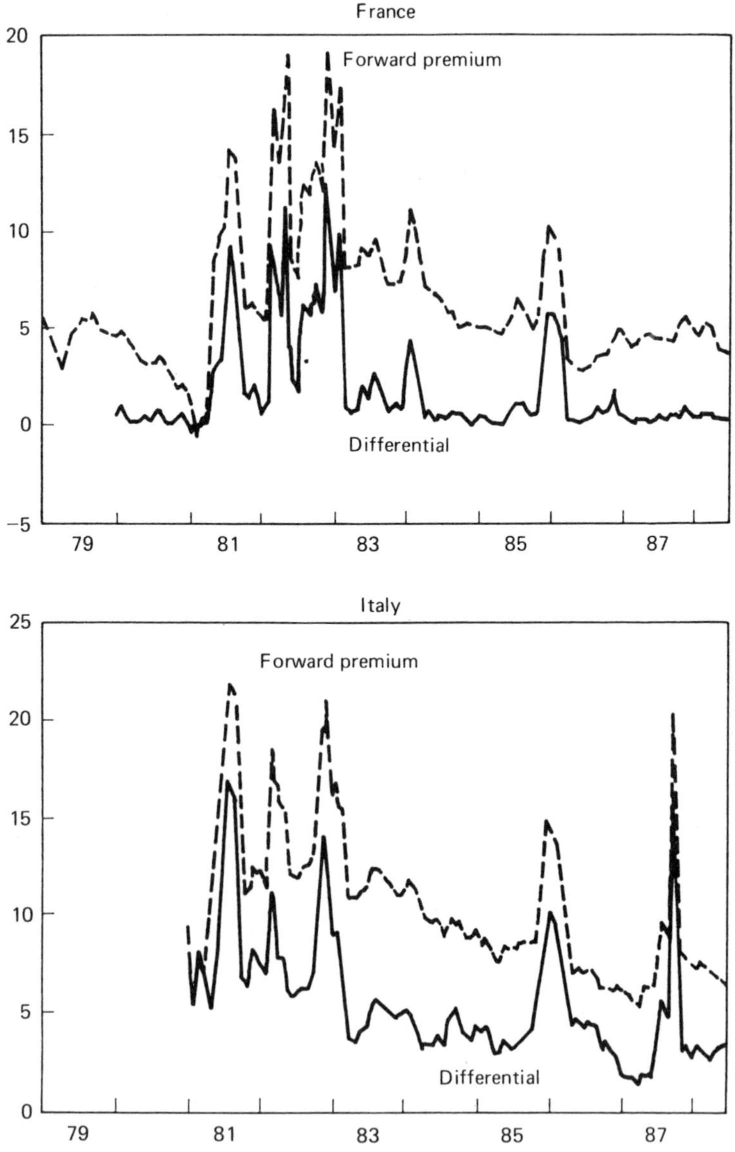

Source: Wharton Econometrics.

Figure 8.5 Differential offshore and domestic interest rates (three-month) and foreward premia

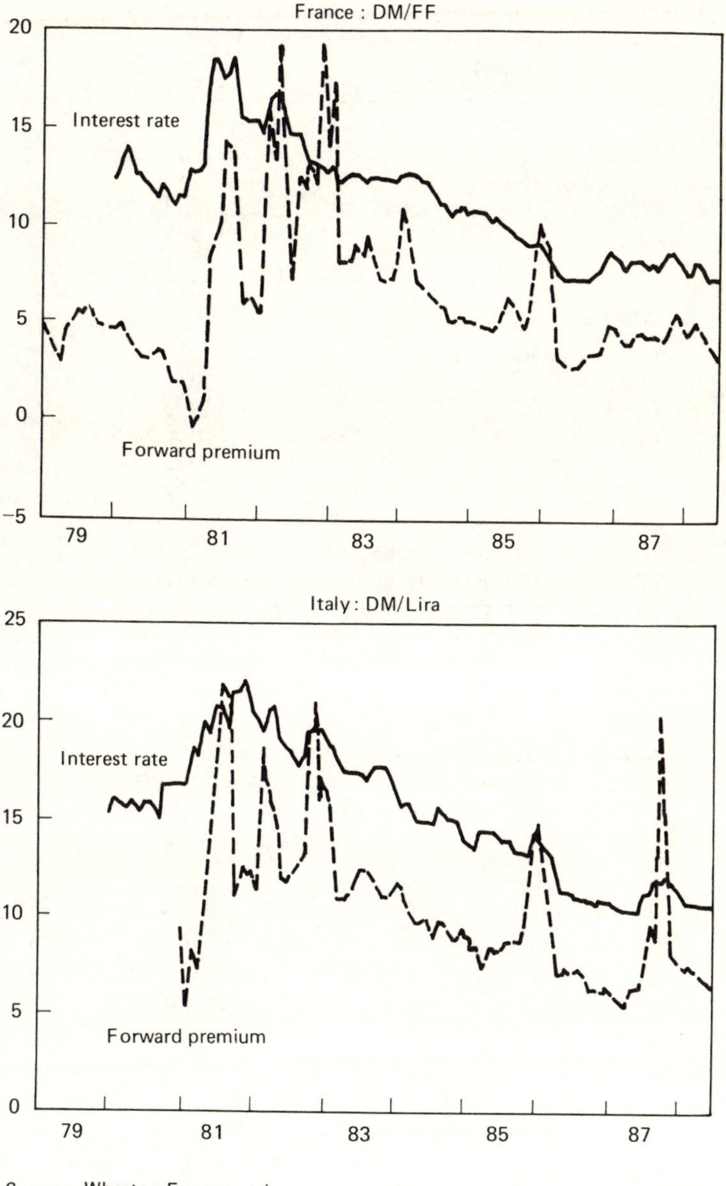

Source: Wharton Econometrics.

Figure 8.6 Domestic interest rates (three-month) and forward premia

Table 8.1 Unconditional and conditional standard deviations of the monthly changes of the offshore and the domestic interest rates in the EMS

	Unconditional	*Conditional*
Offshore interest rates		
France	2.91	2.37
Germany	0.61	0.53
Italy	2.84	2.51
Netherlands	0.55	0.43
Belgium	1.70	1.30
Domestic interest rates		
France	0.81	0.67
Germany	0.61	0.53
Italy	0.66	0.52
Netherlands	0.44	0.55
Belgium	0.64	0.59

Note: The conditional standard deviation was obtained by regressing the changes of the interest rates on their own past changes (with six lags) and on the changes of the US interest rate (present and past). The standard deviation of the residuals of these equations was used as the measure of the conditional standard deviation.

Source: Wharton Econometrics. The domestic interest rates are the treasury bill rates, except for France where we use the commercial paper rate.

What does this evidence teach us about the future relationship between Germany and the other member-states, when capital movements are liberalised? Will this liberalisation weaken the position of Germany and push the system towards more symmetry and cooperation?

There are two reasons to answer the question affirmatively. First, the evidence discussed in this section indicates that the use of sterilisation policies by Germany, and capital controls by France and Italy have allowed the EMS to be a system which is *de facto* relatively symmetric (at least when a speculative disturbance occurs). Of one of the instruments, i.e. capital controls, cannot be used anymore, this will have important implications for the interest rate adjustments following speculative crises. One can expect that when large speculative movements occur, this will put more upward pressure on the domestic interest rates of the weak currencies. It is also likely, however, that the downward pressure on the German interest rate (and the upward pressure on the German money stock) will be more intense than in the past when capital controls could be used by the weak currency countries. In other words, capital controls applied by the weak currency country shield the domestic money market of the weak *and* the strong currency countries from the effects of speculative crises. In its absence the pressure to adjust will be felt more strongly not only in the weak currency but also in the strong currency.

In this connection it should be stressed that the very asymmetric interest rate reactions we have observed in the offshore market are very misleading evidence of the degree of asymmetry of the system. As long as capital controls existed, the Euro-FF and Euro-lira were very thin markets compared to the Euro-DM (which is just an extension of the domestic DM money market). As a result, when speculative shocks occurred, prices in the thin markets moved without much effect on the broad Euro-DM market. When capital controls were completely abolished, the Euro-FF and Euro-lira markets became extensions of the domestic money markets, and therefore they also became broad markets, similar to the Euro-DM market. It is quite unlikely that when speculative shocks occur this will then only move the interest rates of the weak currencies.

A second and more fundamental reason why liberalisation of capital movements is more likely to lead to more symmetry within the system has to do with the political economy aspects of the problem. It was noted earlier that freedom of capital movements will enforce a significantly higher degree of convergence of monetary policies among the major EMS-partners than has been the case up to now. The Dutch–German regime stands as a model of the kind of convergence that must occur.

It is doubtful, however, whether the very asymmetric relation that exists between the Netherlands and Germany can be used to guide the relations between France and Germany. The French economy is comparable in size to the German one. It is, therefore, difficult to conceive that the French authorities would accept the same subordinated role towards Germany, as the Netherlands is willing to do. Put differently, the relative economic power of France relative to Germany is such that an asymmetric functioning of the EMS (with Germany setting the systemwide monetary policy) is not a long run option for the EMS. Sooner or later such a system will lead to open conflicts between the two major EMS countries. These conflicts could jeopardise the whole system.

5 CONCLUSION

In this chapter we have analysed two questions concerning the liberalisation of capital movements within the EMS. First, we studied the issue of the timing of the liberalisation process. We concluded that the liberalisation comes at the right time. The degree of convergence of monetary policies has increased significantly in the last few years. In addition, freedom of capital mobility has the characteristics of increasing the credibility of the fixed exchange rates within the system. It is, therefore, an important step towards monetary unification. It is important, however, that the existing margins of 2.25 per cent be maintained for a while. These margins and the implicit commitment that has evolved in the EMS to limit the size of possible realignments have become an essential feature of the system, allowing for both credibility and flexibility.

A second question analysed in this chapter was the effect the liberalisation of capital movements would have on the degree of asymmetry and the role of Germany in the EMS. We argued that, if anything, freedom of capital movements would make the system more symmetric. One of the features of capital controls in France and Italy was that they not only (partially) insulated the French and Italian money markets, they also reduced the external influences on the German money markets. The abolition of capital controls will, therefore, also open up the German money market to disturbances originating in the French and Italian markets, which after all are comparable in size to the German one.

The liberalisation of capital movements within the EMS poses new challenges. The pressure to coordinate policies following this liberalisation will increase significantly. What form should this cooperation take? The Dutch–German model whereby one country dominates the other in setting monetary policies does not seem to be promising to guide the relations between the major countries in the system. Therefore, more symmetric cooperative decision processes will have to be used. These almost certainly imply some form of institutional integration of the monetary policy-making process. Ad hoc cooperation is likely to be insufficient because such cooperation is prone to conflict and disagreement, and therefore has a low credibility.

The question today is whether the EMS-countries will be able to devise more symmetric decision rules in the system. A failure to do so would put the system under strain, and may jeopardise its future.

Notes

1. For such a view, see e.g. Gros and Thygesen (1988), and Driffill (1988).
2. The total cumulative devaluation of the guilder relative to the DM was 3.8 per cent.
3. See Giavazzi and Pagano (1985), Sarcinelli (1986), Katseli (1987).
4. See Fratianni and von Hagen (1988).
5. For a more rigorous treatment, see Gros (1987).
6. This is the conclusion drawn by Giavazzi and Giovannini (1988), ch. 4, using the same evidence.

References

De Grauwe, P. (1988) 'Is the European Monetary System a DM-zone?', CEPS Working Paper, Brussels.

Driffill, J. (1988) 'Capital Controls and the European Monetary System', in Giavazzi, F., Micossi, S. and Miller, M. (eds) *The European Monetary System 1979–87* (Cambridge University Press).

Fratianni, M. and von Hagen, J. (1988) 'German Dominance in the EMS: The Empirical Evidence', mimeo, Graduate School of Business, Indiana University, April.

Giavazzi, F. and Pagano, M. (1985) 'Capital Controls and the European Monetary System', in Euromobiliare, Occasional Paper.

Giavazzi, F. and Giovannini, A. (1988) *Limiting Exchange Rate Flexibility: The European Monetary System* (Cambridge: MIT Press).

Gros, D. and Thygesen, N. (1988) 'The EMS: Achievements, Current Issues and Directions for the Future', CEPS Paper, no. 35, March.

Gros, D. (1987) 'Capital Controls in the EMS: A Model with Incomplete Market Separation'. CEPS Economic Working Document, no. 32, August.

Katseli, L. (1987) 'Macroeconomic Policy Coordination and the Domestic Base of National Economic Policies in Major European Countries', Paper presented at the Conference on the Political Economy of International Macroeconomic Policy Coordination, Andover, Mass., November.

Sarcinelli, M. (1986) 'The EMS and the International Monetary System: Towards Greater Stability', *Banca Nazionale del Lavoro Quarterly Review*, March.

Thygesen, N. (1988) 'Decentralisation and Accountability Within the Central Bank: Any Lessons from the US Experience for the Potential Organisation of a European Central Banking Institution?', in P. De Grauwe and T. Peeters (eds) *The EMS and European Monetary Integration* (London: Macmillan).

9 Financial Liberalisation and Exchange Rate Policy in the Newly Integrating Countries of the European Community*

Jorge Braga de Macedo

1 INTRODUCTION

Following the latest enlargement of the European Community, there has been a great deal of discussion about the creation of a European financial area. This was seen as an essential part of the single market deadline of 1992. As the tenth anniversary of the EMS has been reached, the liberalisation of capital movements has progressed faster than expected. Until recently only Germany, Denmark and Benelux had been financially and monetarily integrated via the exchange rate mechanism (ERM) of the EMS. Now even ERM countries which traditionally relied on capital controls such as France and Italy have liberalised before the July 1990 deadline. The association of financial integration with monetary policy coordination has not always been welcome, however. This is clear from the experience of the UK, free of controls but avoiding any commitment to the ERM. Ireland and Spain, retaining controls and present in the ERM, provide a third possibility. Greece and Portugal, retaining controls and absent from the ERM, are the fourth possibility. The focus of this chapter is on this fourth category, and on Spain, even though some references to Ireland as well as to Italy will be made in the context of the catching-up process. Economic cohesion is indeed the counterpart of both the single market objective and the wish for a monetary union.

In Greece, Spain and Portugal, financial and monetary integration also interact with trade integration because the countries involved are

* The author writes in his personal capacity, following the views expressed in *European Economy*, no. 36, May 1988.

still adjusting to membership. Greece joined in 1981, and Portugal and Spain followed in 1986. The policy analysis is thus more complex in newly integrating countries. But the countries are also less known, except for the fact that Spain is rightly seen as considerably larger and more industrialised than the other two. The three new members were part of the group of 'newly industrialising countries' (NICs) identified by the OECD in thc early 1970s. They were frequently referred to as European of Mediterranean NICs, along with Israel, Turkey, Yugoslavia, etc. Reversing dictatorships of varying length and intensity, the three new EC member countries restored democratic institutions shortly after the first oil crisis. Now they are just embarking on a process of economic integration with the other nine member countries as well as among themselves. As a consequence, it may be said that the three countries are also NICs in the sense of representing 'newly integrating countries' relative to a well-defined and substantially larger entity.

Grouping the three NICs together – as against the nine older members – may be convenient for some purposes. Mention has already been made of the catching-up process, in which an older member Ireland and a founding member Italy ought to be added to the NICs group. There are other cases where significant differences emerge in describing the economic structure of the three NICs or in discussing the policy-making process. Substantial cleavages appear in attempting to characterise voting patterns on Community matters. The economic structure and the long-run policy pattern towards foreign economic integration is also specific to each one of the NICs.

Greece and Portugal have a history of involvement with steps towards European free trade in manufactures in the 1950s and 1960s, which are lacking in Spain. The domestic effects of lower tariffs on Greek and Portuguese industrial imports were rather limited in the face of both quantitative restrictions and domestic controls. In Spain, even the lowering of Spanish tariffs was in its infancy when the political constraints on integration disappeared. Conversely, the degree of financial development and of budgetary consolidation is higher in Spain than in the other two NICs, let alone Italy. Greece and Portugal share financial underdevelopment, with features particular to each. In Greece it is visible in the use of profit retention as the discretionary source of investment finance for firms. In Portugal, the nationalisation of the banks in 1975 introduced a bias towards riskier projects. The system which froze competition among financial intermediaries until private banks were allowed in 1985, has proved quite fragile. Three years before

1992 the nationalised banking sector has not begun to be even partly privatised. Each country's calendar toward full integration with the EC ranges from 1991 for Greece to 1996 for Portugal. The overlap with the central objective of a unified market in 1992 brings additional pressure on the country to adjust its economic structure. It also introduces an externality in each country's performance, because a misadjustment would cast in doubt the entire programme, especially in terms of the related objective of EC cohesion.

Germane to the desirable extent and speed of financial liberalisation is of course the question of the exchange rate arrangement. The absence of the UK from the exchange rate mechanism of the EMS reduces some of the pressure which might otherwise be brought on the NICs to peg their exchange rates. It also seems to suggest the advantage for the NICs of exploring new forms of association with the EMS. Can the credibility of domestic macroeconomic management be preserved without explicit reliance on the discipline of the EMS? The EMS has been identified as a DM area because of the central role of the Bundesbank in setting monetary policy targets for the area as a whole. This role is likely to remain in the foreseeable future, as it provides a positive externality to the ERM member countries. The characterisation of the ERM as a DM area would certainly become less appropriate if the UK were to take part, however. This effect, due to the worldwide importance of sterling, is specific to the UK. Since Spain joined the ERM, the notion has been that the peseta has become part of the DM area. That being said, to experiment with some form of wider band will certainly facilitate Spanish membership of the system before the UK. This would not dilute the identification of the EMS with the Deutschmark, and it would enhance Spain's role within the NICS.

The major problem has been to find the appropriate level of the peseta. It was necessary to strike a compromise between the current strength of the peseta and the medium-term competitiveness of the Spanish economy. The experience of Italy is relevant not only because of the wider band but also because between 1975 and 1985 the opening was gradual and sustained. The inability to control the public sector borrowing requirement continues to make the perfect openness of the Italian capital market less credible than in other ERM member countries. Nevertheless, the experience of 1988 suggests that this need not provoke capital outflows, much to the contrary. The same lesson can be gleaned from the dismantling of controls in France, ahead of the 1990 deadline.

Preventing a sudden transition towards financial openness among the NICs is certainly consistent with current awareness of the drawbacks of excessive financial liberalisation, as well as with the preference for a sequencing of financial liberalisation after real liberalisation. But this desirable caution should never be used as a defence of the existing financial structure in the NICs. Especially in the small ones, this would be equivalent to condoning financial underdevelopment. It is difficult to attain a cohesive EC without broadening financial development. In turn a cohesive EC would allow a smoother transition towards a monetary union.

The remainder of this chapter is divided into two sections and a conclusion. Section 2 deals with some conceptual issues regarding international capital mobility. Section 3 measures the degree of capital mobility using real return differentials and then discusses possible exchange rate policies for the three NICs. It is suggested that desirable financial liberalisation and exchange rate unification among the members of the EMS should not wait either for the UK or for the three NICs. The requirement is of course that there should be no durable exception to the objective of a cohesive Community. This was stated in the Single Act, and used as a motivation for the doubling of the Structural Funds and for attempting a process of monetary integration. Such arrangements are sometimes called 'minilateral' to emphasise that they are easier to achieve than the more ambitious multilateral negotiations might be. Minilateral solutions towards monetary integration include of course membership in the exchange rate mechanism of the EMS. Other steps should be envisaged, however. Specific arrangements between the three NICs, or between Spain and Portugal, about ways to attain financial integration may also be part of such a minilateral approach.

2 THE EC ENLARGEMENT AND CAPITAL MARKET INTEGRATION

2.1 Welfare effects of international capital mobility

There is now widespread agreement among economists and policy-makers that some form of financial development is the key to economic and social development. The realisation that financial underdevelopment hinders economic progress does not imply, however, that immediate financial liberalisation is necessarily the most appropriate policy response. Analytical results about the order of liberalisation suggest that financial liberalisation without prior dismantling of trade barriers may not be advisable.[1] The idea that relative prices (as captured by the real exchange rate) must be transparent before worrying about their rate of change (given by the real interest differential) makes it clear that real liberalisation should take precedence before financial liberalisation. Even McKinnon (1988), the most enthusiastic defender of financial liberalisation, became a little 'gun-shy' after the resounding failure of various experiments of all-out financial liberalisation in the southern cone of Latin America.[2]

There is an earlier literature which draws on the so-called transfer problem showing that, paradoxically, a capital inflow can hinder rather than help. Suppose trade is distorted and foreign funds are used to buy imported capital-intensive goods for investment. Then the effect of a capital inflow will be negative on the economic welfare of the representative consumer insofar as the distortion will be amplified.

If capital is internationally mobile, welfare would only increase unambiguously in a small open economy if all taxes were uniformly lowered, including both tariffs on goods and taxes on capital movements. Since international capital mobility raises the price–output response in the economy, if imports are capital-intensive, this greater response raises the cost of tariff protection.[3]

The transition towards an integrated European capital market therefore requires not only a lowering of taxes on the international movement of capital but also a substantial lowering of trade barriers by the NICs and by the Community as a whole.

2.2 Macroeconomic effects of international capital mobility

The results summarised above are important for the microeconomics of financial liberalisation but the current caution may have been rather the result of greater awareness about the macroeconomic preconditions for financial liberalisation. The recurrence of banking crises illustrates the so-called 'disaster myopia' of financial markets. The importance of a stable macroeconomic environment was neglected during the prosperous 1960s, at least during the earlier part of the decade. After the turbulent 1970s and 1980s, the requirement of some form of macroeconomic stabilisation was acknowledged. Doubts that financial development may occur without generating bubbles and crashes have become excessive, just as these doubts were all too easily discounted before the October 1987 stock market crash.[4]

In turn, macroeconomic stabilisation requires some form of control over the government budget deficit, a problem that has been pervasive in some of the member countries, including not only the three NICs but also Italy. Without controlling the primary deficit, even the gains on the rate of price inflation will be short-lived, and this lessens the credibility of macroeconomic stabilisation. Macroeconomic success becomes tied to the ability to control the government deficit, but does not necessarily mean full employment. Despite recent improvements in job creation, macroeconomic policy alone has failed to solve the persistent unemployment problem which has been plaguing the EC, including Spain and – to a much lesser extent – Greece and Portugal. Continued reforms at the microeconomic level are required for a sustained improvement in employment. This structural change in turn hinges on the ability to bring about economic efficiency at the firm level, along the lines of the lowering of taxes on international transactions – or at least intra-EC transactions – discussed above.

The conventional answer about the macroeconomic effects of greater capital mobility shows that monetary independence requires flexible exchange rates. Contrast an entirely insulated domestic capital market with a fully integrated one. In the latter, monetary expansion will not be able to reduce interest rates and can only expand output if the exchange rate depreciates. If the exchange rate is fixed, on the contrary, an expansion of domestic credit leads to offsetting capital outflows: monetary policy is powerless. This assumes that domestic and foreign assets are perfect substitutes, so that either imperfect substitutability or imperfect mobility may allow some control of the national central bank upon its monetary base, at least in the short run.[5]

Despite the appeal of this conventional result of the Mundell–Fleming model, recent directions in open-economy macroeconomics provide qualifications to the strong policy implication of loss of monetary independence. Simple examples have been provided by Dornbusch (1987) of how price setting by firms, irreversible investments and expectations modify the analysis. Considerations of industrial organisation and market structure, especially large entry costs and small national markets, may lessen the price discipline induced by opening the economy. Viewing labour as an irreversible investment may induce waiting in the face of small improvements in business conditions induced, say, by favourable real exchange rate developments. If the insight is applied to the return of capital flight, then the immediate payoff must overshadow the prospect of subsequent deterioration. This requires some frontloading which – because it involves higher fiscal incentives – may run counter to fiscal stabilisation. Finally, the role of expectations may be to extrapolate changes in monetary policy in ways that have a strong impact on asset prices. A small increase in money growth, extrapolated into cumulative increases, would lead to a strong immediate depreciation, to be then undone by a gradual appreciation.

Even without incorporating these new insights, whose policy relevance is quite clear, the conventional result must in any event be qualified when capital mobility is not perfect, exchange rates are not fully flexible and there exists some form of monetary cooperation. This may well have been the situation in the EC area in the last ten years, even though the trend toward dismantling capital controls spread from Germany, Denmark and Benelux towards France and Italy in the late 1980s. If the degree of capital mobility is now higher among the major countries, this has immediate implications for the NICs. Should they lower barriers as well, join the ERM, cooperate more effectively, or some combination of these alternatives?

As mentioned, the policy implications drawn below point to 'minilateral' solutions among the NICs and some of the other member countries. In particular, the possible move toward the ERM would have to take into account the absence of the United Kingdom and hold views about the expected duration of Bundesbank leadership among the countries taking part.

2.3 Long-run resource transfer versus capital market efficiency

The difference between the microeconomic and macroeconomic aspects of financial liberalisation can be shown by an analytical distinction between capital movements which may help to show in which way the exchange restrictions are binding in a particular country. The distinction is not however easy to illustrate in practice. Capital movements based on differences in endowments lead to long-run resource transfers. Capital movements based on arbitrage opportunities enforce capital market efficiency. As emphasised by Krugman (1987), this distinction mirrors the distinction between inter- and intra-industry trade. This is important because the source of the gains from trade is different and the distributive consequences are also different. Inter-type capital movements tend to lower the rate of return to capital in less capital-intensive countries such as the NICs, whereas intra-type capital movements would enforce the equality of returns on comparable financial assets.

In relation to long-run flows, the consequences of the enlargement for the unification of the members' capital markets can also be seen as part of the broader question of the flow of international capital into the Community, sometimes referred to as 'new international corporate arrangements'. For example, a Japanese company wishing to manufacture motor vehicles for the EC market needs to locate inside the EC to avoid the external tariff. An enlarged EC gives it more choice, and the cheap labour country may be the most attractive.[6] The NIC's are thus candidates for inter-type flows. The reason why Spain, after joining the EC, was less able to control capital movements than either France or Italy may also be related to intra-type capital movements, when the situation of the NICs is less homogeneous.[7] The importance of interest-rate sensitive remittances into Greece and Portugal may lessen the ability of both governments to depart from interest rate parity, but as we will see below, their capital market is much more closed than Spain's.

3 THE EC NICs AND THE EMS

3.1 Capital mobility and real interest-rate differentials

Attempts at measuring capital mobility under fixed exchange rates which focus on the 'offset coefficients' from domestic credit expansion into capital outflows have already been mentioned. Independently of the exchange rate regime, however, perfect capital mobility equalises real rates of return among identical assets denominated in different currencies, and should be directly testable by looking at the real interest differentials between countries. Given the world rate of interest, then, there should be no correlation between national savings and investment.[8]

If private saving falls, there should be no crowding out of private investment, because the country can borrow abroad at the going interest rate. The same is true for the government saving through a budget surplus. Since the data suggest a high correlation between savings rates and investment rates, the paradoxical conclusion is that capital mobility is not in fact all that high between industrialised countries. There are, again, econometric problems with the results but, even when the endogeneity of national savings is corrected, the correlation remains and actually rises in the 1970s, suggesting that capital mobility declined.[9]

Along the same lines, several studies find higher correlations in the OECD area than in developing countries. The possibility that capital mobility, both official and unofficial (i.e. capital flight), may in fact be higher between countries with different levels of financial development is contrary to the standard presumption. It also casts the desirability of financial liberalisation into a different light, closer to the attempts at whitening black markets.[10]

Tests also suggest that real interest rates are far from perfectly correlated among countries. The rejection of the unbiased nature of the forward rate as a predictor of the future spot rate implies differences in expected rates of return and thus the failure of real interest parity (RIP). Frankel and MacArthur (1987) and Frankel (1989) attempt to decompose the difference between real interest rates into 'political' and 'currency' components, so as to assess where the failure of real interest parity comes from. If it comes from political factors, the notion that there are obstacles to the free movement of capital across nations is confirmed. If the failure comes from 'currency' factors, an alternative explanation for a fall in national savings to crowd out domestic investment via a rise in the real rate of interest will be the failure of purchasing power parity (PPP). Bringing together RIP and PPP is consistent with our earlier emphasis on the sequencing of trade and financial liberalisation.

Differences in expected returns can thus be attributed to 'political' or country factors, leading to departures from covered interest parity, as well as to 'currency' factors, leading to a forward premium or discount over the inflation differential. We write then the real interest differential with the United States as the sum of the covered nominal interest differential and the real forward discount:[11]

$$r - r^* = (i - i^* - fd) + (fd - p + p^*)$$

where r (r^*) = the real interest rate in the EC member countries (the US)

i (i^*) = the nominal interest rate in the EC member countries (the US)

$p(p^*)$ = price inflation in the EC member countries (the US)

fd = forward discount against the dollar.

The real forward discount can in turn be expressed as the sum of the exchange risk premium or forward bias and expected real depreciation:

$$fd - p + p^* = (fd - e) + (e + p^* - p)$$

where e = the expected change in the nominal exchange rate against the dollar.

Given the widespread movements in real exchange rates that have characterised the current international monetary system, PPP cannot be said to be expected even when we are dealing with several years. A major reason for the failure of RIP may thus be the failure of goods-market integration, via tariffs or other barriers to trade. This is shown by expected movements in real exchange rates, rather than by the political premium.

This is indeed one of the conclusions reached by Frankel (1989) in a study of three-month real-interest differentials in 25 countries from September 1982 to January 1988. The local interbank rate is measured relative to the Eurodollar interest rate and they are deflated by realised consumer price inflation during the ex-post three-month period. The sample is divided into five categories of descending financial openness, of which the most open, the least open and the middle (semi-open) category involve EC member countries. Germany, the Netherlands, and the UK are open; Belgium, Denmark, France, Ireland, Italy and Spain are semi-open; Greece and Portugal are closed. In a way the 'open' grouping matches financial development. It includes the two major hard currencies in the ERM and the pound sterling. The role of London as a world financial centre is thus reflected in the UK real interest differential against the dollar independently of the exchange rate regime with respect to its major European partners.

Table 9.1 shows the mean and the coefficient of variation of the components of the three-month real interest differential between the Eurodollar rate and a standard rate in each one of the EC member countries, together with the three relevant group averages. Open countries tend to have a small and stable covered nominal interest differential and exchange risk premium but not necessarily a small and stable real interest differential or real exchange rate change against the US dollar. The sample average shows a negative real interest rate differential of about 2 per cent, with a coefficient of variation twice as high. The mean real forward discount is zero despite a high variability, so this translates into a covered differential of the same amount.

Among the three NICs, Spain shows a small positive differential whereas Greece and Portugal show a negative differential. The high variance of the real differential suggests that the Spanish capital market has not liberalised relative to the other countries with the same mean, Belgium, Ireland and Italy. But Spain is indeed the most integrated of the three NICs. The political premium is five times less than for Greece and Portugal, and the same as for France. The real forward discount in Greece is three times smaller than in Spain but Greece shows a

Table 9.1 Realised real interest differentials (August 1982–January 1988) (% p.a.)

	(1) $r-r^*$		(2) $i-i^*-fd$		(3) $fd-p+p^*$		(4) $fd-e$	(5) $e+p^*-p$
	m.	*c.v.*	*m.*	*c.v.*	*m.*	*c.v.*	*mean*	
Germany	−1	2	0	1	−2	2	4	−5
Netherlands	−1	6	0	1	−1	4	4	−5
United Kingdom	0	9	0	2	1	6	4	−4
Open Group	−1	4	0	2	−1	3	3	−5
Belgium	1	6	0	3	0	8	8	−7
Denmark	−3	1	−4	0	0	50	8	−7
France	−1	6	−2	2	1	0	8	−7
Ireland	1	3	−1	5	2	3	8	−6
Italy	1	1	0	5	1	2	9	−8
Spain	1	12	−2	2	3	2	9	−6
Semi-open Group	0	10	−1	2	1	5	7	−7
Greece	−9	1	−9	1	1	13	3	−2
Portugal	−4	3	−8	1	5	2	11	−7
Closed Group	−7	2	−7	1	1	8	3	−2
All	−2	4	−2	2	0	12	5	−4

Note: The variation coefficient (c.v.) is the standard deviation divided by the absolute value of the mean (m.). The symbols under the column numbers are explained in the text.
Canada and Switzerland are also included in the Open Group.
Bahrain, Mexico and South Africa are also included in the Closed Group.
Austria, Norway and Sweden are also included in the Semi-open Group.
Hong Kong, Malaysia, Singapore, Australia, Japan and New Zealand are also included in All.

Source: Adapted from Frankel (1989), rounded to the nearest per cent.

volatility that is over six times as large. The exchange risk premium in Spain and Portugal is higher than in the semi-closed group and in Greece. This shows the forward market is thin and with a bias toward depreciation. The perceived difference in the openness of the Spanish and Portuguese economies to trade in goods is not reflected in expected departures from PPP against the semi-open group of EC countries. The rate of expected real depreciation was indeed close between the two Iberian countries, whereas in Greece the value was three times smaller in absolute value. The real exchange rate of Greece is thus expected to depreciate against both of the other NICs, and indeed all of the other EC countries.

The pattern in Table 9.1 confirms that currency factors are more relevant in Spain and Portugal than in Greece, whereas the political factors are stronger obstacles to capital mobility in Greece and Portugal than in Spain. These last factors are reflected in the large negative real return differential of Greece and Portugal, clear evidence that the controls on capital outflows are defending a repressed capital market. In Spain the same controls are consistent with a positive real return differential, inducing inflows. These numbers are consistent with our prior remarks that Spain is becoming part of the European and international capital market in a way that has so far not been observed either in Greece or in Portugal. A structural explanation for the greater commitment of the Spanish authorities might be the prior consolidation of public finances. Before a budgetary consolidation a financial liberalisation is more likely to lead to higher interest rates than might otherwise be the case. This has unfortunate consequences. Firms in the preferred sector find themselves in difficulty because they have to compete with firms from the curb market at higher rates. They may go bankrupt and will certainly try to lay off workers. Firms from the curb market are now facing lower rates and they increase borrowing for investment, which also allows them to shed labour.[12] Other explanations for the difference between Spain and the other two NICs range from the degree of industrialisation to the nature of bank regulation.

3.2 Exchange rate and budgetary policy: a 'minilateral' approach

The conduct of monetary policy in the two closed NICs has been subject to the constraint imposed by a high borrowing requirement of the Treasury and a reluctance to raise interest rates so as to keep down interest payments on the public debt. This disguised fiscal policy is also the result of explicit or implicit contracts with the trade unions, to be found in the three NICs. The implied institutional changes should thus be included in the assessments of the costs and benefits from coordination within the EMS framework. Simply put, the central banks of Greece, Portugal and Spain – not to mention Italy – would follow the Bundesbank rather than their national Treasuries let alone their trade unions. The policy implication is that specific arrangements for the three NICs may be desirable, as long as they are open to other member countries along the lines of so-called 'minilateral' negotiations. The open nature of the agreement is particularly important for Ireland and Italy. In fact, the peseta has entered the ERM with a wider band. A characteristic of these countries which is relevant for their exchange rate policy is also the expectation of increased transfers from the Community.

This message is consistent with recent awareness of the drawbacks of excessive financial liberalisation even by its most ardent defenders as well as with the preference for a sequencing of financial liberalisation after real liberalisation. An illustration of the peculiar nature of capital mobility in the NICs is that the effect on the three stock markets of the Wall Street crash of 19 October 1987 was much higher than expected. This serves to remind us that the estimates of the degree of capital mobility reported above must be interpreted for calm rather than for turbulent periods.

Greater capital mobility will affect the availability of financial services to residents of the NICs, or indeed of the lesser financially developed EC members. If there is the presumption that a national bank would do a better job than a foreign one, some degree of monetary autonomy might remain after free trade in financial services comes about. Insurance, banking and the marketing of securities are around 7 per cent of EC GDP and growing strongly. Despite the mobility of capital across national borders, steps toward international harmonisation in banking services or insurance are necessary at the EC as well as at the world level. Yet, even within the EC, the question of how the regulatory and executive powers should be organised in an integrated market is only beginning to be addressed as part of the single market objective.

Rather than thinking in terms of the whole OECD area, as in the banking directives, here we focus on 'minilateral' initiatives involving countries that are relatively underdeveloped financially. With respect to the EMS, the minilateral approach includes not only the informal peg to the ECU, or 'shadow EMS', but also joining the ERM with a wider band.

The lower credibility of an exchange arrangement that would not tie the central bank's hands is to be kept in mind. Nevertheless some experimentation with an informal peg to the ECU, perhaps with a wider band and a separate financial rate, may be appropriate. The UK experience in 1987/8 suggests caution about the timing of the decision. Some believe that joining in 1986 would have been a superior alternative. In countries where inflation is substantially higher than the Community average or where the overhang of bad debts seems most serious for financial liberalisation, the informal peg may be part of a multiannual fiscal adjustment strategy. Since Spain has already joined, it will be more difficult for Greece or Portugal – let alone the UK – not to announce some exchange rate strategy.

4 CONCLUSION

It was argued in this chapter that specific financial and exchange rate arrangements among the three NICs, Ireland and Italy may be desirable, supporting a multiannual fiscal adjustment strategy. These arrangements which are particularly necessary in the two closed NICs, Greece and Portugal, would not run counter to the ultimate objective of economic integration and would be open to another member country with the same structural adjustment problem. The idea of an as-if joining of the EMS seemed the most attractive during the time before the removal of capital controls or before consolidation of public finances, whichever comes last. Such shadow-EMS might involve some form of wider band as in Italy, so as to facilitate early membership in the system. This would prevent a greater financial openness than desirable, given the degree of real liberalisation and financial development of the three NICs.

Once the relationship between capital mobility and the liberalisation of financial services is taken into account, Community practices with respect to harmonisation, mutual recognition and coordinated supervision will have to adapt. The agreement on the most appropriate scope of financial regulation – national, community-wide or worldwide – must be preceded by a credible fiscal adjustment strategy. It is difficult to believe that such structural adjustment will be completed by 1992 in all member countries. Nevertheless some signs that the doubling of structural funds towards the EC periphery has not backfired might be required for the internal market to be accompanied by greater EC wide economic cohesion. This places an especially heavy burden on setting the right macroeconomic environment and correcting it when it is disturbed by shocks. To do so with fewer policy instruments calls for enhanced cooperation on their assignment to jointly agreed policy targets. As this may be facilitated by experimenting sooner rather than later with the EMS, budgetary consolidation can no longer be avoided even in the two closed NICs, Greece and Portugal.

Notes

1. The quote is from a self-assessment of the influential 1973 book where financial liberalisation was enthusiastically endorsed. See Comment in Macedo (1988).
2. See Edwards and Van Wijnbergen (1986), Rodrik (1984), Edwards (1984) and Macedo (1985). The relevance of the Southern Cone experiences for Southern Europe is discussed by Calvo (1985). See also Branson (1984) on Greece, (1985) on Greece and Turkey and (1986) on Portugal.

3. These results are due to Neary (1987a and b), where several forms of trade restrictions are compared with and without capital mobility. The welfare effects of tariffs are opposite to those of quotas when capital mobility is allowed for. The welfare cost of a quota is lowered rather than raised, because of the absence of the price effect. Similarly, the cost of a voluntary export restriction is lowered with capital mobility because the smaller price rise reduces the rents accruing to foreigners.
4. See Diaz (1986) for a classic analysis of the Chilean banking crisis and Macedo (1989) for an application to Portugal.
5. The interest-sensitivity of capital movements was measured to be quite high in Germany, implying that offset coefficients would have been close to one if the Bundesbank had not pusued a systematic sterilisation of reserve flows. The estimate of the offset coefficient of Banco de Mexico by Cumby and Obstfeld (1983) and of Banque de France by Claassen and Wyplosz (1982) suggest a higher degree of autonomy, because of imperfect substitutability as well as imperfect mobility, due in the second instance to the existence of capital controls. The long-run success of the sterilisation policy is highly questionable, according to Obstfeld's (1982) assessment of the evidence.
6. This effect takes the external tariff as given. See Bliss (1988) for a relaxation of this assumption in an enlargement context.
7. Tests of interest-rate parity, which do not work for the franc or the lira, work for the peseta largely due to one-way arbitrage. See Vinals (1986).
8. This is the macroeconomic implication of perfect capital mobility emphasised by Feldstein and Horioka (1980) and Feldstein (1983).
9. Obstfeld (1987). He also develops other measures of capital mobility, with equally poor results. Dooley, Frankel and Mathieson (1986) test the Feldstein–Horioka proposition using data for 49 countries from 1960 to 1984 and correcting for the endogeneity of national savings. This is done with instrumental variables for the private and public savings rates in order to allow for a policy reaction of governments in the face of incipient current account imbalances, such that these will be reduced. Despite all of these refinements, they reach results that contradict the presumption that capital mobility is high. Indeed, as mentioned by Frankel and MacArthur (1989), the results also contradict the associated presumptions that capital mobility has been rising since the 1950s and especially after 1973 and that it is higher for industrialised countries. The contention of Harberger (1983) is of course consistent with this last result.
10. A different rationalisation of these findings, due to Dooley and Isard (1986), comes from the idea that governments are more tempted to renege on their debt to foreigners, the higher such debt is. The implication is that there cannot be a high level of capital mobility in a world of sovereign nations. This emphasis on the country of 'political' factors is standard when applied to LCD debtors. While it is not generally used for industrialised countries, the emphasis on political preferences may be appropriate for countries who joined recently and where the social consensus about European economic integration may still be in the making.

11. The deflators of the real forward discount or premium are indexes of the purchasing powers of the two currencies in Kouri and Macedo (1978).
12. This phenomenon was observed in Korea. Branson (1985) stresses the importance of the curb loan market in Greece. See also Dutta and Polemarchakis (1988).

References

Bliss, C. (1988) 'Optimal External Tariff in an Enlarged Customs Union', draft, Oxford, January.

Branson, W. (1984) 'Financial Reform in Greece', draft, Athens School of Economics, Athens.

Branson, W. (1985) 'Liberalizaçao Financeira e Estabilizaçao Económica: o caso da Grécia e da Turquia', IPSD, A Reforma do Mercado de Capitais, Lisbon.

Branson, W. (1986) 'Portugal's Entry into the European Communities: Challenges and Opportunities', draft of a World Bank Report.

Calvo, G. (1983) 'Lecciones del Monetarismo: El Cono Sud', draft, CEMA, Buenos Aires.

Claassen, E.-M. and Wyplosz, C. (1982) 'Capital Controls: Some Principles and the French Experience', in J. Melitz, and C. Wyplosz (eds) *The French Economy: Theory and Policy* (Boulder, Co.: Westview Special Studies).

Cumby, R. and Obstfeld, M. (1983) 'Capital Mobility and the Scope for Stabilisation: Mexico in the 1970s', ch. 11 in P. Aspe, R. Dornbusch and M. Obstfeld, *Financial Policies and the World Capital Market: the Problem of Latin American Countries.*

Diaz, C. (1986) 'Goodbye Financial Repression, Hello Financial Crash', *Journal of Development Economics*, February.

Dooley, M. and Isard, P. (1986) 'Country Preferences and Exchange Rate Determination', draft, IMF.

Dooley, M., Frankel, J. and Mathieson, D. (1986) 'International Capital Mobility Among Industrialised Countries vs. LDSs: What Do Savings–Investment Correlations Tell Us?', NBER WP no. 2043, IMF Staff Papers.

Dornbusch, R. (1987): 'Open Economy Macroeconomics: New Directions', NBER WP no. 2372, August.

Dutta, J. and Polemarchakis, H. (1988) 'Credit Constraints and Investment Finance: Some Evidence From Greece', paper presented at the IMF–Bocconi Seminar on 'Fiscal Policy, Economic Adjustment and Financial Markets', January.

Edwards, S. (1984) 'The Order of Liberalisation of the External Sector in Developing Countries', International Finance Section, Princeton University, Essay no. 156, December.

Edwards, S. and Van Wijnbergen, S. (1986) 'The Welfare Effects of Trade and Capital Market Liberalisation', *International Economic Review*, February.

Feldstein, M. (1983) 'Domestic Saving and International Capital Movements in the Long Run and in the Short Run', *European Economic Review*, vol. 21.

Feldstein, M. and Horioka, C. (1980) 'Domestic Saving and International Capital Flows', *Economic Journal*, vol. 90.

Frankel, J. and MacArthur, A. (1987) 'Political vs. Currency Premia in International Real Interest Differentials: a Study of Forward Rates for 24 Countries', NBER WP no. 2309, July.

Frankel, J. (1989) 'Quantifying International Capital Mobility', draft, Harvard.

Harberger, A. (1983) 'Vignettes on the World Capital Market', *American Economic Review*, vol. 70.

Kouri, P. and Macedo, J. (1978) 'Exchange Rates and the International Adjustment Process', Brookings Papers on Economic Activity.

Krugman, P. (1987) 'European Economic Integration: Some Conceptual Issues', in T. Padoa-Schioppa (ed.) *Efficiency, Stability and Equity* (Oxford University Press).

Macedo, J. Braga (1983) 'A Portfolio Model of an Inconvertible Currency: the Recent Experience of Portugal', in M. de Cecco (ed.) *International Economic Adjustment: Small Countries and the European Monetary System* (Oxford: Blackwell).

Macedo, J. Braga (1985) 'Experiências de Liberalizaçao do Mercado de Capitais: Relevância para o Caso Português', IPSD, A Reforma do Mercado de Capitais, Lisbon.

Macedo, J. Braga (1986) 'Comment on McKinnon'.

Macedo, J. Braga (1989) 'Banking in a Frozen Public Sector: Portugal 1974–1989', draft, UNL.

McKinnon, R. (1973) *Money and Capital in Economic Development* (Washington, DC: Brookings Institution).

McKinnon, R. (1986) 'Financial Liberalization in Retrospect: Interest Rate Policies in LDCs', paper presented at the 25th anniversary of the Economic Growth Center, Yale University.

Neary, P. (1987a) 'Tariffs, Quotas and Voluntary Export Restraints with and Without Internationally Mobile Capital', draft, Queen's University, August.

Neary, P. (1987b) 'Welfare Effects of Tariffs and Investment Taxes', paper presented at the EEA meeting in Copenhagen, August.

Obstfeld, M. (1987) 'How Integrated are World Capital Markets? Some New Tests', NBER WP no. 2075, November.

Obstfeld, M. (1982) 'Can We Sterilise? Theory and Evidence', *American Economic Review*, May.

Rodrik, D. (1984) 'Why the Simultaneous Liberalisation of the Current and Capital Account Might be Recessionary', draft, Princeton University.

Vinals, J. (1986) 'Spain and the European Monetary System', draft, Bank of Spain, March.

Part V
Problems and Perspectives

10 The European Monetary System Ten Years On: Problems and Perspectives*

Rainer S. Masera

1 INTRODUCTION

Operational experience with the EMS, coupled with theoretical analysis,[1] have convinced me that a system of fixed exchange rates that can be adjusted discretely, and which therefore offers substantial opportunities for speculative profits, will be difficult to maintain in conditions of complete capital mobility, even with unlimited very-short-term reciprocal lines of credit in place. We are faced with a difficult road ahead, but the leitmotif of this chapter is 'keep going and you won't stop'.

In the ten years since the inception of the EMS numerous assessments have been made of its performance with analyses highlighting the strong and weak points. In addition to the study by Professor Ferri published here, there are other recent contributions of notable interest.[2] Since I have already addressed this subject,[3] I have chosen to focus on the problems that I believe will have to be tackled in the near future if the EMS is to develop into an integrated financial and monetary area. On the one hand, this presupposes complete substitutability of financial assets denominated in European currencies and held in member countries and, on the other, increasingly stable exchange rates, leading, in the end, to fixity.[4]

The urgency of these problems is enhanced by the more intense *competition between financial systems* associated with the creation of an integrated market, especially in view of the probability that this will involve the European financial industry in a phase of Schumpeterian 'creative destruction', not only as a result of the quantum increase in

* I am grateful to S. Del Punta, G. Faustini, F. Guelpa and N. Sartor for their comments on an earlier draft of this chapter.

the size of markets but also because it will be necessary to cut costs in a period marked by rapid technological innovation and financial deregulation, coupled with a revision of supervisory operating procedures.

There are three main problems requiring immediate and simultaneous attention if an orderly process of financial and monetary unification is to be possible in Europe. In addition to the integration of monetary and exchange rate policies, it will be necessary to address the issues of harmonising financial and prudential regulations and making the taxation of financial incomes more uniform. Both of these factors contribute to the establishment of an integrated market and their importance is enhanced by complete freedom of capital movements.

I shall only touch briefly on the harmonisation of financial regulations and taxation,[5] and shall devote most of my remarks to the integration of monetary and foreign exchange policies. I shall analyse the problems primarily with reference to Italy in order to bring out clearly the steps that will have to be taken if the Italian economy is to develop in line with the rest of Europe.

2 THE HARMONISATION OF FINANCIAL REGULATIONS

We are currently faced with two very different approaches to financial regulation in Europe: the British approach, in which a key role is played by markets, the development of which determines the structure of the system of intermediaries and their importance; and, at the other extreme, the approach exemplified by Germany, in which banks play a primary role and have very close links with industry.

The freedom to supply financial services, which will become effective on 1 January 1993, implies the right of every licensed bank to engage in a series of predetermined activities in every Community country in conformity with the rules and under the supervision of its home country. This application of the *principle of mutual recognition* – which amounts to a 'Copernican revolution' compared with the previous doctrine of *total harmonisation* – will lead to competition between the various regulatory frameworks and financial systems, with gradual convergence on the model that best meets the needs of the market.[6]

There is thus the problem of suitably dosing minimal harmonisation and mutual recognition: the harmonisation implemented in accordance with Community directives and supranational law will be followed by further harmonisation in response to competition and the need for each credit system to compete on equal terms with those of the other Community countries.

The creation of a core of standard regulations is intended to perform the, anything but easy, task of avoiding excessive deregulation and limiting the danger of instability and distorted competition; while minimal harmonisation of the operational methods of prudential supervision is intended to prevent the less-regulated systems from enjoying an unjustified competitive advantage, which would provoke a downward levelling of regulations to the least strict standards. Ex-ante it is by no means easy to identify the equilibrium point of all these different requirements, especially in view of the substantial disparities between national systems discussed above. In particular, the relationship between institutions and the market appears to be strongly influenced by the *global rules* that govern each system, bearing in mind that the development of financial markets as separate entities is a feature of the economies in which the importance of the banking system is less, in terms of its links with other financial sectors and industry.

The growing interpenetration of the financial and banking markets implies that both should be set within a regulatory framework that will guarantee stability while avoiding rigidity. Otherwise, the effect would be to put a straitjacket on competition between operators in different sectors in the area where it is liveliest, i.e. along the demarcation line between them. Such flexibility in the rules governing operators' behaviour can only be achieved by providing for close and pragmatic concertation between the authorities responsible for developing and carrying out supervisory controls.

The efforts to bring about regulatory convergence, notably in connection with entry requirements, activity-related capital adequacy and pricing, together with those to link the various financial supervisory bodies, both within each country and internationally, are among the most far-reaching problems on the road to an integrated monetary area and require clear decisions. Their solution cannot be left simply to competition between regulatory systems,[7] they will have to be consciously tackled in the light of the indications that economic theory can provide.

Recent analytical studies of regulatory problems reveal the complexity of the factors that interact in the various levels of the decision-making process. Simplified models focusing variously on stability and transparency or on stability and efficiency as the basis for control appear inadequate. What is required is the identification of the cases in which market mechanisms are inadequate and need to be supplemented by regulation.

The asymmetric information approach and reputation theory provide instruments for an innovatory analysis of the problem of regulation in the financial field. In particular, traditional approaches emphasise the static aspects of allocative efficiency and the microeconomic aspects of stability. Today, the 'objective divisions' between banking activities, the securities business and insurance no longer exist. In the new conditions of truly global markets,[8] innovation, the reduction in the technological cost of operations and the resulting economies of scale and scope make dynamic efficiency of paramount importance. On the other hand, the fact that individual operators and informed investors are expected to identify suitable institutions, instruments and operations that nonetheless involve a known element of risk requires that unsound financial institutions and operators be subject to the discipline of the market. Only when this condition holds are savers and final borrowers spurred into making the necessary autonomous assessment of risk and financial operators encouraged to invest in developing their reputations, transparency, capital strength and profitability.

In short, if the primary reason for exercising control is the gap between private and social benefits, competition between regulatory authorities will not be the most effective means of maximising social welfare. The problem of establishing a European supervisory authority that would operate pragmatically and, if necessary, in opposition to national authorities should be tackled at the same time as a central monetary institution is created.

3 THE HARMONISATION OF TAX REGULATIONS

The need for greater tax harmonisation is evident, since disparities in this field would not only be incompatible with a future single currency but are already an obstacle to the creation of an internal market in which there is complete freedom of capital movements.[9]

If they are allowed to remain, the differences in the taxation of the income from financial assets in the various member countries[10] would encourage artificial arbitrage operations. Today's disparities in the taxation of interest, dividends and capital gains would give rise in an integrated capital market to serious distortions both in the location of intermediaries and the size of national markets and in the structure of net yields. Such distortions, moreover, would have undesired effects on exchange rates and lead to calls for the reintroduction of capital controls, thereby moving us away from the objective of monetary unification and the creation of the single market.

Failure to achieve sufficient fiscal uniformity would result in a tendency to bring the taxation of 'unearned' income into line with the least onerous system, with very low or zero rates of taxation and a consequent increase in the burden borne by 'earned' income.

Moreover, the need for greater harmonisation is not restricted to the relevant legislation, since whenever the tax on investment income is not withheld at source or is withheld 'on account' – so that full payment is left to investors' 'fiscal conscience' – there is a very significant difference in many European countries between theory and practice, as described in the Lebègue report on the organisation and prospects of the securities market in France.[11]

Since the *assessment* of investment income also involves considerable difficulties and care needs to be taken to prevent the progressiveness of personal income taxes from discouraging financial saving, a universal system of 'in settlement' withholding tax levied at source might be the easiest and fastest way of ensuring basic fiscal neutrality. As things stand today, such a withholding tax could be levied at a rate of around 20 per cent.

Thus there also appears to be a need for the structures and rates of personal income taxes to be made more uniform, by moving in the direction already taken by the major industrial countries towards a smaller number of tax brackets and thereby establishing de facto a system midway between a fully progressive system and a flat-rate system.

4 THE HARMONISATION OF MONETARY AND EXCHANGE RATE POLICIES

Last, but definitely not least, there are the problems associated with the need for closer coordination of monetary policies and further convergence of economic fundamentals and exchange rates. Failure to move in the direction of enhanced exchange rate stability would severely hinder the orderly competition between member countries' financial assets and the efficient allocation of saving. Financial assets denominated in different currencies would no longer be perfectly substitutable, which is the indispensable precondition for complete integration.

Autonomous control by each member country of its money supply and exchange rate is not compatible, in principle, with the aim of creating a unified European financial market, especially since reaping the benefits of financial integration will ultimately depend on the ability to ensure unchanging exchange rates after a period of enhanced stability and, in the end, a single currency.

The analysis of monetary and exchange rate policy problems can be divided conceptually into two parts: the analysis of the *technical problems* regarding the mechanisms for creating money and determining exchange rates, and the analysis of the '*institutional*' *problems* regarding the identification of the authorities that should regulate these mechanisms. There are analogies with the functions performed in each country by central banks, but there are also significant differences and complications. It needs to be recognised, in fact, that we are dealing with the conditions analysed by coordination theory;[12] even if the cooperative solution is the best overall, there is always the risk that a country will seek to modify the most efficient systemic solution to try and improve its own position.[13]

4.1 Technical systemic problems

As long as there are differences between the policies pursued by EMS countries, and the international situation continues to exert a destabilising influence on the System, the liberalisation of capital movements risks being accompanied by large speculative flows in expectation of realignments of the central rates. On the other hand, the incomplete convergence of the fundamental economic variables means that we cannot yet do without such changes.[14]

Complete monetary unification thus cannot be achieved without a change in the mechanisms of the EMS. The solution I would propose in this connection is two-pronged:

- all the participating countries should undertake to keep the variations in their bilateral central rates within a predetermined range, say 3–4 per cent, in each year; and
- *every* country, including the United Kingdom, Spain and Italy should immediately adopt 3–3.5 per cent bilateral fluctuation margins.[15]

Realignments involving changes in central rates that cause a 'break' in market quotations provide speculators with a one-way bet. By contrast, if the new and the old fluctuation bands (equal to twice the instantaneous margin[16]) overlap, market quotations are not subject to discrete changes when a realignment is agreed, on the assumption that the exchange rate shifts, in the case of a revaluation, from the upper part of the old band to the lower part of the new one.

The determination of a fluctuation band that will satisfy the foregoing condition thus depends both on the variation in central rates required over time to maintain balance-of-payments equilibrium and on the frequency with which it is desirable, on average, to carry out realignments.[17]

As regards the latter aspect, there appear to be two conflicting requirements: on the one hand, realignments cannot be put off for so long that they become obviously inevitable; on the other, the system cannot be tranformed into a *crawling peg* with small but frequent adjustments, despite this having been proposed in some quarters. Such a course would annul the fundamental disciplinary effect and credibility of the system, which are consistent with the objective of gradually achieving monetary unification. In present circumstances an average frequency of between 12 and 18 months would appear to reconcile these requirements.

As regards changes in central rates, I believe that the current inflation differentials – especially with regard to domestic costs in the EMS countries – and the prospective changes in real factors requiring further variations in equilibrium exchange rates would allow member countries to undertake to keep the variations in their bilateral central rates below 3–4 per cent per year. The adoption of this constraint should nonetheless be accompanied, as I shall show below, by an undertaking to modify the main mechanisms governing the development of costs that are not consistent with the objective of monetary stability.

Adequate fluctuation of both exchange and interest rates around a more stable central value, coupled with recourse to intervention on the forward foreign exchange market and a commitment to respect an upper limit on central rate variations, would make it possible to counter destabilising movements of speculative capital and to progress towards the goal of monetary unification. This would be achieved without having to accept the hypothesis of Europe advancing at two different speeds in the process of monetary integration, an approach that I believe to be dangerous and which could face some countries, and especially Italy, with some very difficult choices.

Subsequently, both the constraints – presumptive in the case of central rates and operational in that of the fluctuation band – should be gradually tightened, in conformity with the goal of monetary and financial unification. Notably, the maximum permitted variation in central rates should be reduced to zero over a period of five years or so.

It should be noted here that the exchange rate policies pursued so far within the EMS, implying an upward drift of the real exchange rate of some currencies and the depreciation of others (the strong currencies), cannot serve as a model for the phase of monetary integration that we are now entering.

The pendulum of central rate variations has swung too far in the direction of infrequent intervention and created a situation that is undesirable on balance. In particular, not changing the lira/DM central rate for more than two years has caused current account distortions.[18] Moreover, as the gap between price levels widens, the market becomes subjectively more convinced of the probability of a realignment. The differential between real interest rates thus tends to overestimate the difference between yields expressed in a common currency.[19] In other words, in order to counter the impact on capital movements it is necessary – with reference to the foregoing bilateral example – to keep interest rates in Italy above, and those in Germany below, the domestic equilibrium level. Thus, the distortions in the current account are supplemented by others of a financial nature, which are particularly onerous in Italy's case in view of the large public debt.

4.2 Some remarks concerning Italy

More than any other country, Italy will need to back the double commitment to reduce fluctuation margins and limit changes in central rates with measures correcting the domestic factors that generate upward pressure on costs and prices, notably wages and the budget deficit. In particular, it will be necessary to guarantee a close link between increases in money wages and improvements in productivity, especially in the public sector. Unaffected by international competition and given an employment target, the latter has not improved its efficiency or productivity to the same extent as the private sector and especially industry excluding construction (see Table 10.1), which have clearly been stimulated by the combined effect of Italy's unaccommodating exchange rate policy and fierce international competition.

By contrast, the divergence of nominal costs and real productivity in the public sector has exacerbated the difficulty of controlling the public finances, already aggravated by the burden imposed by the public debt. It is for this reason that the distinction made here is between industry and general government rather than the more usual one between industry, agriculture and services. In reality, while the improvement in agricultural productivity has kept pace with that of

Table 10.1 Productivity and money wages and salaries in industry (excluding construction) and the public sector in Italy (1970 = 100)

	*Productivity in industry (excluding construction)**	*Productivity in the public sector*†	*Per capita money wages and salaries in industry*	*Per capita money wages and salaries in the public sector*
1970	100.00	100.00	100.00	100.0
1971	99.98	103.00	112.3	115.0
1972	107.62	103.90	125.1	126.2
1973	116.59	102.40	148.4	141.4
1974	122.52	101.30	185.8	164.0
1975	113.65	95.60	229.9	183.8
1976	125.94	97.20	284.4	216.2
1977	129.64	95.40	335.0	265.5
1978	135.27	95.30	385.3	318.0
1979	144.31	*99.36*	463.2	388.1
1980	150.89	100.24	544.9	492.7
1981	153.83	99.10	660.7	635.1
1982	156.37	97.52	776.8	728.9
1983	162.72	91.73	909.9	845.4
1984	176.80	92.89	1044.3	939.5
1985	184.09	94.51	1164.1	1025.7
1986	189.52	97.39	1247.2	1106.7
1987	198.43	100.91	1352.7	1236.8
1988	206.05	N.D.	1459.7	1358.6

Notes: * Value added at constant prices per employee.
† Estimates made by Formez for the period 1970–8 (physical indicators regarding the activities of Justice, Education, Museums, Hospitals, State telephone, Post Office, State railways, etc.). The updates for the period 1979–87 were based on physical indicators regarding the activities of the Post Office and the State railways.

Sources: ISTAT, Contabilità nazionale, Annuario Statistico.

industry, productivity in private services has risen no faster than that of public services. As Professor Fiaccavento has shown in a recent study, from which the figures for Table 10.2 were taken,[20] the new national accounts series indicate that the productivity of services actually *decreased* at an average annual rate of 0.06 per cent between 1980 and 1988, while rates of increase of 3.33 per cent and 3.30 per cent were recorded in industry and agriculture respectively.

In the coming years the creation of the single market, and hence the opening of private services to international competition, is likely to

Table 10.2 Labour costs, productivity and prices in Italy (average percentage changes)

	Agriculture	*Industry*	*Services*	*Total*
1970–80				
Labour costs*	22.66	18.77	17.46	18.45
Productivity†	3.40	3.59	1.32	2.76
Prices**	14.64	14.18	15.87	15.06
Consumer prices††				14.15
1980–88				
Labour costs	11.45	13.06	12.39	12.77
Productivity	3.30	3.33	–0.06	1.50
Prices	6.95	9.99	12.32	11.23
Consumer prices				10.61

Notes: * Per employee.
† Value added per worker at constant prices.
** Deflator of value added.
†† Consumer price index for blue- and white-collar households.

Source: ISTAT, Contabilità nazionale (revised series from 1970 on).

produce similar effects to those generated in industry and agriculture.[21] Another reason for focusing on the public sector here is that, in contrast with other EEC countries, the mechanisms for determining public sector wages and salaries are much less rigorous than in the private sector, with a very tenuous link between earnings and productivity that risks causing Italy to be left behind in the monetary integration of Europe.

The difficulty of measuring productivity in the public sector is, of course, well known. While it is reasonable to assume that the prices of goods freely exchanged in the market reflect the value that consumers attach to them (provided market conditions are not too far from perfect competition), the valuation of public services is more complicated. In the national accounts they are valued on the basis of the costs incurred in their production, so that if labour productivity is measured in the conventional way as the ratio of total value added to the number of employees, any increase will not significantly differ from that in real per capita earnings.

It is therefore necessary to have recourse to 'physical' measures of output, which are often either not available or only partially significant unless they are used very carefully. The data with which to carry out such calculations are limited and in any case tend to contain a large subjective component, apart from the fact that they are usually made available with considerable delay. For all these reasons, the analyses in question are restricted to specialist publications and fail to influence economic policy decisions. In this paper I have used estimates of public sector productivity made by Formez[22] and updated them on the basis of physical indicators for the Post Office and the State railways.

Notwithstanding these measurement difficulties, the figures available lead to an unambiguous conclusion: some of the public sector's lower rate of productivity improvement compared with industry can be justified on the grounds that the nature of services prevents more efficient production techniques from being adopted in many sectors (in education, for example, there is obviously a limit beyond which labour intensity cannot be reduced); most of the gap, however, has to be attributed to the greater 'inefficiency' with which public resources are managed, since internal controls are rarely an effective substitute for the stimulus of competition or able to overcome the greater inertia in adopting the optimal combination of the factors of production in the sectors where this is technically possible.

The rate of increase in public sector wages in the 1970s and 1980s has nonetheless not differed significantly from that of industry (see Table 10.1), leading to what Baumol calls an 'unbalanced pattern of growth'. It is worth noting, moreover, that the overall increase in public sector wages during the period in which the EMS has been in operation have actually *exceeded* that of industry, covering the gap accumulated during the mid-1970s, thereby confirming the view put forward in this paper that the exchange rate constraint does not impose discipline on the public sector in the same way as it does on the private sector, which is exposed to international competition.

Focusing on the ten years of the EMS, the data thus reveal two reinforcing scissor-like divergences: on the one hand, earnings in the public sector have grown faster than in industry and, on the other, the virtual stagnation of productivity in the public sector has been accompanied by a significant improvement in that of industry. Between 1978 and 1987 the index of productivity in industry excluding construction rose by 46.7 per cent, while that of the public sector rose by less than 6 per cent. By contrast, the indices of real per capita wages and salaries (compensation of employees) in the two sectors rose by 19 per cent and 32 per cent respectively (see Figures 10.1 and 10.2). These developments are summarised in the *inverse* ratio of the growth in real earnings to productivity in the two sectors (see Figures 10.1, 10.2 and 10.3).

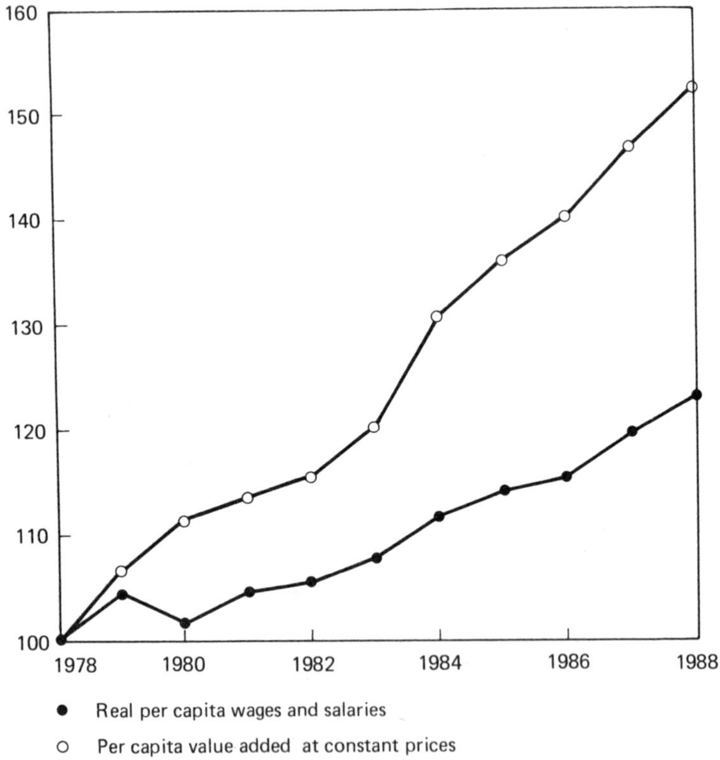

Source: ISTAT, Contabilita nazionale.

Figure 10.1 Real wages and salaries and productivity in industry (excluding construction) in Italy (1978 = 100)

I have compared these results for Italy with the corresponding figures for Germany. The choice of these two countries, apart from the obvious interest of this conference in the Italian case, is designed to provide a clear example of the differences that still exist today between the economies participating in the European Exchange Rate Mechanism. Moreover, if the objective is to achieve monetary and exchange rate integration with Germany, this country has to be considered as providing the base line.

The comparison with Germany accentuates the opening of the 'scissors'. On the one hand, the increase in public sector earnings in Germany was 13 per cent smaller than that recorded in industry (Figures 10.4 and 10.5); on the other, even though statistics on public

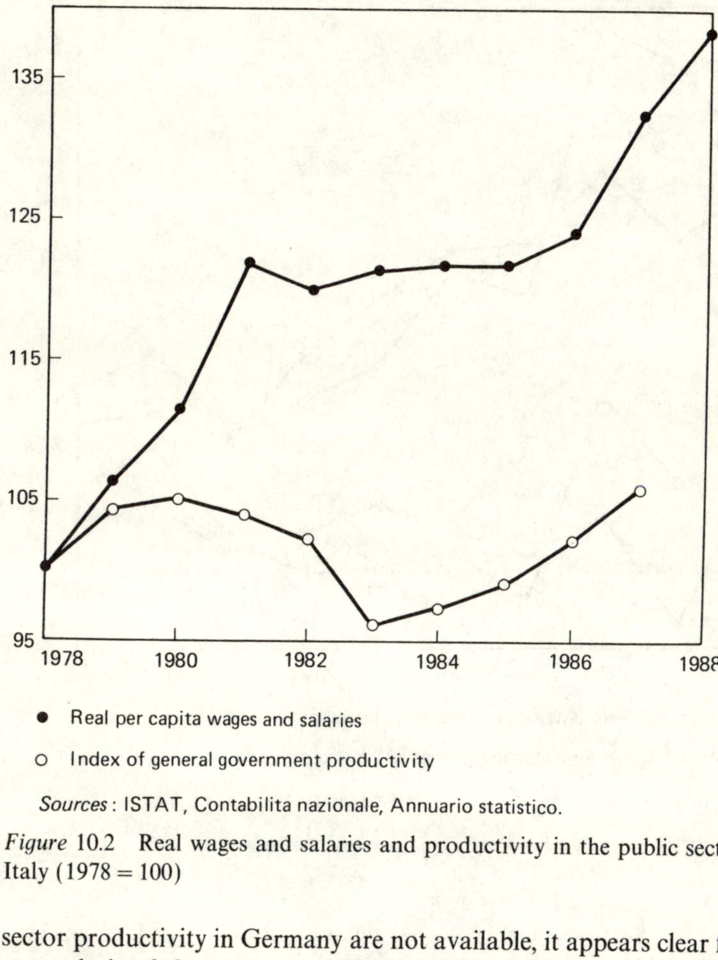

Sources: ISTAT, Contabilita nazionale, Annuario statistico.

Figure 10.2 Real wages and salaries and productivity in the public sector in Italy (1978 = 100)

sector productivity in Germany are not available, it appears clear from an analysis of the services supplied that productivity increased more than in Italy.[23]

This conclusion is supported by the results of a recent survey of the productivity of public services in selected countries.[24] Between 1970 and 1986 the index of railway productivity rose by 36.5 per cent in Germany and only by 0.4 per cent in Italy; as for the postal service, in the period 1975–86 productivity rose by 9.4 per cent in Germany and fell by 9.6 per cent in Italy.

The divergence is also due, however, to the ratio of the index of productivity in industry (excluding construction) to that of real earnings having been higher in Italy than in Germany ever since the inception

Source: ISTAT, Contabilita nazionale.

Figure 10.3 Real and money wages and salaries in industry (excluding construction) and the public sector in Italy (annual percentage rates of change)

of the EMS (Figure 10.6). Between 1978 and 1987 the productivity gains in Italian industry excluding construction exceeded the rise in real earnings by 23 per cent, while the figure for Germany was only 5.6 per cent. The burden of protecting the competitiveness of the Italian economy has thus been borne exclusively by the industrial sector, which has had to compensate for the negative performance of the public sector.

Despite the increases in real earnings in Italian industry having been *smaller* than those in productivity, there was nonetheless a significant divergence between real and money wages (see Figure 10.3). Obviously,

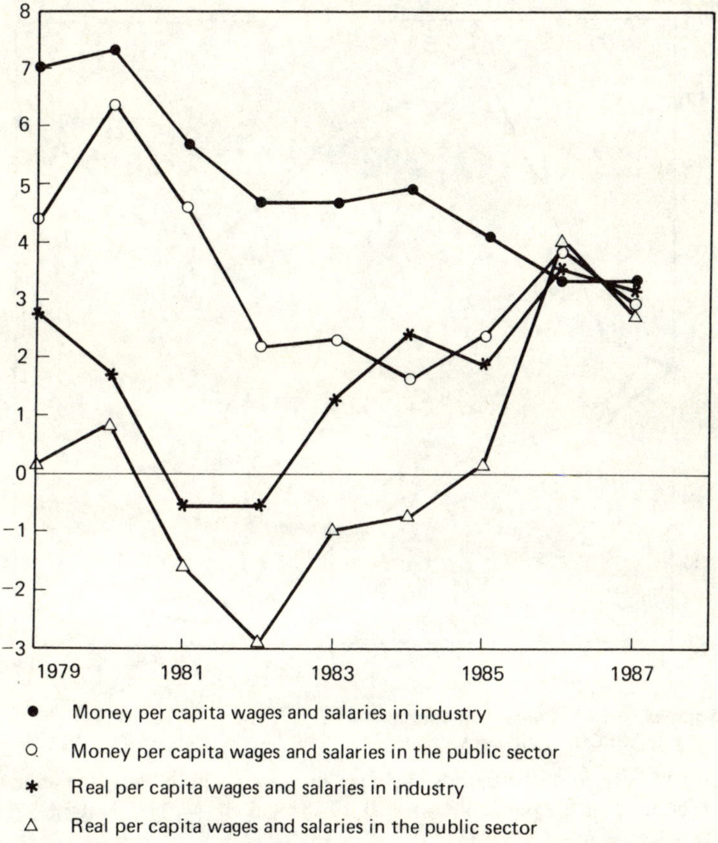

Source: OECD, National Accounts.

Figure 10.4 Real and money wages and salaries in industry (excluding construction) and the public sector in Germany (annual percentage rates of change)

if it were no longer possible to modify the exchange rate, this divergence would inevitably cause a loss of competitiveness.

This international comparison highlights the need for Italy to adopt a policy for public sector incomes that would link increases in money wages more tightly to productivity, a principle that has been extensively ignored in recent years. As I mentioned, while market mechanisms and the exchange rate constraint, coupled with international competition, are sufficient to ensure this linkage in the sectors producing tradeable goods and services, in the public sector it can only be achieved as a

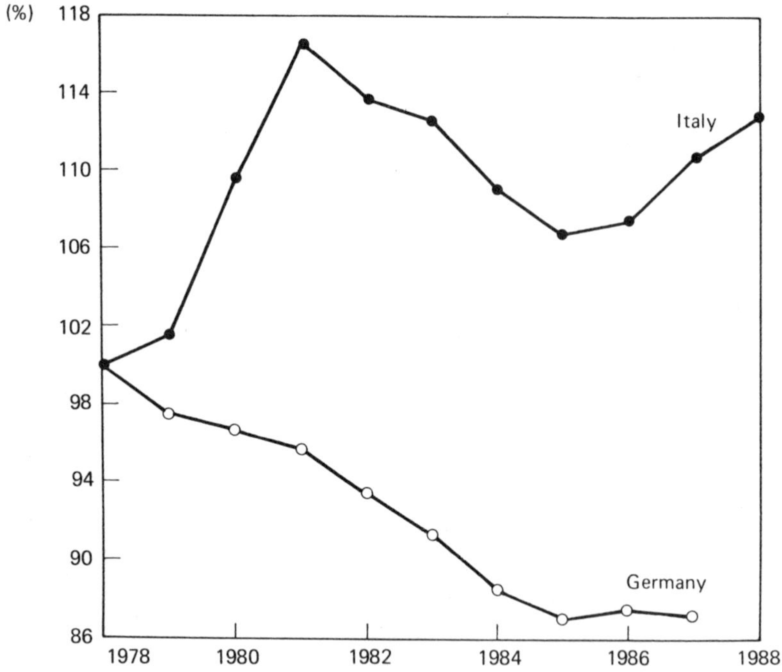

Sources: ISTAT, Contabilita nazionale.
OECD, National Accounts.

Figure 10.5 Ratio of the indices of wages and salaries in industry (excluding construction) and the public sector in Italy and Germany (1978 = 100)

result of explicit political action. In my opinion, it would be the first and the most important demonstration of control over the growth in the current expenditure of the public sector as a whole. It would create the conditions for achieving a degree of monetary stability that would permit the pursuit of objectives for employment and competitiveness without the external restraint returning to suffocate economic growth and the burden of the public debt provoking financial instability.

Even in the private sector of the Italian economy, and especially in industry, a major problem is that of uncoupling wage demands from inflation expectations and strengthening the link between increases in *money wages* and *productivity*. This is indispensable if the competitiveness of industry and market services is not to be undermined by the implementation of the plan to achieve increasing exchange rate stability vis-à-vis countries, such as Germany, that have made a close

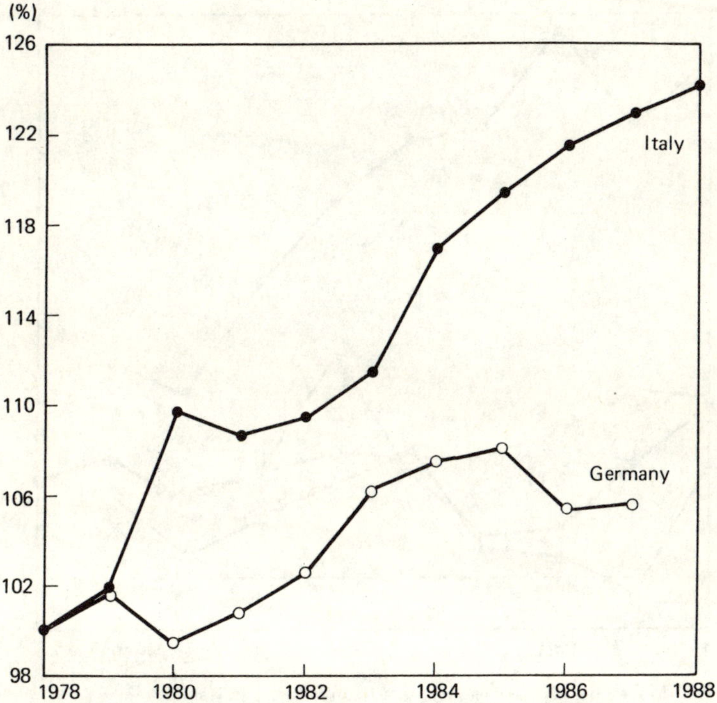

Source: ISTAT, Contabilita nazionale.
OECD, National Accounts.

Figure 10.6 Ratio of the indices of productivity and real wages and salaries in industry (excluding construction) in Italy and Germany (1978 = 100)

relationship between money wage dynamics and productivity the linchpin of their industrial relations. Figure 10.7 clearly shows, in fact, that the gap between the rates of increase in money wages and productivity in Italian industry is still significantly larger than that recorded in German industry, despite its having narrowed considerably since the inception of the EMS.

In the light of the foregoing considerations, there appear to be good grounds for concluding that there will have to be a substantial change in the *mechanisms of wage formation* in Italy. It will only be possible to break out of the vicious circle of inflation fuelled by increases in costs and expectations of inflation if wage demands are made consistent with the hypothesis of zero inflation and earnings are therefore effectively linked to productivity. The scope for greater efficiency in the

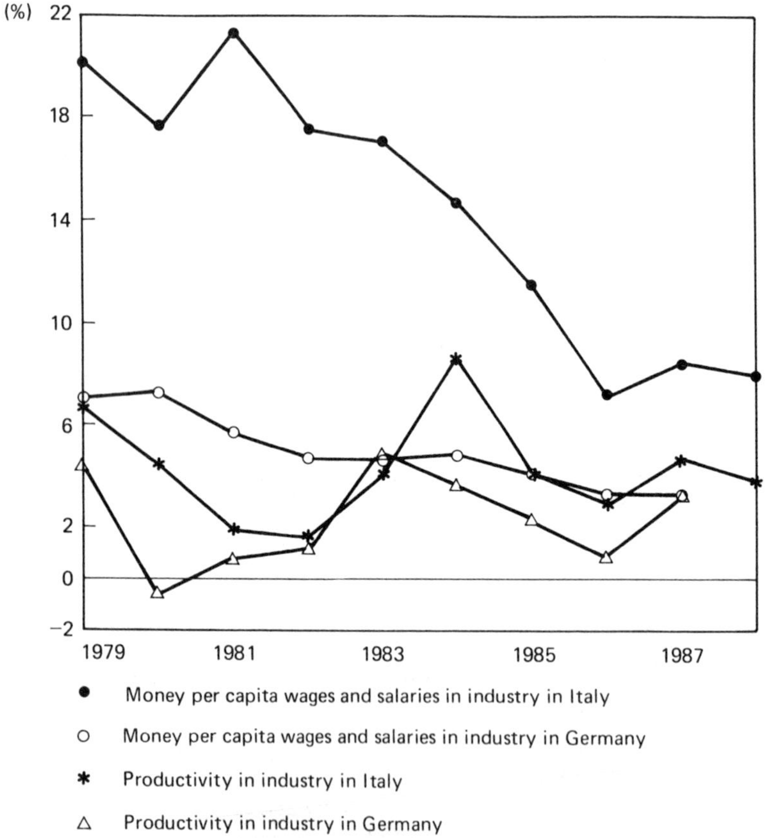

Sources ISTAT, Contabilita nazionale.
OECD, National Accounts.

Figure 10.7 Money wages and salaries and productivity in industry (excluding construction) in Italy and Germany (annual percentage rates of change)

private and public services sectors is considerable, so that plenty of room exists for increases in real earnings, provided these are made dependent on the actual achievement of 'real' results.

The reform of the mechanisms of wage formation, which would contribute significantly to curbing the growth of current government expenditure, could be accompanied by a monetary reform. Italy could precede its European partners (see Section 4.3) and anchor the 'new lira' to the ECU. This would permit the public debt to be converted into 'new lire', with a large saving in interest payments.[25]

Models based on the approach that Barro and Gordon[26] developed clearly indicate that the credibility of the government is the crucial factor in the determination of prices and wages in the private sector. Even more than the commitment to a stable exchange rate, and hence to control over the money supply, it is the action of the government in fixing public sector wages and salaries that determines businessmen's expectations. Taken together, the two measures proposed here would therefore go a long way towards uprooting inflationary expectations. The sectoral adjustment measures already formulated by the government (the Amato plan) would produce synergetically complementary effects and complete the strategy for the restoration of the public finances to a sound footing.

The reduction in public expenditure, both on current account and for interest payments, would have a beneficial effect on the budget deficit and hence on inflation, creating a virtuous circle in which decreases in the deficit in *nominal* terms would be both the condition and the consequence of decreases in *real* terms. Anchoring the 'new lira' to the ECU would set a seal on the elimination of the gap separating Italy from its partners as regards rates of increase in real and nominal wages and prices. The monetary reform would also defuse expectations of inflation and confirm the switch to the new regime.

This virtuous circle would be further strengthened by a mechanism that I have described elsewhere.[27] Briefly, a reduction in the rate of inflation brings an immediate reduction in the debt burden since, in the short term, changes in the cost of servicing the public debt in real terms are related in a directly proportional manner to the rate of inflation.

4.3 Institutional problems

Another problem closely related to that of enhancing the overall disciplinary effect of the exchange rate constraint is that of strengthening monetary cooperation, with the adoption of 'rules of the game' consistent with the goal of unification.

One possible coordination formula involves an 'asymmetrical' solution: the country whose currency is the linchpin of the system ensures that the growth of its monetary aggregates is consistent with domestic price stability. It it up to the other countries in the system to manage their exchange rates vis-à-vis the dominant currency through appropriate changes in interest rates.

This formula has the advantage – which is not to be undervalued – of providing the whole system with a nominal anchor that benefits from the discipline and monetary 'reputation' of the leader country. Particularly in the context of a common economic policy framework based on cooperation and designed to promote the growth of the European economy as a whole, this solution nonetheless appears unacceptable to the other EMS countries, and the leader country itself might be unwilling to accept the constraint inherent in pursuing a passive exchange rate policy within the area and the resulting reduced freedom in the use of anti-inflationary instruments.

Another formula – which is the one that I personally prefer – is based on the coordinated management by the central banks of the Community of the growth rates of both the domestic component of monetary base and domestic credit. In the aggregate, this would imply a joint decision on the total creation of monetary base in the area.

The steps to be taken to achieve these objectives without weakening the fundamental commitment to monetary stability could be as follows:

- the present powers of the Committee of Governors of the EEC central banks would be enlarged to permit the joint ex ante fixing of monetary aggregates and the coordinated management and control of financial and credit aggregates. In order to strengthen the control of intramarginal exchange rate fluctuations, the impulses generated by the foreign component of monetary base would have to be promptly reflected in changes in interest rate differentials. More generally, liquidity and credit creation would have to be carefully controlled and coordinated in the context of overall portfolio equilibrium;
- the Committee of Governors would develop a common policy vis-à-vis third currencies leading to intervention concerted at the European level; and, most importantly,
- all the European currencies making up the ECU would have to participate in the exchange rate mechanism on an equal footing.

If these steps were accompanied by guarantees regarding the exercise of unaccommodating control over individual countries' monetary and exchange rate policies, the Committee could initially act as a European Monetary 'Board' and subsequently turn into a European Monetary 'Fund' (of which member countries would be the shareholders) with an organisational structure permitting it not only to govern the credit mechanisms needed to ensure balance-of-payments adjustment but also to manage on its own account the related exchange and interest rate risks.

This approach requires the *Fund* to have legal personality and to be administratively and operationally autonomous, so as to constitute the nucleus of a *European central bank* and to enjoy institutional guarantees analogous to those of the central banks that have the most independence in ensuring monetary stability. It is also necessary to stress the importance of the continuous monitoring of monetary and exchange rate policy in conjunction with the central banks of the member states.

At this point, it would be only a short step to arrive at a federal central bank with full 'constitutional' guarantees of its independence, in line with the recent suggestion of the President of the Bundesbank. It is worth recalling in this connection that the US Federal Reserve System was conceived in the context of the gold standard as a 'system' of twelve federal banks that were coordinated but enjoyed a considerable degree of autonomy in their 'domestic' credit markets.

Within this framework it would also be desirable to cast the ECU in a central role,[28] both as an international reserve asset and as a European currency in parallel with national currencies. In my opinion this will require not only the removal of the restrictions on the acceptability of official ECUs but also the creation of a link between the official and the private ECU markets allowing central banks to transform their official ECU assets into private ECU balances and vice versa. This can be done through an institution, such as the BIS, that would act both as a clearing house for private ECUs and as the recognised holder of official ECUs.

The Committee of Governors (and subsequently the *European Monetary Board*) would be responsible for supervising ECU creation, subjecting it to controls analogous, especially as regards reserve requirements (preferably dominated in high-powered ECUs), to those in force for national currencies and taking account of the growth in the latter. This organisation would also be responsible for the centralised management of a part of Europe's foreign currency reserves as well as the actual creation of official ECUs and the operation of the short-term credit support mechanisms serving to discourage and counter speculative attacks on participating currencies.

The development of the ECU would encourage the necessary harmonisation of the taxation of financial assets in the Community. In the situation described above the ECU, if necessary redefined, could in the end become the European currency. The separate national currencies would be gradually anchored to the ECU and become identified with *the* European currency. The ECU liabilities of the Board would constitute Europe's monetary base. Account would naturally have to be taken of the gradual increase in the ECUs in circulation and of their distribution within the Community in order to ensure the control of total monetary assets and credit flows.

The assumption that the Board will have to become a 'sovereign' body raises the question whether it should also be made responsible for monetary supervision at the supranational level, of which I have already underscored the importance in an integrated market for capital and financial services.

Personally, I am of the view that these functions should be performed by a different organisation that, while working in close contact with the *Board*, would be autonomous. Such a body should provide the necessary, and appropriately dialectic, link between the Board and the various national supervisory authorities.

5 CONCLUSIONS

In this chapter I have focused on three problems that will have to be tackled in the short term to enable the financial integration of Europe to proceed in an orderly manner: national regulatory systems, the taxation of financial assets and enhanced exchange rate stability in a context of closely coordinated monetary policies are the issues. Though there are, of course, other problems, I have attempted to identify the nature of these three and to indicate possible ways of overcoming them.

Today's general move towards greater exchange rate cohesion and monetary stability, set within the framework of a system that is rigorous but nonetheless able to forestall and counter destabilising currency speculation, means that domestic costs will have to be stable if integration is to provide the foundation for economic growth and a gradual reduction in unemployment.

If European financial integration is to make progress, there will have to be greater convergence of economic fundamentals. In Italy's case, the challenge of 1992 is inextricably related, on the one hand, to the rehabilitation of the public finances and, on the other, to changes in the mechanisms for determining money wages that will make Italian earnings rise at a 'European' rate and link increases to 'real' improvements in productivity and efficiency. Market mechanisms and the exchange rate constraint will oblige the private sector to move in the desired direction, and the intensification of competition in services as a result of the single market will sharpen the spur. In the public sector, by contrast, appropriate action by the political authorities will be necessary.

Notes

1. M. Obstfeld, 'Competitiveness, Realignments and Speculation: the Role of Financial Markets', in Giavazzi, F., Micossi, S. and Miller, M. (eds) *The European Monetary System* (Cambridge University Press, 1988) and C. Wyplosz, 'Capital Controls and Balance of Payments', *Journal of International Money and Finance*, June 1986.
2. In particular, see F. Giavazzi, 'The Exchange-Rate Question in Europe', *Discussion Paper Series*, no. 298, CEPR, January 1989; CER, *Lo SME dieci anni dopo*, Rome, December 1988; Proceedings of the Conference organised by the Ministry of Foreign Affairs and IMI on 'The European Monetary System Ten Years after its Inception: Results and Prospects', Rome, 5 December 1988.
3. *L'unificazione monetaria e lo SME – l'esperienza dei primi otto anni* (Bologna: Il Mulino).
4. P. Kenen, 'Capital Mobility and Financial Integration: a Survey', *Princeton Studies in International Finance*, no. 39, 1976.
5. I have addressed these issues on other recent occasions and refer the reader to the following publications for a more detailed, and I hope convincing, discussion of the views set out here. The tax issues are examined in *Finanza, moneta e risparmio: la prospettiva del'92* (Rome: Luiss University) forthcoming; the regulatory issues in 'Monetary and Financial Markets in Europe: Regulation and Market Forces', *Review of Economic Conditions in Italy*, Banco di Roma, forthcoming.
6. Cf. A. Steinherr and P. Gilbert, 'The Impact of Financial Market Integration on the European Banking Industry' *Research Report* no. 1, Centre for European Policy Studies, January 1989; Banca d'Italia, 'Intermediazione finanziaria non bancaria e gruppi bancari plurifunzionali: le esigenze di regolamentazione prudenziale', *Temi di discussione*, no. 113, 1989; 'Il mercato unico degli enti creditizi', prepared by the Community Affairs section of IMI, February 1989.
7. Cf. M. Sarcinelli, 'L'integrazione finanziaria europea e la sfida politica del 1992: è l'approccio di mercato sufficiente?', *Moneta e Credito*, December 1988.
8. Cf. BIS, *Recent Innovations in International Banking*, April 1986.
9. On this issue, see Commission of the European Communities, 'Mésures fiscales à adopter par la Communautée en liaison avec la libéralisation des mouvements de capitaux' (Commission Communication to the Council), and the Hannover European Council, 27 and 28 June 1988, 'Conclusions of the Presidency'.

10. For a detailed analysis of these differences, see Banca d'Italia, 'La tassazione delle rendite finanziarie nella CEE alla luce della liberalizzazione valutaria', *Temi di discussione*, no. 114, February 1989; and 'Il trattamento fiscale dei proventi delle attività finanziarie', published by *Studi Finanziari*, February 1989.
11. Conseil National du Crédit, *La fiscalité de l'épargne dans le cadre du marché intérieur européen*, June 1988.
12. See, for example, K. Hamada, 'A Strategic Analysis of Monetary Interdependence', *Journal of Political Economy*, no. 4, 1976; and M. Canzoneri and J. Gray, 'Monetary Policy Games and the Consequences of Non-Cooperative Behaviour', *International Economic Review*, no. 3, 1985.
13. For a systemic approach to the problem of the efficiency of international monetary systems, cf. G. Basevi, 'Il sistema dei cambi', in T. Padoa-Schioppa (ed.) *Il sistema dei cambi oggi* (Bologna: Il Mulino, 1986).
14. Cf. P. Baffi, 'Due momenti del negoziato sullo SME: la banda larga e l'adesione del Regno Unito', Proceedings of the Conference organised by the Ministry of Foreign Affairs and IMI on 'The European Monetary System Ten Years after its Inception: Results and Prospects', op. cit.
15. At present the instantaneous margin is equal to 2.25 per cent for every currency except the lira (6 per cent) and the pound and the peseta, which formally have infinite margins.
16. See, for example, R.S. Masera, *L'unificazione monetaria e lo SME*, op. cit., ch. 3, app. 2.
17. Denoting the maximum bilateral realignment by Δe_{ij} the frequency of realignments in annual terms by f and the fluctuation band common to every country by b, the considerations set out in the text enable the desired width of the band to be expressed in terms of the following disequality: $b \geqslant \Delta e_{ij}/f$. If the band were narrower, a realignment would probably cause a discrete 'jump' in market quotations. In practice, it would be preferable for the band to equal rather than exceed the second term, since, provided it remains credible, the narrower the band, the greater its stabilising effect on expectations.
18. The last realignment in the EMS took place on 12 January 1987. From the end of 1987 to now (April 1989) the lira/DM has remained virtually unchanged at around 735.
19. For an analytical treatment of this problem, see L. Bini Smaghi and R. Masera, 'L'evoluzione degli accordi di cambio dello SME: marzo 1979 – marzo 1987', in *L'unificazione monetaria e lo SME*, op. cit., ch. 4.
20. C. Fiaccavento, 'L'economia italiana tra ciclo e trend', paper presented at a conference held at IMI on 16 March 1989. Indices in Table 10.2 have been updated on the basis of the last available data.
21. Cf. C. Dell'Aringa, 'Produttività e retribuzioni: esperienze di relazioni industriali', *Rassegna di statistiche del lavoro*, no. 1, 1989.
22. Formez, *La produttività nella Pubblica Amministrazione* (Rome: Edizioni Il Sole 24 Ore, 1987). The Formez estimates (available up to 1979) are based

on physical indices regarding the activities related to both non-marketable (justice, education ...) and marketable (Post Office, State railways ...) public services.

23. It is interesting that the applications made both in Germany, to the federal institutions, and to international organisations for estimates of the development of public sector productivity indicate that such statistics are not available.
24. Nomisma, *Produttività e competitività*, December 1988.
25. With the current levels of interest rates, there would be a reduction of nearly three points in the rate paid on the public debt as a result of its conversion into ECUs. Every one point reduction implies a corresponding decrease in a full year of nearly 10 000 billion current lire in the borrowing requirement.
26. R.J. Barro and D. Gordon, 'Rules, Discretion and Reputation in a Model of Monetary Policy', *Journal of Monetary Policy*, July 1983.
27. R.S. Masera, 'The Balancing of Public Finance in Italy: Four Arguments', *Rivista di Politica Economica*, no. 20, 1986.
28. L. Dini put forward new proposals in 'A Single Currency for Europe: Economic Policy and Financial Choices', a paper presented at the conference organised by the Confindustria on 'A Single Currency for Europe', Rome, February 1989.

11 Macroeconomic Policy Coordination and the European Monetary System

Richard Portes*

Macroeconomic policy coordination is a major topic in the Report of the (Delors) Committee for the Study of Economic and Monetary Union. Indeed, its treatment of fiscal policy coordination immediately became one of the more controversial aspects of the Report. The academic literature in theoretical and applied macroeconomics over the past few years has also emphasised policy coordination (see Buiter and Marston, 1985; Bryant and Portes, 1987). This literature stresses the strategic interaction among national governments, between national central banks and finance ministries, and between the domestic policy authorities and their private sectors.

These interactions are often analysed formally or informally with the tools of game theory, which are particularly helpful in understanding cooperative and non-cooperative behaviour. The latter, whether strategic or passive, can generate inefficiencies. Explicit or tacit coordination can make all participants ('players' or partners) better off. But 'coordination' need not be full cooperation. Some degree of coordination can be enforced by a commitment from each participant to play by a given set of rules applicable to all. The overall framework in which these rules are set is often called a policy 'regime', of which the EMS is an example (the concept of an international monetary regime is elaborated by Aglietta, 1989).

The rules, either as written or as applied in practice, need not be symmetric among the participants, just as full cooperation may involve

*I have benefited greatly from discussions with David Begg, Daniel Cohen, Barry Eichengreen, Francesco Giavazzi, Alberto Giovannini, Jacques Melitz, Marcus Miller, Massimo Russo, Lars Svensson, Charles Wyplosz, and participation with them and others in the CEPR International Macroeconomics research programme, supported by grants from the Ford and Alfred P. Sloan Foundations. I am grateful to George Alogoskoufis for comments. None is implicated by my free use of their ideas, nor is the Centre for Economic Policy Research.

bargaining in which the participants may have different bargaining power. Even if the rules do not embody any asymmetry, it may arise from the different characteristics of the participants. One theme of this essay is asymmetry among countries in the EMS and its implications for policy coordination.

Even if all the EC countries join fully in the EMS, and the System itself progresses further towards economic and monetary union with whatever policy coordination this may require internally, the EC will still be only a coalition of players in a broader 'game', the world economy. Fashioning and implementing appropriate strategies in this global context – agreed EC external macroeconomic policies – may also require specified forms of coordination of the policies of individual EC countries. This will be the second particular theme of the paper.

A basic premise of the discussion here is that it refers to the EMS *in transition* and managing that transition over the next several years, not to full economic and monetary union itself. Research is only now analysing the conditions under which, in a monetary union with irrevocably fixed parities and (ultimately) a common currency, fiscal policy coordination among political units may be unnecessary – it is, after all, unheard of among American states or Canadian provinces. A central fiscal policy for the Community may then be desirable for distributional and other reasons, but I shall not discuss that here, except in relation to the Community's external economic policy (Section 4).

1 POLICY COORDINATION IN A FIXED EXCHANGE RATE SYSTEM

Rules are at least partial substitutes for the bargaining in full, directly cooperative policy-making. That bargaining is often difficult, time-consuming, conflictual in process, and even sometimes inconclusive after all that. So if the rules function fairly well – countries do not often deviate from them and the outcomes are generally satisfactory – it is not obvious that there should be any strongly felt need for policy coordination, at least in respect of policies covered by the rules.

Policy coordination is neither necessary nor sufficient for exchange rate stability. If the rules specify fixed exchange rates, and the premise is that imbalances in national macroeconomic policies are the prime source of exchange rate instability, then appropriate policy coordination is of course a sufficient condition for following the rules. But this is a strong premise – it ignores inefficiencies in financial markets, for example. Nor is it clear that optimal, internationally coordinated macroeconomic policies are required to sustain exchange rate stability – weaker measures that are easier to specify and implement may be enough for that (common monetary targets, intervention rules, reserve pooling, etc.).

Moreover, full policy coordination is not obviously desirable, even if it is feasible. One need not be so negative as Feldstein (1988) to question whether the benefits of international policy coordination outweigh the costs. There is significant disagreement over the size, and even the likely sign, of the benefits (see Currie *et al.*, 1989, for a survey). And even if our understanding of the national and international economies were enough to make fully coordinated policies desirable in principle, they would at the very least be hard to calculate, as the academic literature demonstrates.

That is why some recent work assesses how a fixed exchange rate system functions as a simple rule that imposes some degree of policy coordination, comparing the outcome with what full coordination would (if feasible) have offered. Here, too, the results are not unambiguous (compare Levine *et al.*, 1989, and Hughes Hallett *et al.*, 1989), but there does seem to be some basis for arguing that fixed rates provide many of the benefits the full coordination could achieve. A recent study group report opts on different grounds for 'a rule-based system of coordination, with the emphasis on a more managed exchange rate system', as opposed to discretionary coordination or rule-based coordination focusing on various policy targets or instruments (Group of Thirty, 1988).

None of this denies that fixed rates are often sub-optimal: without substantial international factor mobility and fiscal redistribution, adjusting parities will be the efficient short-run mechanism to compensate for country-specific shocks and imbalances or asymmetries in wage-price behaviour (Giavazzi, 1989). The point is merely that the EMS may go quite far enough already to reap the potential gains from macroeconomic policy coordination.

Another argument based on strategic considerations virtually identifies the EMS itself with policy coordination. It stresses that a key feature of policy coordination is the commitment to maintain it. In the absence of agreed and effective international enforcement (punishment) mechanisms, there will often be an incentive to 'free ride' or a domestic political reason to renege, no matter how desirable sustained cooperative behaviour may be for the group as a whole and, in the longer run, for the potential 'deviant' itself. Joining the EMS is in this view a precommitment to whatever degree of policy coordination is needed to stay in, a political investment in the credibility of the country's commitment not to renege.

2 POLICY COORDINATION IN THE DELORS COMMITTEE REPORT

Even on a less extreme interpretation, exchange rate management in the EMS does already provide or enforce a substantial degree of policy coordination. It is maintained partly because of the economic benefits of that policy coordination, partly because of structural features of the European Community as well as domestic and international political considerations. Without any further specific measures, it is likely to deepen anyway as the EMS widens, goods and capital markets become more integrated, and realignments diminish. So why did the Delors Committee put so much emphasis on extending policy coordination – in particular, for fiscal policy?

The Committee might have taken the view that the absence or ineffectiveness of policy coordination caused the demise of the Gold Standard system or of the Bretton Woods exchange rate system. But there are more plausible alternative explanations. More and better macroeconomic policy coordination might have been necessary but would not have been sufficient to avoid the financial crisis of the 1930s, although 'beggar-thy-neighbour' strategic behaviour did make it worse (Eichengreen and Portes, 1987). The prime cause of the breakdown of Bretton Woods was the inability of the institutional structure to withstand the pressures of growing and more volatile capital flows. This would suggest we should focus now on dealing with short-run portfolio shifts in the EMS – on intervention rules, pooling reserves, the width of bands, the timing and size of realignments – rather than on any substantial extension of macroeconomic policy coordination. To the extent that US fiscal and monetary excesses added to the problems of the early 1970s, we may observe that no country in the EMS could now escape from the fixed exchange rate discipline as did the US as the issuer of the reserve currency.

The Delors Committee were surely conscious of this historical background. They were doubtless aware that macroeconomic policy coordination is neither necessary nor sufficient for exchange rate stability; that its benefits are not demonstrably great; that exchange rate management is itself a surrogate for policy coordination; and that the constraint of adhering to the EMS has already brought more joint and coordinated decision-making as well as some degree of macroeconomic convergence (Thygesen, 1989). So starting from the fixed-rate EMS, why stress more policy coordination, in particular on the fiscal side, beyond what more rigid exchange rates could be expected to bring? Political considerations might have suggested that this call would in fact be divisive.

There are several conjectural answers to this question that bear directly on our chosen topics of asymmetry and EC external macro policy. But first we should state a fundamental premise behind the Report and the creation of the Delors Committee itself. The EMS has not been sufficient, in the ten years in which it has survived and developed, to bring any appreciable progress towards the *monetary unification* it had prefigured. Some thought it necessary to force the pace; the Report's emphasis on extending policy coordination may reflect this underlying motive.

We can be more specific. First, the Committee enunciated a desire for more 'convergence of economic performance' (paragraph 11) as an end in itself, to which policy coordination might be a means. But the Report did not explain why we should want convergence of the 'fundamentals'. This is not an obvious goal, unless interpreted as the highest growth rate, lowest inflation rate, best income distribution, etc., among EC countries. There will be no agreement, however, on which single country has the best combination of these desiderata, so support for this sort of 'convergence' is a non-operational tautology.

On the other hand, there is a clear underlying fear of threats to EC cohesion from '*divergence*'. Since it would be difficult to make Germany become more expansionist (inflationary), fiscal 'coordination' might be seen as (i) a way of exerting pressure on Germany to compensate for its dominance of EC monetary policy (the asymmetry); (ii) a way of forcing fiscal authorities in other countries to become more German, i.e., to 'put their houses in order'. Seen in this way, we have an echo of the global macroeconomic policy attitudes of 1979–85 – the very antithesis of policy coordination (Group of Thirty, 1988, Section 2.4). This too is an implicit recognition and acceptance of asymmetry. In any case, the non-German fiscal authorities will be forced to adapt: without exchange controls, budget deficits will directly affect current-account balances, which will then exercise an unavoidable long-run constraint on fiscal policies.

Second, the Report suggests that coordination makes countries less rather than more constrained – cooperation with the collective sets the individual free. Paragraph 12 asserts that greater interdependence in goods and financial markets entails that the 'attainment of national policy objectives will become more dependent on a cooperative approach to policy-making'. The source in political philosophy is not cited, and the economic argument is also unclear. One political interpretation is practical, not philosophical: it will be necessary to gang up on Germany to get it to be more flexible, and 'policy coordination' is a shorthand for such a process. In any event, the opposite economic proposition seems more plausible: closer monetary union will mean that countries will want more fiscal freedom, not less, although increasing market integration will constrain them.

A third argument is that policy coordination is necessary to deal with international spillovers or 'repercussions' of national policies (paragraph 13). But these are partly controlled by exchange rate stabilisation itself. Moreover, the thrust of the fiscal policy rules suggested by the Report seems directed at countries with 'lax' policies, whose errors are not likely to have great spillover effects on Germany; and the proposed rules would limit only longer-run rather than short-run excesses, so the stress is in any case not on stabilisation problems. All these points in fact relate to the serious, difficult issue of asymmetry among the countries in the System. Germany is not expected to change its preferences nor its underlying economic structure, under which German growth is seen as export-led while being limited by monetary conservatism and demographic constraints.

There is a less fundamental but equally important feature of the Report's attitudes to fiscal coordination. Fiscal laxity in some countries and 'incompatible national policies' are seen to put an excessive burden on monetary policy (paragraphs 5, 12). We might interpret these remarks as a justification by the central bankers' club of their ganging up to support each other in their battles against national treasuries. Should they not find it sufficient, however, to prescribe that deficits should not be financed by central bank credit and let the capital markets discipline the fiscal authorities? The Report offers no contrary argument, and further research is doubtless necessary on this key point.

A final argument for fiscal policy coordination in the Report raises the second of our two themes: that the EC as a whole needs a fiscal and monetary mix appropriate to internal and external balance for the Community (paragraph 30). The earlier points relate to what has been called 'relative coordination' (Currie *et al.*, 1989), which focuses on exchange rate relationships and balance of payments interactions. 'Absolute coordination' refers to the overall stance of policy and the avoidance of collective or global errors of economic management. The basis of reference changes if we shift from the G-7 or G-3 to the EC, but the distinction is still valid and clear. 'Absolute coordination' and the EC's external macro policies are not unrelated to 'relative coordination' and the issue of asymmetry. One justification of asymmetry is that it is an efficient way of providing the System with a 'nominal anchor', which is an element of absolute coordination (one we shall not discuss).

3 ASYMMETRY AND HEGEMONY

Giovannini's (1989) distinction between a symmetric and an asymmetric exchange rate system rests on characterisations of the preferences of participating countries. The structure of bargaining is symmetric throughout. In the context of a simple model, we have a symmetric system when each central bank has a domestic target, say the nominal interest rate, and a foreign target, say reserves. In an asymmetric system, the central country targets its domestic nominal interest rate, while the others (periphery) target reserves. The peripheral countries give up domestic targets, and international portfolio shifts affect their interest rates but not that of the centre country.

'Hegemonic stability theory' is the related simple hypothesis that international economic stability requires a single dominant power. It conventionally starts from the alternative view that hegemony derives from unequal economic and political strength which gives the policy interaction 'game' an asymmetric structure: there is a leader that acts on the assumption that other countries will adjust to its policies, and the other countries, followers, that do in fact adjust on the assumption that the leader will not respond to their actions.

For the EMS, it is usually maintained that Germany does not have the economic or political weight vis-à-vis France and Italy to dominate as a hegemon; nor does the DM function as an important reserve currency, another possible source of hegemony. Hence the operational hypothesis is that Germany trades off growth against monetary stability, and its targets are real effective exchange rate stability and the inflation rate; while the others trade off growth against balance-of-payments equilibrium, so their targets are exchange rate stability and reserves.

Capital controls then play a key role. The strict 'rules' of the asymmetric system require peripheral countries to follow the centre's monetary policy fully, but capital controls give them some degree of monetary independence. In practice, they avoid full monetary policy 'coordination' with the centre by maintaining different degrees of sterilisation of intervention, which would not be possible with full capital market integration (Mastropasqua *et al.*, 1988). Some suggest that since the others do maintain domestic monetary independence now with capital controls, while Germany too may lose some of its autonomy when it can no longer sterilise so freely, there is in fact no asymmetry, now or prospective (De Grauwe, 1989). I cannot accept this reasoning, because there evidently does exist a difference between the two cases.

A proposition analogous to the hegemonic stability hypothesis is that fixed exchange rate regimes always operate asymmetrically. Giovannini (1989) tests this proposition. He investigates the timing of discount rate changes under the Gold Standard; uses event studies of interest rate behaviour around devaluations in the Bretton Woods and EMS periods; and tests how domestic targets varied with reserve flows under each of the systems. The data accept the asymmetry hypothesis for only two of the three – surprisingly, the evidence on Bretton Woods is weak.

Others have tested for asymmetry in the EMS: Giavazzi and Giovannini (1987, 1989); Artis and Nachane (1989); Cohen and Wyplosz (1989); and De Grauwe (1989). These tests look at relations between forward premia and offshore interest rate differentials, as well as between forward premia and domestic interest rate differentials; cross-country transmission effects between domestic interest rates and between money supplies; and cross-country relations between inflation rates and wage-setting behaviour. The evidence is mixed. I would assess it overall as supporting the centre-country role of Germany and the interpretation of it above, although the data cannot reject the hypothesis that there is some reciprocal influence of the 'periphery' on Germany.

Yet there is no such asymmetry in the rules governing the operation of the EMS – indeed, the 'divergence indicator' and the prescribed responses to its movements were specifically intended to act symmetrically. They were never implemented. The evidence shows asymmetry, and this is clearly the general perception among practitioners and the informed public. If the asymmetry lies not in the rules, nor in German hegemony, it must lie in preferences regarding policy targets.

Giavazzi and Pagano (1988) have pushed this further to suggest that the peripheral countries (or at least their central banks) wish to 'tie their hands' to fixed exchange rates in the EMS so as to be forced to follow the German monetary lead, or at least to maintain that appearance – in this way, they can 'import' the anti-inflation credibility of the German monetary authorities. (Most recently, the extreme anti-realignment position of France since mid-1988 might be so interpreted.) This may be efficient, too, insofar as it counteracts the strategic interaction (and consequent time-inconsistency problems) in the relation of domestic monetary authorities with their own public, which otherwise would generate inflation.

This is a strong form of monetary policy coordination. It would not be regarded as exceptional, however, by those observers of 'economic summitry' who have noted that there is often greater cross-country cooperation between officials in the same domain than internal cooperation between officials with different responsibilities (central bank international cooperation contrasted with domestic conflict between central Bank and finance ministry).

Melitz (1988) argues that 'monetary discipline' is not a sufficient attraction for the peripheral countries to stay in a System led by Germany; a convincing explanation must go back to the direct gains from policy cooperation. Conversely, one must also ask what are Germany's motives to stay in the EMS, apart from the initial political impetus. Giavazzi and Giovannini (1988) assert that the main benefit has come in the form of a stable real effective exchange rate for the DM. Others (e.g. Rieke, 1989) suggest German satisfaction with the general adoption of anti-inflationary policies and the role of the DM as an anchor.

Do we want asymmetry in the longer run? Herr Poehl amusingly spoke of the 'Franc fort' just at the time that the French became totally determined to keep it so. Others have less facetiously suggested everything from modelling a European central bank on the Bundesbank's structure to locating it in Frankfurt and giving it a German president; the latest version has the operational arm in London, consciously recalling the American analogy. All this confirms that asymmetry does indeed transfer an anti-inflation reputation and general conservative rectitude from Bundesbankers to other central bankers.

Perhaps this is just symbolic and short-run – surely if credibility is borrowed long enough, it is ultimately perceived as being on permanent loan, and the actual convergence of inflation rates to low levels should support a corresponding shift in attitudes. That the EMS has been asymmetric need not mean it must remain so, even if one accepts the contention that all past fixed-rate systems have been asymmetric, since according to that argument they have all been maintained by capital controls (Giovannini, 1989). These are to go. Some aspects of asymmetry must go with them – in particular, there will be less scope for sterilised intervention all around. The consequence may nevertheless be asymmetric: there is nothing to preclude total surrender of monetary sovereignty by the periphery to Germany. In a sense, however, this would have to be a much more conscious and transparent decision than tacit following of Germany hitherto. And it is not impossible that Germany will adjust somewhat too – one role for explicit policy coordination would be to bring that about.

Although discussions of asymmetry have so far focused on monetary policy, it is highly likely that the Internal Market programme will limit some aspects of German fiscal policy freedom like that of all other EC countries and hence give less scope for asymmetry. Goods market, capital market and labour market integration will enforce some degree of convergence of VAT, capital taxes, and possibly even income taxes, even without any Brussels-inspired harmonisation. But this can be overstated, as it often is by both proponents and opponents, for different reasons. We need much more research in this poorly understood area.

The major fear that must be faced squarely is that any remaining asymmetry will limit the growth potential of the periphery. The growing current account imbalances in Europe – in particular, the inexorable rise of the German surplus – may indeed motivate initiatives for explicit fiscal policy coordination (if not a substantial realignment – or perhaps both). If this were asymmetric, it would be unacceptably deflationary in its overall impact. Policy coordination and 'convergence' cannot act as a permanent drag on the growth of the periphery.

This line of argument assumes, however, that the imbalances cannot be financed indefinitely by voluntary capital flows. Financial integration may offer an escape from the constraint – a full substitute for policy coordination – if it facilitates the 'automatic' accommodation of current account imbalances by private capital flows, as in a monetary union with sufficiently flexible factor prices. We know very little about how to promote this outcome consciously, other than with relatively crude tools of 'regional policy'; this should be a high priority topic for research and policy discussions.

To the extent that asymmetry does persist as (we assume) exchange rates become more rigid, will not progressive currency substitution tend to eliminate it? Indeed, we might conjecture this will affect both the internal policy of the Bundesbank and its long-run capacity to exercise leadership in the EMS. Currency substitution, too, is a key area for future research on the evolution of European monetary institutions.

Finally, the greatest imponderable: the effects of the eventual entry of sterling into the exchange rate mechanism of the EMS. At a stroke,

Frankfurt is no longer the dominant financial centre of the System, at least in the short run; and conscious monetary and fiscal policy coordination both become much more complex. Asymmetry disappears, at least in its existing form. This might be a decisive argument for letting exchange rate targetting serve indefinitely as the surrogate for explicit policy coordination.

4 ABSOLUTE POLICY COORDINATION AND EC EXTERNAL MACROECONOMIC POLICY

This is a much less well explored area, and we can be correspondingly brief, although the issues are of great importance for research and policy-making. A fixed exchange rate system may enforce policy coordination within a regional bloc like the EC, but the EMS is not global for any practical purpose. We must still consider how policies at the aggregate level interact with those of countries external to the system. This raises problems of both relative and absolute policy coordination within the EMS and in a global context.

The EMS is just one component of a wider set of agreements on trade, industrial and agricultural policies among EC member countries. It is often argued that many of those other agreements themselves require exchange rate stability to function properly, hence the need for discipline and the EMS. An alternative view is that it is easier to get agreement in the EMS (or on any other single area of policy) when it is possible to offer trade-offs in other areas – this is the sort of bargaining that led, for example, to the Bonn summit accord in 1978. It is relevant not only within the EC but also in its dealings with the rest of the world. EC exchange rate policy is closely related to EC trade and agricultural policies, and any intra-EC policy coordination needed to get a common external macro policy must take this into account, as well as the possibility that EC/US/Japan negotiations might do so too.

One reason for absolute policy coordination is simple and clear. Tighter economic integration will make uncoordinated responses to external (from outside the EC) shocks more costly, because the spillovers that are ignored in framing those responses will be greater (Wyplosz, 1989). In general, both fiscal and monetary policy coordination will be desirable.

A second argument is somewhat more involved. Aggregate EC monetary policy will have to be devoted to fixing the aggregate EC effective exchange rate. Therefore a more active fiscal policy will be needed to give internal balance (stabilisation), and it will have to be used consistently, with coordination if not necessarily convergence (Kenen, 1988).

A third reason is subtle and requires formal demonstration, to which the reader is referred (Cohen and Wyplosz, 1989). The essential point is that the need to take account of the trade balance of the exchange rate union as a whole generates an externality in the interaction among its members as they adjust to external (from outside the EC) shocks. Monetary union and the constraints it imposes set only the aggregate inflation rate of the Community. If external shocks affect members asymmetrically, or if such shocks are transitory, responses to them taking account only of the exchange rate rules and corresponding monetary constraints will result in an inappropriate real exchange rate and trade balance for the union as a whole.

There have been some detailed discussions of the 'assignment rules' that the EMS might use to bring about both internal and external balance (Russo, 1989; and Russo and Tullio, 1988). These follow similar lines to those considered in the literature on international monetary reform and exchange rate management (see Miller, Eichengreen and Portes, 1989).

Both the 'trade balance externality' and EC assignment rules need further study. Such efforts should not ignore, however, the fact that one impulse behind calls for absolute policy coordination among EMS members is the same as a fundamental motive for moves towards economic and monetary union itself: the desire that the EC should be able to negotiate as a macroeconomic unit with the US and Japan, just as it does as a trading partner; and that it should thereby increase its negotiating strength, create a currency that will function jointly with the dollar and yen as a reserve currency, etc.

Any such approach towards comparable bargaining power will mean, however, that the EC will not be *able* to set the ECU/$ or ECU/yen rate unilaterally. That too will have to be the subject of a direct bargain, which may be quite symmetrical. There is no '(n-1) rule' in a symmetrical game as it is played in practice.

References

Aglietta, M. (1989) 'Stabilité dynamique et transformation des regimes monetaires internationaux', paper presented to EHESS colloquium, Paris.

Artis, M. and Nachane, D. (1989) 'Wages and Prices in Europe: a Test of the German Leadership Thesis', CEPR Discussion Paper no. 296.

Bryant, R. and Portes, R. (eds) (1987) *Global Macroeconomics* (London: Macmillan).

Bryant, R., Currie, D., Frenkel, J., Masson, P. and Portes, R. (eds) (1989) *Macroeconomic Policy in an Interdependent World* (Washington, DC: IMF).

Buiter, W. and Marston, R. (eds) (1985) *International Macroeconomic Policy Coordination* (Cambridge University Press).

Cohen, D. (1989) 'The costs and benefits of a European currency', in M. de Cecco and A. Giovannini (eds) *A European Central Bank? Perspectives on Monetary Unification after Ten Years of the EMS* (Cambridge University Press).

Cohen, D. and Wyplosz, C. (1989) 'European Monetary Union: an Agnostic View', CEPR Discussion Paper no. 306, in R. Bryant *et al. Macroeconomic Policy in an Interdependent World* (Washington, DC: IMF).

Currie, D., Hughes Hallett, A. and Holtham, C. (1989) 'The Theory and Practice of International Economic Policy Coordination: Does Coordination Pay?', in R. Bryant *et al. Macroeconomic Policy in an Interdependent World* (Washington, DC: IMF).

De Cecco, M. and Giovannini, A. (eds) (1989) *A European Central Bank? Perspectives on Monetary Unification After Ten Years of the EMS* (Cambridge University Press).

De Grauwe, P. (1989) 'Is the European Monetary System a DM-zone?', CEPR Discussion Paper no. 297.

Eichengreen, B. and Portes, R. (1987) 'The Anatomy of Financial Crises', in R. Portes and A. Swoboda, *Threats to International Financial Stability* (Cambridge University Press).

Feldstein, M. (1988) 'Thinking about International Economic Coordination', *Journal of Economic Perspectives* 2, 3–13.

Giavazzi, F. (1989) 'The Exchange Rate Question in Europe', CEPR Discussion Paper no. 298, in R. Bryant *et al., Macroeconomic Policy in an Interdependent World* (Washington, DC: IMF).

Giavazzi, F. and Giovannini, A. (1987) 'Models of the EMS: Is Europe a Greater Deutsch mark area?', in R. Bryant and R. Portes, *Global Macroeconomics* (London: Macmillan).

Giavazzi, F. and Giovannini, A. (1988) 'Can the EMS be Exported? Lessons from Ten Years of Monetary Policy Coordination in Europe', CEPR Discussion Paper no. 285.

Giavazzi, F. and Giovannini, A. (1989) *Limiting Exchange Rate Flexibility: the European Monetary System* (Cambridge, Mass., MIT Press).

Giavazzi, F., Micossi, S. and Miller, M. (eds) (1988) *The European Monetary System* (Cambridge University Press).

Giavazzi, F. and Pagano, M. (1988) 'The Advantage of Tying One's Hands: EMS Discipline and Central Bank Credibility', *European Economic Review*, 32, 1055–82.

Giovannini, A. (1989) 'How Do Fixed Exchange Rate Regimes Work? Evidence from the Gold Standard, Bretton Woods and the EMS', in M. Miller *et al.*,

Blueprints for Exchange Rate Management (New York and London: Academic Press).

Group of Thirty (1988) *International Macroeconomic Policy Coordination* (New York and London).

Hughes Hallett, A., Holtham, G. and Hutson, G. (1989), 'Exchange Rate Targetting as Surrogate International Cooperation', in M. Miller *et al.*, *Blueprints for Exchange Rate Management* (New York and London: Academic Press).

Kenen, P. (1988) Panel discussion, in F. Giavazzi *et al.*, *The European Monetary System* (Cambridge University Press).

Levine, P., Currie, D. and Gaines, J. (1989) 'The Use of Simple Rules for International Policy Agreements', in M. Miller *et al.*, *Blueprints for Exchange Rate Management* (New York and London: Academic Press).

Mastropasqua, C., Micossi, S. and Rinaldi, R. (1988) 'Interventions, Sterilisation and Monetary Policy in EMS Countries 1979–87', in F. Giavazzi *et al.*, *The European Monetary System* (Cambridge University Press).

Melitz, J. (1988) 'Monetary Discipline and Cooperation in the European Monetary System: A Synthesis', in F. Giavazzi *et al.*, *The European Monetary System* (Cambridge University Press).

Miller, M., Eichengreen, B. and Portes, R. (eds) (1989) *Blueprints for Exchange Rate Management* (New York and London: Academic Press).

Portes, R. and Swoboda, A. (eds) (1987) *Threats to International Financial Stability* (Cambridge University Press).

Rieke, W. (1989) Panel discussion, in M. De Cecco and A. Giovannini, *A European Central Bank?* (Cambridge University Press).

Russo, M. (1989) Panel discussion, in M. De Cecco and A. Giovannini, *A European Central Bank?* (Cambridge University Press).

Russo, M. and Tullio, G. (1988) 'Monetary Policy Coordination within the European Monetary System: Is There a Rule?', in F. Giavazzi *et al.*, *The European Monetary System* (Cambridge University Press).

Thygesen, N. (1989) 'Panel discussion, in M. De Cecco and A. Giovannini, *A European Central Bank?* (Cambridge University Press).

Wyplosz, C. (1989) Discussion of Cohen, in M. De Cecco and A. Giovannini, *A European Central Bank?* (Cambridge University Press).

12 The EMS, the Dollar and the World Economy

J.A. Kregel

1 INTRODUCTION

Despite the sayings of savants, history does seem to repeat itself. Or at least it must seem so to anyone familiar with international economic conditions in the late 1950s when the two principal problems facing the United States in the international sphere were its international payments deficit and the threat the creation of the European Common Market posed to its elimination. The US is still struggling with the problems surrounding the adjustment of its foreign accounts and in this regard is still concerned about the impact of the Common Market, now under the fear that the 'Single Market' will become a 'Fortress Europe'.

The relation of the development of the EEC and US payments imbalances appears as a perennial cause of difficulty, in particular as far as European Monetary Union (EMU) is concerned. This was certainly true for both the late 1960s when adherence to the Bretton Woods Agreements hampered discussion of an independent EMU, and then again in the late 1960s when events in the US impeded implementation of the Werner report, and finally in the late 1970s when fear of exchange rate and monetary instability caused by dollar weakness led to the creation of the European Monetary System (EMS). However, the current debates over the continued monetary and financial integration required for implementation of the Single European Act seem to be dominated by purely domestic European concerns. After dominating discussion and action, the problem of formulating a common European dollar policy seems to have become a secondary issue. One explanation is that given the present, or any of the likely future, form of the EMS there is little likelihood of formulating a common dollar policy.

As already noted, the problems which are being discussed today are not much different from those faced by the Bretton Woods system at the end of the 1960s, when the US sought to adjust its external position in order to avoid internal policy adjustment and the EEC countries failed to agree on a common response, other than refusing exchange rate adjustment the US requested, and which it could thus achieve only by dissolving the System. Today, the EEC economies are still in a fixed-rate system, the US is still trying to adjust its external position without change in domestic policy, and the problem is still the appropriate rates of exchange of the EEC countries relative to the dollar.

The breakdown of the Bretton Woods System thus postponed the envisaged EMU and led to two ersatz Bretton Woods-type systems, the Snake and the EMS. Although the latter has been more successful than the former in promoting convergence of economic performance, neither seems to have been any more successful in providing the basis for a common dollar policy. This raises the question of whether the problem is not to be found in the framework of the monetary system adopted as much as in the willingness of the EEC countries to act conjointly relative to the dollar.

The source of the problem may be found in the role of capital flows, both within the community and between the community and the rest of the dollar world. This was the main source of difficulty faced by the Bretton Woods system, it has been a source of differential impact on the EEC countries, and it is perceived to be the main difficulty that the reform of the EMS will face. From this point of view the possibility of a common dollar policy becomes intimately linked with the possibility of creating a system in which a high degree of regional and international capital mobility might serve to stabilise exchange rates and cause economic performance to converge rather than the opposite. There seem to be two ready examples: the pre-First World War gold standard and the pre-1979 US financial system. Aspects of both will be drawn on to try to identify an alternative system.

2 EUROPEAN MONETARY INTEGRATION AS A RESPONSE TO US POLICY

It must be presumed that the original Treaty of Rome did not foresee any formal European Monetary Union or European Monetary Fund or monetary authority because of a possible conflict with the already existing international commitments of the member countries to the Bretton Woods Agreements. Nonetheless it did make ample provision for free movements of capital within the Community (in 1957 none of the member countries had yet satisfied Article IV, section 4 of the Bretton Woods treaty) although these were not part of the original philosophy of Bretton Woods.

Despite the fact that capital flows had by then come to cause great disruption, the Werner Report reiterated this commitment to free capital flows, but also recognised that this could be achieved only through the creation of a single community currency or a formal monetary union administered by some sort of regional European IMF.

At the same time, the EEC moved towards its first formulation of a common dollar policy through the reduction in fluctuation margins relative to the dollar which produced the Snake.[1] The argument in favour of reducing fluctuation bands was based on the fact that a fixed band relative to the dollar produced a band of European cross rates which was twice as large. By stabilising relative to the dollar European central banks were thus making the dollar less variable and thus more attractive to hold than their own currencies as a means of payment and in reserves. The reduction of intervention margins relative to the dollar to 0.6 per cent was agreed in March 1971, before the declaration of dollar inconvertibility. Neither the Werner recommendations, nor the reductions in margins, were undertaken; the events of May and August 1971 and October 1973 produced a series of expedient serpentine monetary structures representing a joint EEC float relative to the dollar with enlarged margins (of which the current EMS must be considered as one). All of them bore high resemblance to the exchange rate regime of Bretton Woods and none of them imposed free movements of capital, nor created a European IMF. Oddly enough, the conflict between regional and international monetary commitments remained, for the IMF anachronistically continued to live on after the death of Article IV which was its raison d'être.[2]

Thus the EEC may be simply repeating the Bretton Woods experience as it attempts to create a European monetary organisation to manage a fixed exchange rate system as part of its attempt to achieve free capital movements by mid-1990 and a single market in financial services by 1993. Indeed, most of the discussion of the restructuring of the EMS necessary to facilitate the completion of the Single Market Act concerns the question of the possibility of free capital flows within the community and a system of reduced fluctuation bands in the absence of a central institution or of a common currency. As Paul De Grauwe has reminded us, the arguments recall the division of 'economists' and 'monetarists' within the Werner Committee, or those who consider policy convergence the prerequisite for monetary union versus those who consider monetary union as the prerequisite for policy convergence. The former position is held by the Bundesbank which considers that a European Central Bank which would centralise the decision over money creation in each member country would violate German law requiring it to stabilise the internal value of the Mark, while the UK rejects a common currency because it would require a centralised Community fiscal policy to offset regional (national?) discrepancies in economic performance implying both 'government interference' in the market and loss of national sovereignty in fiscal policy.

Now the striking thing about these discussions from an historical perspective is that they are centred almost totally on problems internal to the EEC and the EMS, and fail to recall the basic fact that the EMS was born as a reaction to the breakdown of the Bretton Woods System which was in large part the result of US-European conflicts over policy objectives on the one hand and the changes in the ranking of US internal objectives which led to changes in the United States' monetary policy in the 1970s on the other.

3 A COMMON DOLLAR POLICY? – THE TRADITIONAL VIEW

Despite a long tradition of critical analysis of the operation of the Gold Standard, economists' thinking about the structure of the International Monetary System tends to be dominated by the paradigm of the traditional price-specie-flow adjustment mechanism based on a 100 per cent gold-based domestic money supply and the quantity theory of money as expressed in the so-called 'rules of the game'. But central banks, who usually have the responsibility for operating international payments systems, seem never to have either believed or followed these rules. This is not surprising, if, as De Cecco (1987) suggests, the stability of the gold standard was in fact maintained by the actions of private banks such as Rothschilds and Morgan.

In most interpretations, modern fixed exchange rate systems are considered to be replicas of the Gold Standard. The necessity of preserving fixed rates in the presence of limited foreign exchange reserves provides the 'policy discipline' required to make central banks adjust their domestic money supplies as if they followed the Gold Standard 'rules of the game'. Both Bretton Woods and the EMS are thus considered to preserve the 'rules of the game' adjustment system.

The stability provided by the operation of this adjustment mechanism implies variability of each country's supply of money. But, if prices are determined by money growth, international stability precludes price stability as a domestic policy target. Domestic price stability as an objective of policy can then be achieved in two different ways.

- Eliminating the external constraint of fixed exchange rates, and substituting an internal monetary growth rule. If all countries adopt the same money supply rule (or agree to the same target rate of growth of international money), then exchange rates and the international system will be stable. This is the basis of McKinnon's (see e.g. 1979) position on international monetary reform.
- Maintaining fixed exchange rates, but substituting a 'price rule' or price 'anchor', such as gold was presumed to play, for the 'quantity rule' on the growth of the money supply. This was the reasoning behind the 'supply-siders'' call to reintroduce gold in the United States at the beginning of the Reagan administration (cf. Miles, 1984).

  It would be possible, however, to eliminate this internal price anchor[3] by keeping a fixed price rule against the *n*th currency if that currency had stable prices. In this case if the *n*-1 countries in the system all fix to the *n*th country they all have variable, but constrained, wages and prices which 'converge' on the stable norm set by the *n*th country as the *n*-1 countries in the system must still abide by the 'rules of the game'.

In the end the first (monetarist) solution won favour in the US which embraced flexible interest rates and exchange rates and money control, while in Europe the second solution was adopted in the form of the EMS experiment of an island of fixed exchange and interest rates with the Bundesbank providing the anchor in a sea of dollar turbulence.

An interpretation of the operation of the EMS along these lines has recently been given by Russo and Tullio (1988), who describe it as a system of fixed exchange rates in which 'the money supply cannot be exogenously determined by the monetary authorities of individual countries without interfering with the balance of payments adjustment process. This is the more true the greater the degree of capital mobility in the system'. Such 'a properly functioning fixed or adjustable exchange rate system needs a rule governing inflation', which in the case of the EMS is provided by the '*n*th country (the "leader")' i.e. Germany, which has 'provided an anchor' and enjoys 'a greater degree of monetary autonomy than the other members' (ibid., p. 36). They conclude that when the EMS has functioned well, it is because Germany has used this autonomy to follow a fixed monetary growth rule, imposing the operation of the 'rules of the game' adjustment mechanism on the other members.

This is the interpretation of the EMS as a DM zone, in which asymmetry allows the Bundesbank to follow a money supply rule because the *n*-1 ERM central banks relinquish control over their domestic price and monetary policies. In exchange for increased monetary autonomy and control over the 'price anchor', Germany (just as the US under Bretton Woods) gives up control over its exchange rate within the ERM. But while the *n*-1 countries take on responsibility for intervention to fix prices relative to the DM, it is the Bundesbank which determines the rate of exchange of each of them relative to the US dollar. In such conditions it is impossible to have a 'common' EEC policy relative to the dollar other than that determined by the Bundesbank which determines the divergence between EMS and US inflation rates.

But, if the other EMS ERM central banks accept the central role of Germany because it provides the stable price anchor which ensures the efficient operation of the balance of payments adjustment process within the EEC, this implies that, given US policy, Germany cannot have an independent dollar policy since any attempt by the Bundesbank to influence the DM/$ exchange rate will mean giving up strict adherence to its money growth rule which will damage its credibility and its ability to play the role of the price anchor within the EMS. In this interpretation of the 'rules of the game' with an internal price anchor based on a quantitative money supply rule, the only possible common policy is no policy at all: a free float against the dollar.[4]

On this view a common policy could be achieved only by replacing the German internal 'quantity' anchor with an external 'price' anchor, such as the adoption of a single European currency or a European monetary authority determining policy vis-à-vis the dollar. There would then no longer be a conflict between community monetary growth and dollar policy, since both would by definition be 'common'. The reason that this is impossible is that the Bundesbank could not accept it, being caught in the bind of having at one and the same time to abide by legislation that requires it to participate in the EMS and to control the internal value of the currency. The only way the Bundesbank can satisfy both requirements, i.e. control its money supply and remain part of a fixed exchange rate system, is if it is the *n*th country 'leader' without responsibility for supporting its exchange rate relative to the other members.

If this were the only interpretation of the operation of fixed rate systems that would be the end of the story; the conclusions would be that under the current structure of the EMS ERM there is no possible 'common' dollar policy, and there is no reform of the system which the Bundesbank could legally accept which would allow a common dollar policy. If the EMS is to be judged on its ability to stabilise the variations in the dollar by formulating a common dollar policy, it is condemned to follow in the footsteps of Bretton Woods.

Yet, just as most central banks under the gold standard, it is quite clear that at the very least the Bundesbank does not behave as if it believes this traditional account; it does actively intervene to influence the DM/$ exchange rate in conflict with the application of a monetary rule, and in order to affect the exchange rate of the DM within the ERM. This is most probably because the tradition of monetary policy built up in Germany in the 1960s is based on what Giersch (1970) has called the 'direct mechanism' of international price transmission in contrast to the impact of the 'liquidity inflow through the balance of payments surplus' which had been the official position until convertibility at the end of the 1950s. In this view there are direct and indirect influences of a balance of payments surplus on domestic prices. The direct effect comes through the operation of the law of one price: if demand for domestic goods rises it is because they are cheaper than those abroad and their prices will thus increase; a revaluation allows their prices to rise in foreign currency terms without impact on prices in home currency. The indirect effect is through the increase in demand due to an export-led boom which will eventually increase wages and prices. It is easier to cut off this excess demand by revaluing the exchange rate quickly rather than by raising interest rates, which only aggravates speculative flows and produces an even larger revaluation.

But this suggests that it is the exchange rate and not money growth which is the instrument which is the preferred intermediate target for the policy objective of price stability. But if the Bundesbank is controlling exchange rates, it is not controlling monetary policy. And, if this is the case, the automatic adjustment assumed to occur with the Bundesbank setting the money growth rule is brought into question.

4 A COMMON DOLLAR POLICY? AN ALTERNATIVE VIEW

Long ago, Robert Triffin (1946–7) observed that the Gold Standard system, as interpreted by proponents of the 'rules of the game', was incompatible with a domestic policy objective of price stability. The point had already been made by Hume when he pointed out in contrast to mercantilist doctrine that in free markets and in the absence of controls on the export of gold, a country could not control its domestic gold supply; if prices are determined by the supply of gold, then the inability to control gold implied an inability to control domestic prices.

Triffin also noted that domestic price stability only became an explicit objective of policy with the creation of the modern policy-active central bank, in part because application of the 'rules of the game' in a modern gold-backed fractional reserve banking system produces greater variability in the money supply and greater instability in the price level.[5]

This suggests an increasing conflict between domestic price stability and the operation of the international adjustment mechanism which is supposed to produce international stability as financial systems become more sophisticated. Or, turning the proposition around, a central bank which attempted to keep to a fixed money growth rule would find that it was faced with increased variability in its payments position and thus increased variability in domestic incomes creating increasing pressure to abandon strict adherence to the 'rules'. Now this is precisely the paradox which would be faced by a central bank with a legal obligation to stabilise the domestic purchasing power of the currency in a country that is part of a fixed exchange rate regime: either it cannot participate in a fixed exchange rate regime or it cannot follow the rules of the game.

But we also know that under the gold standard, discretionary monetary policy was employed, or at least, as Triffin notes, it was used in the 'leader', the UK, in a period in which active countercyclical fiscal policy was unknown. Triffin argues that this is because the gold standard adjustment mechanism did not function as suggested by the traditional description of the 'rules of the game' which was based on a fallacy of composition, analysing the disequilibrium conditions of one country relative to those of the rest of the world presumed to have remained in equilibrium, and which failed to recognise the role of financial institutions in counteracting the forces leading to relative money supply and price adjustment before they occurred.

Triffin instead suggests that adjustment took place via improvements in the top country terms of trade (e.g. a rise in export prices relative to import prices) rather than vice versa, while financial factors directly offset the impact of money on prices envisaged by the traditional rules of the game. Thus a deterioration in the UK payments position would bring about a rise in interest rates and capital inflows which more than offset the fall in the money supply due to the deterioration on trade account. In such conditions, even if one believes that prices are influenced by changes in the money supply, they move in the opposite direction to that suggested in the 'rules of the game'. Instead of prices and current accounts moving in opposite directions internally and internationally, prices, incomes and foreign balances in all countries in the system tended to move together, as the fall in British overseas lending following on the rise in interest rates reduced international investment and incomes in a cycle coordinated from the centre (cf. Triffin, 1964).[6]

The rise in interest rates would have a larger effect on prices in the periphery and on prices in international commodity markets, bringing about a fall in import prices relative to export prices and an improvement in the British terms of trade which brought an improvement in the trade account.[7]

5 AN ALTERNATIVE PROPOSAL

Under the traditional interpretation of the gold standard adjustment mechanism generally applied to fixed rate systems, capital flows impede operation of the rules of the game because they offset the automatic impact of current account balances on the domestic monetary conditions. Free movement of capital, due to be introduced in mid-1990, is also seen to be a threat to the stability of the EMS system because it will impede the supposed automatic adjustment mechanism imposed by the monetary discipline implied by observing fixed rates.

But the alternative interpretation of the Gold Standard looks upon capital flows as an aid to international adjustment. This view, which grew out of the scepticism first expressed by Taussig and Whale concerning the traditional operation of the gold standard and developed by, among others, Knapp (1943), Triffin (1946–7), Bloomfield (1959), Morgenstern (1959), Ingram (1962) and De Cecco (1974), is based on the observation that the gold standard functioned under conditions of a high degree of international financial integration, free movements of capital, stable exchange rates and the absence of exchange controls, while there was no strict adherence to the 'rules of the game' and 'no definite evidence that "monetary discipline" exerted significant "longer run" effects of an equilibrating sort upon the balance of payments ... as is so often attributed to it' (Bloomfield, 1959, p. 61).

This suggests that there is some difference between the Gold Standard system and both Bretton Woods and the EMS. For present purposes two are of importance. The first is that the gold standard was not a 'fixed exchange rate' system in the same sense as Bretton Woods because countries fixed the mint price of gold in terms of their domestic currencies, not the price of foreign currencies. This was a purely domestic guarantee, similar to the legal responsibility of the Bundesbank; it was not an international guarantee. Guaranteeing fixed price convertibility into gold and convertibility into the dollar, Bretton Woods' ersatz gold, are not the same thing. There was no necessity for the central bank to set a fixed price for foreign currency and to support it out of reserves of foreign currency. Indeed, it has often been observed how little gold the Bank of England actually held for this purpose, relying instead on short- and long-term capital movements to stabilise the exchanges. Instead, the guarantee to foreign exchange stability was the primary responsibility of, and carried out by, the private international banking system. This observation forms one of the main points of the alternative interpretation – a system with free capital flows can only produce stability if it is the private banks, rather than the central bank, which bear primary responsibility for exchange stability.

It is currently popular to look to the US Federal Reserve System for the model for the European Central Bank, with each EC Central Bank becoming the equivalent to a US Federal Reserve District Bank. After all, the US has a unified currency system without regional balance of payments difficulties: the monetary liabilities issued by each district bank are freely convertible at a fixed rate of exchange, and thus perfect substitutes. But this would be to miss the point of the US system, which, like most monetary systems, is a composite system of 'public' banks (the district banks), which issue 'public liabilities' (central bank or base money), and private banks, which issue private liabilities (deposit accounts) which are not perfect substitutes either for each other, or for public liabilities. But they are considered to be near-perfect substitutes by the public because the private banks guarantee a one-to-one parity or exchange rate between their own private currency (private deposit liabilities) and the public liabilities (central bank money) which means that they are also perfect substitutes for other private liabilities which offer the same guarantee. The perfect substitution or fixed 'rate of exchange' of major importance in the US financial system is not that between the 'public' liabilities issued by the various District Reserve banks (e.g. between the dollars issued by the New York Fed and the San Francisco Fed); it is the fixed rate of exchange (the one-for-one parity) between the private liabilities of Citibank in New York and Bank of America in California.

How do banks assure this one-to-one parity? By guaranteeing the convertibility of their private liabilities at a 'fixed' one-to-one rate for public liabilities. To be able to make good on this guarantee private banks hold reserves of public liabilities (their primary reserves) or of assets readily convertible into public liabilities (secondary reserves). It is the free movement of these assets between commercial banks within the US which assures the perfect substitution of private liabilities as a fixed exchange rate system.

If the EMS is to replicate the US system it will then be necessary to guarantee not only the convertibility of the 'public' liabilities of the EEC central banks at fixed rates, it will also require guaranteeing the convertibility of the private liabilities of the commercial banks at fixed rates of exchange. As already noted, within the US system this latter fixed partity is not guaranteed by the District bank (except as the lender of last resort), but by the commercial banks themselves. Neither should it be guaranteed by EEC central banks, but should be the responsibility of the commercial banks through investment in primary and secondary reserves composed of the public and private liabilities of all the EEC countries.

This raises the second basic difference. It is often said that gold served as the primary means of international settlement and thus as the primary reserve asset under the Gold Standard and that the dollar simply took over this dual role. But, under the gold standard system a purely private liability (although it was as good as gold or gilt edged), the foreign exchange bill, served this purpose. Indeed, not only did governments not guarantee the value in terms of foreign currency of their domestic money, there was no market for foreign currency or deposits other than the market for a particular short-term financial asset – the foreign exchange bill. Gold was neither the major source of reserves, nor means of payment in the system; it was the foreign exchange bill which provided an endogenous, perfectly flexible, privately supplied means of payment for the international system. It was only to the extent that the conditions in the foreign exchange bill market affected the domestic convertibility of bank notes that gold reserves were necessary.

It was the role of the foreign exchange 'finance' bill to provide the short-term capital movements which assured that the rules of the game were never followed, since any deterioration of the foreign exchanges (an excess supply of sterling bills in the foreign exchange bill market) could be offset by small movements in international interest rate differentials in favour of London which would make it more attractive to hold funds in London. This would reduce the bills drawn on London, which reversed the excess supply of sterling bills in the foreign exchange bill market. It was profit motivated arbitrage, not price fixing, that provided the basis of stability.

If these changes were not sufficient to restore equilibrium they would work through the discount market, eventually driving the banks to the Bank of England, which raised the discount rate, and drove up long-term lending rates. This would have two effects, the rise in long rates reduced long-term capital outflows and thus financing for foreign investment; the rise in short rates reduced the bills drawn on London and thus reduced short-term outflows as well as raising the financing costs for importers and the holding costs for commodity speculators, reducing the inflow of imports and releasing speculative commodity stocks, driving down international commodity prices – thus the reduction in the international level of investment and the improvement in the UK terms of trade observed by Triffin.

This is only a sketch of how the system operated; in the present context the important factor is the role of the exchange bill as the primary short-term financial asset which provided the initial equilibrating (non-rules of the game) capital flows in the adjustment mechanism.

There are thus two elements that we may take from the alternative view of the operation of the gold standard and which we find partially reproduced in the US regional system. First, it is private financial institutions, and the liabilities they issue, which form an important part of the mechanism that insures exchange stability, and second, this mechanism functions because financial institutions hold stocks of privately produced short-term financial liabilities of institutions in other currency regions.

To introduce these factors into the EMS, private banks in each country would be required to offer transactions accounts which could serve as means of payment in any ERM country. They would then have to guarantee the parity (not a one-to-one parity, but that given by the bilateral rate, or by the ECU rate) of their private deposits with private deposits of banks in other ERM countries. How might they insure this parity? Precisely as US banks do, by holding reserves which can be converted into those liabilities (reserves at central banks or correspondent deposits with foreign financial institutions) or foreign government securities. Thus, a typical Italian bank would hold, as part of its primary reserves, deposits with a German correspondent, and as secondary reserves, German short-term government debt or other liquid DM paper. More importantly, German banks would hold Italian deposits and government short-term debt as secondary reserves.

Alternatively, the banks could guarantee the parity of their liabilities in ECU, holding reserves of the basket of currencies making up the ECU, or private ECU or Italian government ECU assets (interestingly, the majority of foreign purchases of Italian government debt has been in ECU-denominated debt).

An imbalance in payments, say an Italian deficit relative to Germany, would mean that Italian banks would sell German financial assets to meet the excess of Italian payments in Germany over German payments in Italy. This would increase deposits at German banks and reduce them in Italian banks, shifting the short-term interest rate differential in favour of Italy. German banks would then be expected to increase their holdings of Italian short term assets, creating a demand for lira deposits to offset the initial excess supply. Central banks need not be directly involved in supporting the fixed exchange rates, but would always have to be present to support their own domestic banks' ability to preserve their one-to-one parity with the domestic currency by borrowing and lending domestic debt in the open market. In this way capital flows could be part of an automatic, profit-driven arbitrage mechanism which would allow free capital flows at fixed rates of exchange.

This mechanism implies that monetary unification should include active measures to diversify the asset portfolios of private financial institutions at the same time as moves are made permanently to fix rates with zero fluctuation bands. This can be achieved not by forbidding but rather by encouraging domestic banks to offer deposit accounts suitable as a means of payment throughout the EEC. Initially banks may offer guarantees of convertibility within the existing 2.25 per cent bands (or perhaps even slightly greater initially). Absolutely fixed rates did not even exist under the gold standard; convertible deposits might be expected to be traded within 'deposit points', similar to the gold points and to represent bank changes.

Banks would not have direct access to central banks' reserves which means that the central banks could no longer intervene in official fixings, although they might want to trade at zero fluctuation bands among themselves. Foreign exchange reserves could be applied for at the 'reserve window', just as domestic reserves are applied for at the 'discount window', at a penalty rate over the fixed rate. In order to meet foreign commitments banks would then either have to sell their foreign assets or increase their borrowing abroad. This should bring about changes in interest rates which produce stabilising capital flows.

This proposal is in its essentials very similar to one that was proposed by Ingram (1962) for the Atlantic Community and it is in this respect that it is interesting for its application to the problem of the common dollar policy. All that needs to be added to Ingram's original proposal is the recognition of the role played by endogenously-created private financial liabilities (the foreign exchange bill) in the gold standard adjustment system, and the suggestion that this role might be played by private ECU-denominated liabilities within an EMS revised as suggested above.

If all private financial institutions restricted their bilateral parity commitments for their private assets to domestic EEC transactions, and carried out all their extra-EEC transactions in private ECU it would be possible to concentrate dollar policy on the ECU/$ exchange rate. This could be done in two ways. Either by allowing the private and the official ECU/$ rate to diverge, producing private arbitrage possibilities, or by operating in the forward market for the ECU to influence private bank holdings. In this way the entire financial resources of the EEC would be involved in any movements of US monetary policy and it would have similar impacts on all EEC countries.

6 CAVEATS

This proposal still does not meet the main difficulties of the Bundesbank, but it does limit its responsibility to preserving the internal rate of exchange between German banks' private liabilities and its own liabilities. It also provides the possibility of monetary union without introducing either a European Central Bank or a unified currency, although it would certainly be more efficient to do so. The possibility of creating a common policy in this case comes by recognising that if portfolio integration of dollar assets were as complete as that of EEC assets the resulting dollar rate would then be a truly common response of a unified and fully integrated European financial market.

Notes

1. In fact the snake had its origin in the European Monetary Agreement which replaced the European Payments Union in 1958 and set fluctuations relative to the dollar at plus or minus 0.75 per cent.
2. It is also important that throughout this period there was marked divergence between France and Germany in terms of their willingness to take measures which might have an impact on the Atlantic Alliance and make the US hesitant to play an active role in European defence.
3. The most sophisticated proposals, cf. Miles (1984), call for both a spot and a forward price anchor, or a composite commodity or index anchor.
4. This is, of course, no different from the problems originally caused by dollar instability in terms of the differential effects caused by international speculative flows on Germany's exchange rate relative to the other EEC

countries and which led to the creation of the EMS in order to form a 'European' dollar policy. It is not surprising that it continued under the fixed rates within the ERM of the EMS; Giavazzi and Giovannini (1986) eventually gave statistical expression to the German concerns on this point.

5. This is because under the gold standard the change in the domestic (gold) circulation would be exactly equal to the size of the payments surplus or deficit, while in a modern fiduciary system the total means of payment will increase or decrease by a multiple of the surplus or deficit which depends on the proportion of gold backing for the note issue and the size of the money multiplier. This point as far as it relates to the money multiplier had already been made by Hayek in his *Monetary Nationalism* (1937).
6. This is, of course, a very similar experience to that of Germany after 1960, when attempts to tighten monetary policy simply brought capital inflows which more than offset the initial restrictive policy. It was this experience which led to the adoption of exchange rate policy as a substitute for monetary policy. Giersch notes that the Bundesbank could only control monetary conditions when the US was acting in the same direction. This also helps to explain why a strong dollar makes the EMS more stable: it makes it easier for the Bundesbank to operate an independent monetary policy, given acceptable movements in exchange rates. But it is not the effect of the strong dollar as such, rather the fact that when monetary policy is tighter in the US than in Germany it gives the Bundesbank the possibility to tighten without offsetting capital flows. It also explains why the weak dollar of 1987 onwards has not produced greater difficulties for the EMS, since for most of this period US monetary policy has been tighter than in Germany and Germany has only moved when the US has tightened first. Thus the impact of the German money supply rule on the other members depends crucially on international monetary conditions. The common dollar policy thus depends on the success of German monetary policy, which in turn depends on whether US monetary policy is compatible or contradicts that in Germany. This is a very weak foundation upon which to build a common European policy to deal with undesirable movements in US policy.
7. This gives an explanation of Germany's post-1973 success in adjusting to the oil crisis by using revaluation to offset deterioration in the terms of trade as well as the persistent German surpluses despite continued nominal revaluations.

References

Bloomfield, A. (1959) *Monetary Policy Under the International Gold Standard – 1880–1914* (Federal Reserve Bank of New York).

De Cecco, M. (1974) *Money and Empire* (Oxford: Blackwell).

De Cecco, M. (1987) 'Gold Standard', in J. Eatwell, M. Milgate and P. Newman (eds) *The New Palgrave: A Dictionary of Economics* (London: Macmillan).

Giavazzi, F. and Giovannini, A. (1986) 'The EMS and the Dollar', *Economic Policy*, 2.

Giersch, H. (1970) *Growth, Cycles, and Exchange Rates – The Experience of West Germany* (Stockholm: Almquist & Wiksell).

Hayek, F. (1937) *Monetary Nationalism and International Stability* (London: Longman).

Ingram, J. 'A Proposal for Financial Integration in the Atlantic Community', in *Factors Affecting the United States Balance of Payments* (Washington, DC: Joint Committee Print, US Government Printing Office).

Knapp, J. (1943) 'The Theory of International Capital Movements and its Verifications', *Review of Economic Studies*, 10.

McKinnon, R. (1979) *Money in International Exchange* (Oxford University Press).

Miles, M. (1984) *Beyond Monetarism* (New York: Basic Books).

Morgenstern, O. (1959) *International Financial Transactions and Business Cycles* (Princeton University Press).

Russo, M. and Tullio, G. (1988) 'Monetary Policy Coordination within the EMS: Is there a Role?', *EC Economic Papers*, 63.

Triffin, R. (1946–7) 'National Central Banking and the International Economy', *Review of Economic Studies*, 14:36.

Triffin, R. (1964) 'The Myth and Realities of the So-Called Gold Standard', in *The Evolution of the International Monetary System* (Princeton University Press).

Index